CATHOLIC RECORD SOCIETY
PUBLICATIONS
(RECORDS SERIES) VOLUME 66

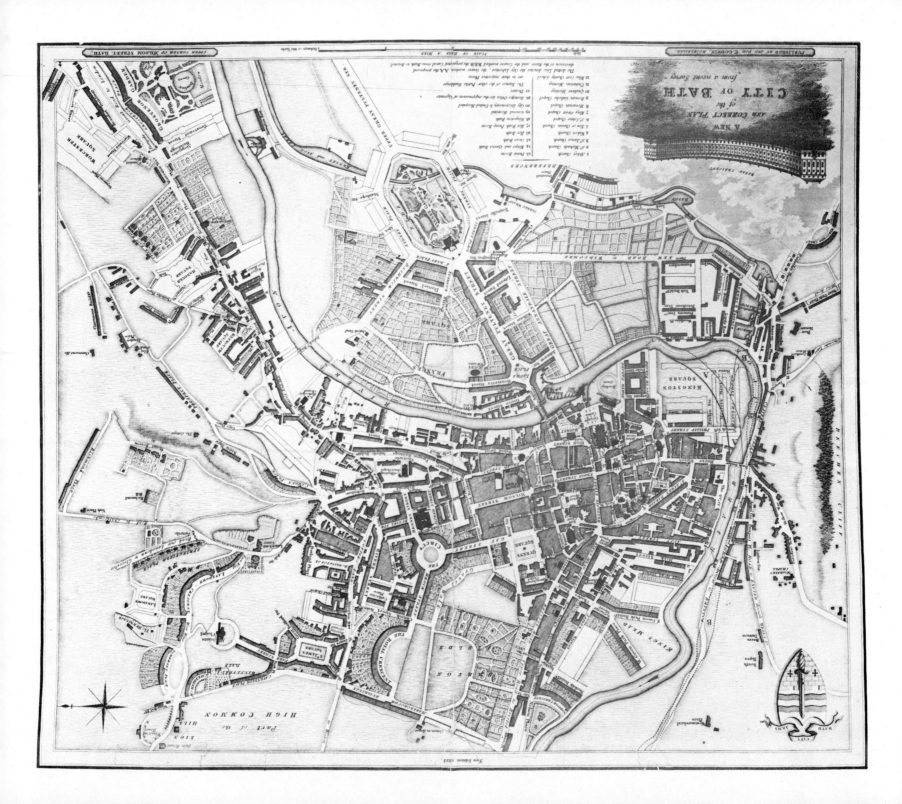

A NEW
AND CORRECT PLAN
of the
CITY OF BATH
from a recent Survey.

REFERENCES

1 Abbey Church
2 S.t Michaels Church
3 S.t James Church
4 Walcot Church
5 New or Christ Church
6 S.t James Chapel
7 King Street Chapel
8 Margaret Chapel
9 Trinity Chapel
10 Quakers Meeting
11 Catholic Chapel
12 Blue Coat Charity School

13 Pump Room
14 Kings and Queens Bath
15 Cross Bath
16 Hot Bath
17 Hot Bath Pump Room
18 Kingston Bath
19 General Hospital
20 City Dispensary
21 United Hospital
22 Theatre

The Names of the other Public Buildings
are in their respective Places

The dotted Line denotes the City Liberties; the Courses marked AA the proposed
diversion of the River; and the Course marked BBB the projected Canal from Bath to Bristol.

SCALE OF HALF A MILE

Furlongs or 80 Yards

New Edition 1805

HIGH COMMON
Part of the

SION

THE ROYAL CRESCENT

FIELDS

THE CIRCUS

BATH ARMS
CITY

POST-REFORMATION
CATHOLICISM IN BATH
VOLUME II : REGISTERS, 1780-1825

Edited by

J. ANTHONY WILLIAMS

CATHOLIC RECORD SOCIETY
1976

Typeset and printed in England by
Lowe & Brydone Printers Limited,
Thetford, Norfolk

CONTENTS

* Followed by *Corrigenda* to *C.R.S.*, 65.

FRONTISPIECE: The plan of Bath in 1825 shows places mentioned in this volume and its predecessor, which contains an earlier plan (1776) antedating the registers here printed. The originals of both are in the Reference Library, Queen Square, Bath.

MEMORIAL INSCRIPTIONS: These exist for a longer period than is covered by the registers here printed; see relevant footnotes, also *C.R.S.*, 65, p. 83, note 425; Davey, *passim,* and "Memorial Inscriptions in Bath Abbey", (i) transcribed by C.P. Russell (MS. with drawings and plan) and (ii) by J. Dunn (typescript), both in Bath Reference Library.

INTRODUCTION and ACKNOWLEDGMENTS

This is the second of two volumes relating to post-Reformation Catholicism in Bath. Its predecessor contains an account-book covering thirty years of the eighteenth century — "that obscure time", to quote Pollen and Burton, when, "again and again, the clue is lost"[1] — as well as material on the rioting of 1780, a variety of other eighteenth-century documents and the journal (1817-8) of Peter Augustine Baines, later bishop and Vicar-Apostolic of the Western District, prefaced by a sketch of the historical background from the Elizabethan settlement to the restoration of the Catholic hierarchy in 1850. Each work is separately indexed but as a number of names occur in both it will sometimes prove profitable to consult the index to the companion volume. Printed here are the first two registers of the Bath Catholic mission, the originals of which, like many others, were not forwarded in 1840 to the Commissioners enquiring into non-parochial registers[2] but are preserved at St John's presbytery, South Parade, Bath. They date only from 1780 because the older records of the mission were burnt during the Gordon Riots in June of that year.

The earliest surviving register covers in detail the period from 27 June 1780 to 28 November 1809 (with one baptismal entry dated 1759,[3] one dated 6 February 1810, relating to a baptism in November 1809, two mortuary-entries for October 1812 and a marriage-entry for December 1813); it measures 8 inches in height and 6 inches across and is now bound in quarter leather with marbled boards and titled in gold on the spine, not quite accurately, "Baptizatorum, Confirmatorum, Matrimoniorum, Status Animarum. Bell Tree 1781-1812". This fails to indicate that deaths and conversions (mostly grouped towards the end, but some entered earlier) are also included. Previously the register was

---

[1] Kirk, p. viii.

[2] See J.O. Payne, *Old English Catholic Missions* (1889) for extracts from Catholic registers forwarded to Somerset House in 1840 and now in the Public Record Office. For a copy of the printed certificate accompanying such registers, see *C.R.S.,* 4, p. 318. The most informative and up-to-date guide is D.J. Steel (ed.) *National Index of Parish Registers* (Society of Genealogists, in progress) especially vol. 3: *Sources for Roman Catholic and Jewish Genealogy and Family History* (1974).

[3] Baptism of William Day. Many years later a William Day, surgeon, of Westgate Buildings, Bath, took the oath laid down in the second Catholic Relief Act, 1791 (*C.R.S.,* 65, pp. 76, 108) and he also occurs in this volume (see index). He attended Bishop Walmesley on his deathbed and was asked by Dr John Kirk, lately president of Sedgley Park School, to intercede with Walmesley over the latter's condemnation of the Staffordshire clergy and their "creed" (for which see B. Ward, *The Dawn of the Catholic Revival in England,* 1909, *passim.*). Day's pleading was unavailing, as is shown by the following letter from him to Kirk, dated 23 November 1797, which is interesting both in revealing a layman acting as intermediary between Walmesley and other clerics and in supplementing "the only particulars which we have" of the bishop's last days (he died on 25 Nov.) printed by Ward, *op. cit.,* II, p. 150. The original is in Birmingham Archdiocesan Archives, C.1415:-

"stoutly bound in leather" with "a very considerable portion" of its pages blank and with some in a different order, as can be ascertained from an earlier transcript with which the present version has been compared and from which have been copied four items headed "Loose sheets in the register" which are no longer in it.[4]

The second register, a long narrow volume measuring 15 inches by 6 inches and similarly re-bound, is worded on the spine, "Baptizatorum, Confirmatorum, Matrimoniorum, Status Animarum. Catholic Church Bath. 1809-24" and runs from 13 December 1809 to 1 January 1825. The titling is again misleading since there are no *Status Animarum* lists, whereas there are mortuary-entries (to 1819 only) and records of converts.

Some use has been made of these registers in the Historical Introduction to the previous volume, but much remains to be extracted from them. Bath's popularity as a fashionable resort in the final decades of the eighteenth century and the opening decades of the nineteenth — for part of which period the Revolutionary and Napoleonic Wars hampered continental travel and deflected additional tourists to the city — gives them a particular significance; their genealogical value is considerable; their importance from the standpoint of historical demography is enhanced by the lengthy *Status Animarum* lists (but also affected by the fact that Bath registers, Anglican as well as Catholic, are liable to include far more visitors and temporary residents than will be found in most other places) while the comprehensive and meticulous

"Rev. Sir,
　　I was in hopes all religious disputes amongst us had subsided; and am sorry to have been the medium of any altercation between Bp. Walmesley and yourself; and it gave me some pain to trouble his Lr. on the subject which has given him so much trouble; particularly seeing his bodily afflictions such, that he can neither stand, move, or turn in his bed; and as he tells me today, can get no sleep at night; add to all which, some unlucky person, some little time since, overset him in his chair in which his servant wheels him about the town, from every appearance wilfully, and very much injured his right shoulder, so as to deprive him in great measure of the use of that arme or hand: so that if we contemplate a 'Jobe' on a dunghill, covered with ulcers (for he has ulcers several) we see but little short of a Jobe in the person of our most worthy Bishop. However, to comply with your request and paying due attention to your letter, I have this day waited on his Lr. with your inclosed to him; and find that he has received your exposition aluded to; and sais it has been fully answered before: that in all propositions we should attend to the obvious sense of it; not to foreign ideas that people may take into their heads: so that if you go upon ideas different from what is the obvious sense of the thing all further reasoning must be in vain.
"This being his L.'s answer, I have only to subscribe myself
Your most Obt. Hble. St.
W. Day
"I have only time to put my letter in the post but should be glad with a letter from my nephew Charles."
Note: Charles Day, of Bath, was at Sedgley Park School from April 1797 to April 1801 (information from Father J.D. McEvilly).

[4] Somerset County Record Office, Taunton: DD/X/LA, C/467: here referred-to as "Taunton transcript", contains a few errors and a good many differences in pagination; the latter are noted as they occur. See also Chronological Table, *infra*, pp. xiii-xiv.

entries by French émigré priests, contrasting with the much briefer English items, are instructive both in their form and in their content.[5]

The five years, 1781-5, written on the flyleaf of the first register evidently relate to Father Michael Pembridge's first pastorate in Bath and figures inserted against names in some of the lists are rough running totals, not wholly accurate. In the original some pairs or groups of names in *Status Animarum* lists are followed by horizontal lines, distinguishing households, but in this printed version spaces serve the same purpose. Other rulings in both registers — e.g. vertical columns — are also omitted while the occasional crossing-out or underlining is mentioned in an editorial note. Only the first eight pages and pp. 45-7 of the first register are numbered; elsewhere I have sometimes indicated pagination where this clarifies the layout. In the French entries apostrophes and accents have been added where omitted, personal and place-names have been given capital first letters where necessary, while punctuation and capitalisation throughout have been rendered more consistent than in the original. Spellings remain unaltered. In all entries dashes are reproduced as such and blank spaces are denoted by the word *blank* in square brackets. Variant readings are similarly bracketted, as are some editorial notes, all of which are italicised. As entries in the first register are neither arranged in strict date-order nor grouped systematically under baptisms, marriages, deaths etc., I have classified them chronologically in the Table preceding the printed version of that register. Further particulars of clergy who made entries in these registers will be found in the first part of this work; i.e. volume 65 of the Catholic Record Society

For permission to reproduce these documents, grateful thanks are due to Canon J.J. Kelly of Bath, and for facilitating their annotation I am indebted to His Lordship Bishop Rudderham of Clifton, the Abbot of Downside and Dr Peter Lunn, Mr. V.J. Kite F.L.A. and the staff of the Reference Library, Queen Square, Bath; the County Archivist and his staff at the Somerset Record Office, Taunton. I am also greatly obliged to Father J.D. McEvilly (Birmingham Archdiocesan Archivist) for a copy of the letter printed in note 3 to this Introduction and for other relevant information, and to Sister Margaret Henson for kindly "vetting" my transcripts of French entries. For valuable editorial assistance in the production both of this volume and of its predecessor I am most grateful to Mr Philip Harris of the Council of the Catholic Record Society. Their publication was also furthered by my late cousin Ethel Carleton Williams and, crucially, by my wife.

J. Anthony Williams,
October 1974.

[5] Most of these occur between pp. 63 & 92. For a useful introduction to French parish registers, see D. J. Steel, *Sources for Nonconformist Genealogy and Family History* (vol. 2 of the *National Index of Parish Registers*, 1973) pp. 760-3; also p. 779 ("Registers" section of Bibliography).

ABBREVIATIONS

Baines's journal:	The journal (1817-8) of Peter Augustine Baines, printed in *C.R.S.*, 65.
Birt:	H.N. Birt, *Obit Book of the English Benedictines, 1600-1912* (Edinburgh, 1913; London reprint, 1970)
Clifton Archives:	Archives of the diocese of Clifton, housed at "St Ambrose", Leigh Woods, Clifton, Bristol.
C.R.S.:	Publications of the Catholic Record Society, London.
Davey:	E.C. Davey, *Notable Catholics who lived and died at Bath between 1678 and 1823* (no date; ? 1912).
Foley:	H. Foley, *Records of the English Province of the Society of Jesus* (7 vols. in 8, 1877-83).
Gillow:	J. Gillow, *A Literary and Biographical History, or Bibliographical Dictionary of the English Catholics* (5 vols., 1885-1902).
Kirk:	J. Kirk, *Biographies of English Catholics, 1700-1800* (ed. J.H. Pollen & E. Burton, 1909).
Oliver:	G. Oliver, *Collections illustrating the History of the Catholic Religion in Cornwall, Devon, Dorset, Somerset, Wiltshire and Gloucestershire* (1857).
R.B.A.:	*The Registers of Bath Abbey, 1569-1800* (ed. A.J. Jewers, 2 vols., Harleian Society, 1900 & 1901, paginated consecutively).
R.H.:	*Recusant History: A Journal of Research in Post-Reformation Catholic History in the British Isles.*
1819 Directory:	*Gye's Bath Directory, corrected to January 1819* (Bath, 1819).

FIRST BATH CATHOLIC REGISTER: CHRONOLOGY

FIRST BATH CATHOLIC REGISTER: CHRONOLOGY (cont.)

Date	Type of entry	Page	Date	Type of entry	Page
1802	Marriages	66, 72	1808	Baptisms	109-12
	Deaths	124		Marriages	71
	Converts	117		Deaths	128-9
	Confirmation	68		Converts	112, 119
1803	Baptisms	95-8		Confirmation	69
	Marriages	66, 69	1809	Baptisms	112-5
	Deaths	125		Marriages	71
	Converts	117-8		Deaths	129
	Confirmation	68		Converts	113-4, 119
1804	Baptisms	98-100	1810	Baptisms	115
	Marriages	70		Converts	119-20
	Deaths	125-6	1812	Deaths	129
	Converts	118	1813	Marriage	71
1805	Baptisms	100-4			
	Marriages	70	—	Undated list of	
	Deaths	126-7		children, ?1781	8-9
1806	Baptisms	104-6			
	Marriages	70	—	"Converts at	
	Deaths	127-8		Different times"	47
	Converts	118			
	Confirmation	68	1772-	Transcript of Horton	
1807	Baptisms	106-9	1787	(Glos.) register-	
	Marriages	70-71		entries.	45-6
	Deaths	128			
	Converts	107-9, 118-9	1791;	"Loose sheets in	
	Confirmation	68-9	1846	the register"	130

Note: "Converts" includes a few adult baptisms.

FIRST REGISTER

In Pembridge's handwriting until page 9.
[flyleaf] Mr Pembridge came to settle at the Bell Tree House, Bath,
Jany 8, 1781/1782, 1783, 1784, 1785.

Catalogus

Baptizatorum, Confirmatorum, Matrimoniorum, Status Animarum et
Defunctorum, Congregationis Bathoniensis apud Bell-Tree, ab Anno D.
1781.

p.1   Status Animarum
                                    or
     Number of R.C. belonging to the Chapel at Bath, 1781.

Men	Women	
	Gent. Families	
David Nagle[1] Esqr.	Mrs Nagle	
Mr Mich. Haney the Butler	Mrs Harold[1] mother	
	Honora Harogan	
	Miss Greenway	10 [sic]
	Margaret Welch	
	Mary Dean	
	Anne Austen	
Joseph Nagle Esqr.	Mrs Nagle	
James Macauley the Butler	Mrs Malpas Mother	
	Miss Fitzgerald	
	Mary Goodacre	
	Mrs Fitzmoris	
	Miss Stoker	
John Stoner Esqr.	Mrs Stoner[2]	20
Edward Parsons the Butler	Miss Plowden	
	Mrs Cowdery	
	Mary Davies	
	Mary Baldwin	
	Joanna Dean	

[1] For the related families of Nagle (or Neagle) and Harrold, see *C.R.S.*, 27, p. 136
& note. David Nagle was one of a group of Bath laymen who sided with Dom
Joseph Wilks O.S.B. against Bishop Walmesley. Their petition of November 1791,
from which his name and that of Pierce Walsh were subsequently deleted, is in
Clifton Archives, IV, no.198. The signatories were Thomas Canning, Henry Dillon,
Philip Howard, Henry Fermor, Pierce Walsh, David Nagle and John Tobin. See also
B.Ward, *The Dawn of the Catholic Revival in England* (1909) I, p. 330 & *passim*.
A letter relating to these families (Archives Nationales, Paris: S.4619, *liasse* 5,
no.126) is printed in *C.R.S.*, 65, p. 178.

[2] For this family see J. Stonor, *Stonor: A Catholic Sanctuary in the Chilterns*
(Newport, Mon., 1951). The wife of John Stonor of Bath was Mary, daughter of
Sir Berkeley Lucy, Bart. of Broxbourne, Herts., and Charles Stonor's wife was
Mary Eugenia, *née* Blount of Mapledurham, Oxon., who, after his death at Grave-
lines in 1781, married the Thomas Canning mentioned in the previous note
(*Stonor*, genealogical tables facing pp. 240 & 320). For Charles Stonor's death-
entry in the Bath register, marked "Rouen", see *infra*, p. 46.

1

p.2 Men		Women	
Charles Stoner Esqr.		Mrs Stoner[2]	
Mr Buckley the Butler		Miss Pendrell	
Thomas Pasey Footman		Esther Allen	
		Eliz. Harris	
		Anne Cook	
		Lucy Norris	
		Mrs Fitzherbert	
		Miss Fitzherber [sic]	
		Mrs Duval	
		Mrs Johnson	40
Walter Smythe Esqr.[3]		Mrs Smythe	
John Owen the Butler		Miss Smythe	
Mr Suliard		Mary Filyin	
		Mrs Hussey	
		Mrs Butler, Maid	
		Mrs Southcote	
		Miss Plunket	
William Stevens, Servt.	to 30 [sic]	Mrs Chetwynd	
		Winefride Albert, Maid	
		Miss Margaret Porter	50
		Miss Sarah Stringfellow,[4] Maid	
Mr Blake		Mrs Blake	
John Fallons, Servt.		Miss Blake	
		Honora Henelly, Servt.	
Sir Richd. Acton[5]		Mary Power, Servt.	
p.3 Men		Women	
Mr Robinson		Mrs Robinson	70
		Mrs Day	
Mr Hugo		Mrs Hugo	
		Elizabeth Green, Servt.	

[3] Father of Mrs Fitzherbert, widowed in 1781, who married the future George IV in 1785 (probably not the "Mrs Fitzherbert" in this and subsequent *Status Animarum* lists; see *infra*, note 41). He died at his Bath house on the Queen's Parade on 14 Jan. 1788 and was buried in the Abbey (Davey, p. 97). See also note 72. His daughter, Mrs Fitzherbert, was present at his death-bed and was again in Bath in 1798 and 1826-7; cf. W. H. Wilkins, *Mrs Fitzherbert and George IV* (1909) II, pp. 61-3, 188, 192-3.

[4] Perhaps connected with the Wiltshire family of that name, in the service of the Catholic Lord Arundell of Wardour; see *C.R.S. Monograph 1*, p. 251.

[5] Sir Richard Acton (d.1791), 5th Bart., of Aldenham Hall, Salop.

Mr Dowling		Mrs Dowling	
		Mrs Catharine Burn	
		Mrs Martha Burn	
Mr John Kendal		Mrs Kendal	
Mr Butt	60	Mrs Butt	
		Betty Green, Servt.	
Mr Mich. Conner		Mrs Conner	80
Mr Butler		Mrs Butler	
Mr Edmund English[6]		Mrs English	
Mr Moland		Mrs Moland	
		Mrs Neal Mother	
Mr Daniel Ryan		Mrs Ryan	
Mr Day Senr		Mrs Day	
Mr Day Junr		Mrs Day Junr.	
Mr N. Day		Miss Day	
Edward Canning Esqr.		Miss Fleming	
		Miss Catharine Fleming	90

Men		Women	
p.4			
Joseph Love		Mrs Love	
James Donelly		Helena Donelly	
Mr Woogan		Miss Dale	
Mr Dean		Miss Thornton	
Ditto Son		Miss Theodosia Benland	
James Dowding		Miss Mary Anne Benland	
George Amesbury		Miss Elizabeth Barrick	
Mr Dun		Mrs Dun	120
William Laythem		Julietta Laythem	
Mr Lowndes	100	Mrs Lowndes	
William Norris		Ms [?] Norris	

[6] A prominent Bath Catholic family; see Davey, pp. 63-4; Oliver, p. 297, *sub* Lewis Bernard and Ferdinand Edward English (later Archbishop); J. S. Roche, *History of Prior Park* (1931) *passim*; P. A. Allanson, Ms. "Biography of the English Benedictines" (at Downside) *sub* John Jerome Jenkins O.S.B. See also note 12 to second Bath register (*infra*, p. 142).

Willm. Howell

[blank] Howell
Edward Howell [sic]

Jeremiah Lions

[blank] Lions

George Hughes

[blank] Hughes

Mr Philip Lynch

Mrs Lynch

Mr James Quigley

Mrs Quigley

Mr [blank] Murphy

Mrs Murphy   130

Mr Thomas Short

Mrs Short

Giles Hall

[blank] Hall

Alexander Macavey   110

Margaret Macavey

Christopher Lieb

Mrs Nadall

Richard Maddox

[blank] Maddox

p.5
Isaac West   Mrs Matthews   160
Mr Gale   Mary Dean
Richd. Hubberston   Anne Dean
Thomas [blank]   Mrs Trainor (Judith)
George Brookshire   140   Mrs Tudor

Mr Hughes   Mrs Hughes

Mr Peter Smith   Charlotte Smith

Thomas More   [blank] More
                                        Catharine More, Daught.

George Burt   [blank] Burt

Mr Kagan   Mrs Keagan   170

                        Women
Anne Hughes   Amy Castle
Elizabeth Haney   Miss Mary Burrell
Mrs Sheuard   Mrs Payne
Mrs Frances   Elizabeth Henderic
Helena Casey   150   Anne Shimeld
Hannah Hughes   Mary Murphy
Dorothy Tracey   Celia Dun
Mary Dory   Mrs Gray
Mrs East   Mrs Knowles
Mrs Whitlock   Sarah Madden   180
Mrs Martin   Bridget Martin

Martha Blake
Anne Ashton
Mary Prosser

Mary Ashton
Mary Ashton Junr.
Frances Prosser

p.6   Women

Louisa Lieb
Anne Watts
Hannah Haney
Mary Jenkins
Mrs Brown
Mrs Leech   190
Mary Stevens, Bradford[7]
Betty Baxwel
Mrs Ready
Elizabeth Russell
[blank] Hutchinson
Anne Rogers
Elizabeth Davies, Stourton[8]
Mrs Crabb, Philips Norton[9]
Anne Haxeland [?]
Mrs Church   200
Jane Robinson
Mrs Price
Mrs Banks
[blank] Twigg
Rose Cosgrove
Jane Magra
Lady Palmer
Betsey Carlas
Walbury   210
Mary Sullivan
Anne [Mrs Crabb deleted]
[Mrs Martin deleted] Miss Cuppa

Mary Lieb
Betty Cottarell
Eliz. Manning
Betty Peddil
Mrs Macnamara
Mrs Pettingal
Mary Welch
Frances Gallis   220
Mrs Catharine Conner – WasherWm[?]
[blank] Russell Daughter
Mary St George
Anne Trimmells
Mrs Thornton, Philips Norton[9]
Flora Coombe
Mary Ross
Penelope Price
Mary Eyre
Mrs Randal   230
Jane Barry
Mrs Pearce
Margaret Foresight
Rachel Baker
Catharine Dowdell
Mrs Darcy
Mary Edwards
Elizabeth Brannan
[blank] Trevors
Sarah Hagerty   240

p.7 1781   Men   Women

Mr Maubache
[blank] Kelly
[blank] Scanlon
[blank] Fenraine
[blank] Hartland
[blank] Hagler

Mrs Maubache
[blank] Kelly
[blank] Scanlon   270
[blank] Fenraine
[blank] Hartland
[blank] Hagler Wife

[7]   i.e. of Bradford-on-Avon, Wilts.

[8]   The strongly Catholic parish of Stourton, Wilts., where "at least a hundred" papists were reported in 1783 (*Wilts. Record Society*, 27, p. 205). No names were asked-for on that occasion and none are given in the 1767 and 1780 returns of papists in this parish (in Salisbury Diocesan Archives) nor do any Stourton papists occur in surviving lists of those taking the oaths between 1778 and 1830 (*C.R.S. Monograph 1*, pp. 248-52 & *passim*) but in August 1784 the burial of "Elizabeth Davis (62), a Papist" was entered in the Anglican register, which contains several other Davis burial-entries marked "a papist" (J. H. Ellis, ed., *The Registers of Stourton, Wilts.*, 1887, pp. 80-86).

[9]   i.e. Norton St Philip, Somerset.

Mich. Brannan[10]
Mr O'Burne
James Collins
James Keys   250
James Macauliff
Ralph Langley
[blank] Maugie
[blank] Brickman
[blank] Foret
[blank] Roberts
Mich. Brian
Mich. Murtery
Joseph Edwards
James Farill Senr   260
[blank] Farrill Junr
[blank] Keasbery
Willm. Macpherson
Sam. Dillon
[blank] Shaw
[blank] Casey
[blank] Casey

[blank] Hagler Daughter
[blank] Pearce
Hannah Baker
Lady Palmer's Maid
Margaret Macauliff
[Anne Rogers deleted]
An Irish Maid Servt.
Catharine Butler   280
Elizabeth Boswel
Elaenora Dunnohaugh W [sic]
Miss Plunket, Walcot[11]
[blank] Murtery wife   280[sic]

[blank] Macpherson

p.8   Men   Women
[blank] Vivier
[blank] Corlas   Elizabeth Corlas
[blank] Robins
Thomas Dutten
George Jackson
[blank] Jolly
Henry Wheland
Robert Jaques   Elizabeth Jaques
Barth. Hayes
[Joseph Savage, deleted]   [Anne Savage deleted]
Thos. Clark
Thomas Perry   [Joanna Perry deleted]
[blank] Mcquire

[Whitsuntide deleted]   1782
[Lake deleted]   Lady Mannock
[Anne Austen deleted]   Martha Bulbeck
[Eleanora Donnohough deleted]   Mrs Mills
[More deleted]   Catharine Gregson
Andrew Fitzgerald   Thos. Waring
Thomas Day, Forscoat[12]

[10]   Michael Brannan of the Pack-Horse Inn, Claverton St., occurs in the *Bath Directory* for 1792, p. 98.

[11]   i.e. the parish of Walcot, Bath. Possibly the letter W, after the preceding name, also stands for Walcot.

[12]   Forscote, or Foxcote, midway between Bath and Frome (about 7 miles from each), not to be confused with Foxcote, Warwicks., seat of the Canning family; see J. S. Hill, *Place Names of Somerset* (Bristol, 1914) p. 184.

Jane Radigan
Mrs O'brian
Eleanor Casey
Mrs Poole

[Followed by blank page]

p.10   Status Animarum A.D. 1782

Resident Families

David Nagle Esqr.   Walter Smythe Esqr.
Mrs Nagle   Mrs Smythe
Mrs Harold   Miss Smythe
Michael Haney   Miss Flyn
Honora Harogan   Mr Suliard
Miss Greenway
Margaret Welch   Robert Dalton Esqr.
Mary Dean   Mrs Dalton
Anne Austen   Miss Dalton
                                 [Mary *deleted*] Catharine Cowdrey
Joseph Nagle Esqr.
Mrs Nagle   Mrs Chetwynd
Mrs Malpas   Catharine Eyre
James Macauliff   Winefrid Albert
Mrs Fitzmorris   [Willm. Stevens *deleted*] Joseph Taylor
Mary Goodacre
                                 Mrs Hussey
John Porter Esqr.   Catharine Butler
Mrs Porter
Rd. Mr Jennison[13]   Maurice Blake Esqr.
                                 Mrs Blake
John Stonor Esqr.   Mr Anthony Blake
Mrs Stonor   Honora Henelly
Miss Plowden
Eliz. Cowdrey   John Lawson Esqr.
Mary Baldwin   Luke Stevenson
Mary Davies
                                 Mr Robinson
Lady Mannock   Mrs Robinson
Mrs Mills   Mrs Day   54
[Mary Cotton *deleted*] Martha Bulbeck Eliz. Harvey
Catharine Gregson
Thomas Waring

p.11
Mr Hugo   Mrs Nadall
Mrs Hugo   Anne Watts
Mary Hugo   Mr Christoph Lieb
Genevieve Hugo   Louisa Lieb
Eliz. Green, Servt.   Mary Lieb
                                 Mrs East

[13]   James Jenison, ex-Jesuit (see *C.R.S.*, 65, p. 73).

Mrs Catharine Burn
Mrs Martha Smith
Mr Smith
Catharine Camplin
Mary Camplin

Mr Giles Hall
Mrs Hall and Sally Do.

Mr John Quigley
Mrs Quigley

Mr Butler and Mrs Butler

Mrs Trayner

Mr John Kendal
Mrs Kendal

Mary Ross [3 children *deleted*]

Mrs Trimmells

Mr Butt and Mrs Butt

Mr James Donelly
Mrs Pettingal

Mrs Donelly and [Daughter *deleted*]

Miss Fleming and Miss Cath. Do.

Mary Prosser
Thos. Prosser and Fanny Do.

Mrs Fitzherbert
Mrs Charlotte Duval
Mrs Johnson
Esther Allen

Mrs Russell

Mrs Matthews
Mary Dean
Mr and Mrs Lynch
Anne Dean

Mr and Mrs English

Mrs Poole
Mrs Welch
Mr and Mrs Lowndes
Mrs Knowles
Mr N. Smith and Mrs Charlotte Do.
Sally Maddin
James Smith

Mrs Marg. Porter
Mr and Mrs Howell and Edward Do.
Sarah Stringfellow

114

*End of page. This list is continued on p. 64 and the following list of
children, undated, may or may not be a further instalment of the same
list. The ink and handwriting, and the separate heading "Children",
appear to make it a continuation of the 1781 list, in which men and
women are grouped separately, though the children's surnames include
two, Ross and Donelly, whose inclusion in the following list may explain
why "3 Children" and "Daughter" are crossed out after being written
originally as part of the parents' entries in the 1782 list above.*

p.12
Children

Boys	Age	Girls	Age
Thomas Murphy	14	Frances Prosser	14
John Quigley		Anne Ashton, 1 Com., Ap. 8, 1782	
Thomas Prosser	15	Mary Anne Bowland	
Charles Baker	14	[*blank*] Thornton	
Edward Howell		Elizabeth Barrick	
James Smith	12	Mary Hugo, 1 Com., Ap. 8, 1782	

Thomas Jenkins	14	Helena Hugo Ditto
Willm. Jenkins		Catharine Murphy, 1 Com., Ap. 5
Robt. Jenkins		Margaret More, 1 Com., Ap. 5, 1782
Peter Carey		Barbara More, 1 Com., Dec. 1784
James Carey		Judith Carey
John Dun		Catharine Camplin, 1 Com., Ap. 8, 1782
John Ross		Catharine Macauliff
John Seifred		Margaret Macauliff
John Brown		Sarah Hall, 1 Com., 20 Aug., 1784
John Donnohough		Mary Donelly
Willm. Tracey		[blank] Scanlon
Edward Woogan		[blank] Ross
Edward Tabor		[blank] English
James Tabor		[blank] Connor
[blank] Foresight		
[blank] Harrill [? Farrill]		
John Roper, 1 Com., 20 Aug., 1784		

p.13 [in Pembridge's hand].
Anno Domini 1759, Die 19 Octobris, Baptizatus est apud Inglisbatch, Gulielmus Day, Natus 14 Oct., Filius Thomae et Susannae Day Conjugum. Patrini Joannes Kendal et Winefrida Kendal,

pr. D. Placidum Nayler

The above is the only entry on its page. Those which follow, from June 1780 to November 1781, occupy the next eight pages, unnumbered in the original register. The next nine entries are in the handwriting of Dom John Bede Brewer O.S.B.

Catalogus Baptizatorum in Capella Catholica Bathoniae.
Anno Dni. 1780. Die Junii vigesimo septimo baptizata est, pridie vero nata Anna, filia legitima Josephi et Annae Savage Conjugum. Sponsoribus Michaele Mathew et Catharina Scandlin.

Joannes Brewer

Anno Domini 1780. Die Julii decimo nono nata est, baptizata vero die vigesimo secundo ejusdem mensis, Catharina Maria, filia legitima Gulielmi et Maria Norris, Conjugum. Sponsoribus Richardo Dean et Maria Mathews.

Joannes Brewer

Anno Domini 1780. Die duodecimo Augusti natus et in periculo mortis sine ceremoniis baptizatus est Georgius, filius legitimus Thomae et Joannae Perry Conjugum.

Joannes Brewer

Anno Domini 1780. Die Septembris vigesimo secundo nata est, baptizata vero Die vigesimo septimo ejusdem mensis Elizabetha, filia legitima Roberti et Elizabethae Jakes Conjugum. Sponsoribus Josepho et Elizabetha Corlas.

Joannes Brewer

Anno Domini 1780. Die Septembris vigesimo quinto natus est, baptizatus vero die primo Octobris sequentis Michael, filius Patricii Kelly et Margaritae Bentley. Sponsoribus Michaele Brian et Elizabetha Serle.

Joannes Brewer

Anno Domini 1780. Die Octobris octavo, suppletae sunt Ceremoniae
Baptismi in Georgium, filium legitimum Thomae et Joannae Perry
Conjugum, natum die duodecimo Augusti ultimi et baptizatum die
decimo septimo ejusdem. Sponsoribus Thoma Moore et Rosa Cosgrove.

Joannes Brewer

Anno Dni. 1780. Die Octobris nono natus est, baptizatus vero die
duodecimo ejusdem Thomas,[14] filius legitimus Gulielmi et Elizabethae
Robinson Conjugum. Sponsoribus Thoma et Susanna Day.

Joannes Brewer

Anno Dni. 1780. Die Novembris vigesimo octavo nata est, baptisata vero
die decimo Decembris Catharina, filia legitima Hyacinthi et Elizabethae
Manuel Conjugum Italorum. Sponsoribus Ambrosio Peregrine et
Catharina Stone.

Joannes Brewer

Anno Dni. 1780. Die decimo sexto Decembris natus est, baptizatus vero
die Januarii sexto Anni Dni. 1781 Edmundus, filius legitimus Edmundi
et Margaritae English Conjugum. Sponsoribus Jacobo Murphy et
Dorothea Moland.

Joannes Brewer

Henceforth in Pembridge's hand, until p. 19.
Pembridge, Jany. 8, 1781.
Baptized
1781 + Jany. 14, Elizabeth Connor,[15] the Daughter of Michael Connor
and Mary Connor alias Stone, his lawful wife. God Father Edmund
English, God Mother Martha Burn.

Michael Pembridge

3. 1781, Jany. 28, Michael Smith, the Son of N. Smith and N. Smith
    his lawful Wife.
    God Father Michael Connor.

Michael Pembridge

4. 1781, Feby. 4, Alexander Ross, the Son of Ross and of Anne
    Ross his lawful wife. +
    God Father Silvester Macavoy, God Mother Mary Connor. Dead.

Michael Pembridge

5. 1781, Feby. 27, Mary Macpherson, the Daughter of William
    Macpherson and of Mary Macpherson alias Daniels his lawful
    Wife. God Father John Kendal, God Mother Anne Price.

Michael Pembridge

6. 1781, March 4. Baptized conditionally, Sinones etc. Dominic
    Anthony Quintas, the Son of Dominic Anthony Quintas and of
    Mary Quintas his lawful Wife. God Father Thomas More, God
    Mother Sarah Hagarty. Died Augst 10 1781. +

7. 1781, March 5, Francis Stoner, the Son of Charles Stoner and
    [*blank*] Stoner alias Blount his lawful Wife. God Father Mr

---

[14] Later a Benedictine (Birt, p. 141).

[15] Baptisms marked with a cross can in some instances be linked to mortuary
entries elsewhere in the register; some have the note "dead" added.

Charles Biddulph by proxy of Mr Mich. Blount, God Mother Lady Nuburgh[16] by proxy of Miss Plowden.

Michael Pembridge

8. 1781, March 19, Mary Jenkins, the Daughter of Thomas Jenkins and of Mary Jenkins his lawful Wife. God Mother Elizabeth Green. Dead.

Mich. Pembridge

9. 1781, Ap. 16, Charles Parsons, born Ap. 13, the Son of Edward Parsons and of N. Parsons alias Gaveston, his lawful Wife. God Father George Brookshire, God Mother Martha Burn.

Michael Pembridge

10. 1781. Baptized May 6, Cornelius Dowding, born the 20 April, the Son of James Dowding and Mary Dowding alias Hawkins his lawful Wife. God Father George Hughes, Godmother Mary Ashton, Died Augst 10 1781. +

Mich. Pembridge

11. 1781, May 9. Baptized Margaret Walbury, the Daughter of John Walbury and Mary Walbury his lawful Wife. Godmother Margaret Lions.

M. Pembridge

12. 1781, June 8, Mary Anne Hughes (born June 6), the Daughter of George Hughes and Mary Hughes alias Short, his lawful Wife. God Father Thomas Short, God Mother Anne Cliff by proxy of Mary Short.

13. 1781, July 18, Mary Bird, the Daughter of Lydia Bird (born July 16), God Mother [blank] Jaques.

Michael Pembridge

[This entry is partly crossed-out and "Died Ap.23 1782" is written against it in Pembridge's hand.]

14. 1781, July 22, Mary Payne (born 21 July), the Daughter of Edward Payne and Mary Payne his lawful Wife. God Father Richard Dean and God Mother Catharine Randall. + Died Sept. 29 1781.

Michael Pembridge

15. 1781, July 24, Elizabeth Church, born July 23, the Daughter of James Church and Anne Church alias Lowndes his lawful Wife. God Father James Slane, God Mother Esther Alden. + Died Sept. 3.

Michael Pembridge

16. 1781, Septber. 2. Baptized Thomas Hayes (born Augst. 26), the Son of Bartholomew Hayes and Martha Hayes his lawful Wife. God Father Thomas More, God Mother Mary More.

Michael Pembridge

17. 1781, Sept. 9, Anne Billington (born [blank]), the daughter of

---

16 Barbara (née Kemp, of Slindon, Sussex) wife of James Bartholomew Radclyffe, 4th Earl of Newburgh ("G.E.C", *Complete Peerage*, IX, pp. 515-6). For the mother's Christian names, see note 2.

John Billington and Christina Billington his lawful Wife. God
Father Jeremiah Lions, God Mother Mary Prosser.

Michael Pembridge

18.   1781, Sept. 23. Baptized John Scanlon (born 11 Septber), the
Son of Patrick Scanlon and Catharine Scanlon his lawful Wife.
God Father Patrick Kelly, God Mother Margaret Kelly.

Michael Pembridge

19.   1781, Sept. 25, was Born and Baptized William Thomas Michael
Vaughan, the son of William Vaughan Esq. of Court Field, Mon-
mouthshire, and of Frances Vaughan his lawful Wife. God Father
Thomas Weld Esqr. of Lulworth Castle, by proxy of David Nagle
Esqr., God Mother Mrs Mary Nagle.

Michael Pembridge

20.   1781 Baptized Nov. 4, Thomas Dutton (born Oct. 26), the Son
of Thomas Dutton and Elizabeth Dutton his lawful Wife. God
Father Thomas Short, God Mother Mary Norris.

M. Pembridge

21.   1781, Novber. 12 Baptized Elizabeth Ryan (born the same day),
the Daughter of Michael Ryan and Elizabeth Ryan alias Barr his
lawful Wife. God Father [blank] Haley.

22.   1781, Novber. 12. Baptized Mary Ryan, twin Sister of the aforesaid Elizabeth (both in danger of death, without the Ceremonies),
the Daughter of Michael and Elizabeth Ryan aforesaid. God
Father [blank] Haley aforesaid. (Both died Dec. 7.)

M. Pembridge

23.   1781, Nov. 30. Baptized John MicMurtry, born 19th Ditto, the
Son of William MicMurtry and Rebecca MicMurtry his lawful
Wife. God Father Giles Hall, God Mother Martha Dowden. Bath.

Michael Pembridge

24.   1781, Novber. 21. Baptized Richard Lanagan (born the same day),
the Son of James Lanagan and Mary Lanagan his lawful Wife (by
private baptism). Supplied the rest Dec. 8. God Father Owen
Macguire, God Mother Anne Monks.

M. Pembridge

For entry no. 25, apparently misplaced when the Register was rebound,
see p. 46.

Easter 1782.

David Nagle Esqr.	Miss Marg. Porter
Mrs Nagle	Sarah Stringfellow
Mrs Harold	
Michael Haney	Mrs Chetwynde
Margt. Welch	Cath. Eyre
Honora Harrogan	Winefride Albert
Miss Greenway	Willm. Stevens
Joseph Nagle Esqr.	Miss Plunket
Mrs Nagle	Mrs Southcot
Mrs Fitzmorris	Miss Dalton

10

Mrs Goodacre	⎰ Mrs Bathoe	40
James Macauliff	⎱ Black Hopperkin[17]	
Mary Elliot	⎰ James Weldon Esqr.	
	⎱ Miss Weldon	
John Stonor Esqr.	Lady Palmer	
Mrs Stonor	⎰ Mr Butler	
Miss Plowden	⎱ Mrs Butler	
Mrs Cowdrey	⎰ Mr English	
Mary Baldwin	⎱ Mrs English	
Anne Davies	⎰ Mr Robinson	
Fanny Prosser 20	⎨ Mrs Robinson	
	⎱ Miss Day Senr.	
Lady Mannock	⎰ Mr Day, Ingsbach[18]	
Mrs Mills	⎪ Mrs Day	
Martha Bulbeck	⎨ Miss Day	
Cath. Gregson	⎱ Mr Willm. Day	
Thos. Waring	Maurice Blake Esqr.	
	Mrs Blake	
Mrs Smythe	Anthony Blake	
Mr Souliard	Eliz. Pollard	
Mary Flynn	Honorah Henally	60
John Porter Esqr.		
Mrs Porter 30	[End of page]	
⎰ Mr Thomas Day, Forscot	⎰ Mrs Nadall	
⎱ Mrs Day	⎪ Christ. Lieb	
Miss Cath. Fleming	⎨ Anne Watts	
Mrs Lowndes	⎱ Mary Lieb	
Mrs Church	Louisa Lieb	
Owen Maguire	Lucy Stone	
⎰ Mr Smith	Mary Burt	
⎨ Mrs Smith	Alice MacDermant	
⎱ James Smith	Mrs Ryley	
Mary Prosser 70	[Mrs Realy deleted]	
Mary Russell	⎰ Mr Kendal	
Mr Smith-Webb	⎱ Mrs Kendal	
Luke Stevenson	⎰ Mr Butt	
⎰ Mr Rian	⎨ Mrs Butt	
⎱ Mrs Rian	⎱ Eliz. Green	
⎰ Mrs Burn	Mary Jenkins	
⎪ Mrs Smith Burn[19]	Giles Hall	
⎨ Mr Smith	Mrs Hall	
⎪ Eliz. Camplin	⎰ Thos. Brown	
⎱ Cath. Camplin 80	⎨ Jane Robinson	
Mrs Martin	⎱ Penelope Price	110

[17] Mrs Bathoe's maid-servant; see Easter penitents list, 1785 (*infra*. p. 32).

[18] i.e. Englishbatch in the parish of Englishcombe on the outskirts of Bath; cf. Hill, *Place Names of Somerset*, p. 46.

[19] Perhaps Martha (*née* Burn) who married Anthony Smith on 20 June 1781 (see *infra*, pp. 47-8) and who appears as Mrs Martha Smith in the 1782 *Status Animarum* list (*supra*, p. 8). See also baptismal entries nos. 40 & 57 (printed on pp. 17 & 20) and note 42.

Thos.[?] Short
Mary Short
Mr O'Burn
Mr Coombs
Flora Coombs
Joseph Love
Mrs Love
Mr Donelly
Mrs Donelly   90

[*End of page*]

Mrs Knowles
Sally Madan
Mary Dennohough
Mary Carlis
Patty Dowdell
Martha Dowden
Anne Austen Senr.
Mrs Matthews   160
Mary Dean   130
Anne Dean
Mary Ross
Mrs Magrar
Thos. Lovet
Barth. Coffill
Eliz. Cottall
Hannah Hughes
Eliz. Peddle
Margt. More, 1 Comm., Ap.5.   170
Thomas More   140
James Collins
Mrs Thornton
Mr Hugo
Richd. Maddox
Richd. Hubberston
Andrew Fitzgerald
Mrs Trainer
Martha Blake
Anne Miles
Eliz. Boxall   150   180
Eliz. Harris
John Dunn

Willm. Howell
Mrs Howell
Edward Howell
Diana James
Mrs Sheward
Mrs Jenkson
Mrs Duval
Anne Johnson
Mrs Birts
Mrs East
Mrs Pool   120

Mary Curwen
Mrs Randal
Mary Twigg
Celia Dunn
Mary Harland
Madeisell[?] Hodges
Hannah Baker
Sarah Baker
Eliz. Barnes
Mr Keagan
Anthony Brasil
Henry Baggs
Mrs Saunderson
Thos. Slade
Mrs Norris
Mrs Welch
Willm. Kelly
George Dutton
John Casey
          Low Sunday
James Smith, 1 Com., Ap.8.
Mary Hugo
Genevieve Hugo   Children
Anne Ashton
Samuel Dillon
Mr Lowndes
Anne More
Mary Hughes
Mrs Murphy   14
Mrs Pettingal   Ap.14
Mr Lynch   15
Mr Anthon Gale   21
Mary Ashton Junr.   21
Elizabeth Jakes   21

        (Children)
Anne Church
Henriet Church
Anne Ross
Eleanor Scanlon
Helen Adams

        (Strangers)
Honble Mr Clifford
Mrs Clifford
Mrs Hussey
Ditto   Maid
Peter Lannan

{ Mary Anne Donelly
{ Sarah Hall +

Lady Mostynn
[Willm. Kelly *deleted*]
Sr. Richd. Acton
John Morris
Mary McNamara
John Efferlyn
Cath. Derrick
Mrs Riely

Mary Parsons
Ap.22, Eliz. Barnes
May 5, Willm Norris
Edward Quin

1782. Received into the Church a Convert, Diana James, Feby. 23, 1782 in the presence of Willm. and N. Howell.[20]
Received into the Church a Convert, Miss Mary Proctor, March 14, 1782: present Mrs Martin and Mr Blake. And Received into the Church a Convert, Mary Elliot: present Mrs Goodacre.
May 16, 1782, Peter Green of Dunkerton, a Convert: present Thomas Brown.
1782, Dec. 8, Charles Francis of Wellow: present Mrs Martin
1782, Dec. [*blank*], John Mills of Bath.

Mortuary List of 1782. [*For the 1781 mortuary-list, and for a copy of part of the 1782 list, see pp. 46-7.*]

Jany.	5	Hannah Haney, Ir., aged 58, Bath, R.P.
	16	John Daman, Frenchman, Bath, R.P.
Feby.	23	Margaret Rian alias Kelly, Ir., 28, Bath, R.P.
	26	Mary Lynch, Ir., 54, Bath, R.P.
March	16	Bridget Martin, 61, Bath, R.P.
April	12	Elizabeth East, 86, Bath, R.P.
	15	Elizabeth Crabb, 92, Philips Norton, R.P.
May	18	Mrs Margaret Reily, Ir., 32, Littleton,[21] R.P.
	19	Anne Pool, 77, Bath, R.P.
June	21	Mrs Catharine Malpas,[22] Ir., 73, Bath, R.P.
	26	Mr Anthony MacHugo,[23] Ir., 54, Bath, R.P.
Oct.	5	Mrs Mary Lucy Stonor,[24] 84, Bath, R.P.
Oct.	13	James Dean, 28, Bath, R.P.
Nov.	17	Judith Kegan, Ir., 42, Bath, R. in P.
Dec.	4	Vincent Bullen, 44, Bath, R. in P.

[20] Christian name Mary (see *infra*, p. 116).

[21] Perhaps High Littleton, Som. She was buried in Bath Abbey on 22 May (*R.B.A.*, p. 468).

[22] Buried in Bath Abbey, 28 June, as "Mapus" (*ibid.*).

[23] Buried in Bath Abbey, 1 July, as "Hugo" (*ibid.*).

[24] See note 2. She was buried in Bath Abbey on 10 October "In Mr Berresford's grave" (*R.B.A.*, p. 469).

Catalogus Baptizatorum in Capella Cathaloca Bathoniense, A.D. 1782
[*continued from p. 12*]

26. 1782, Jany. 21. M. Pembridge baptized Robert Baker, born 19,
the Son of William Baker and Hannah Baker his lawful wife. God
Father Thomas Brown, God Mother Penelope Price.

27. 1782, Jany. 30. Baptized John Dun. Born Jany 15, the Son of
James Dunn and Mary Dunn alias Ellese [?] his lawful Wife. God
Father James Murphy, God Mother Celia Dunn.
M. Pembridge

28. 1782, Feby. 10. Baptized Mary Anne Miles, born 21 Dec. 1781,
the Daughter of Charles Miles and Anne Miles his lawful Wife.
God Mother Elizabeth Cottle.
M. Pembridge

29. 1782, Feby [? Feb 7]. Baptized at Foscott Frances Day (born 4
Feby.), the Daughter of Thomas Day and Mary Day alias Fleming
his lawful Wife. God Father Mr Edward Canning, God Mother
Miss Anne Fleming.
Mr. Coombe[25]

30. 1782, March 17. Baptized Charles Jakes. Born 14 March, the Son
of Robert Jakes and Elizabeth Jakes alias Bird his lawful Wife.
God Father Edward Parsons, God Mother Anne Willisthorp.
M. Pembridge

31. 1782, March 18. Baptized Richard Gregory. Born [*blank*], the
son of Thomas Gregory and Jane Gregory his lawful Wife. God
Father James Murphay, God Mother Mary Murphay.
M. Pembridge

32. 1782, April 19, Anne Robinson born 18 Ap., the Daughter of
+   Mr Willm. Robinson and Mrs Elizabeth Robinson his lawful Wife.
God Father Rd. Mr Andrew Robinson[26], God Mother Miss
Susannah Day, Ingsbach.
M. Pembridge

33. 1782, May 6, John Stone, born 30 March, and May 10, Richard
Stone (twins), born 30 March. Both died May 23rd. God Mother
Mrs Martha Smith.
M. Pembridge

34. 1782, July 9, Anne Haily, born June 25, the Daughter of Patrick
Haily and Rebecca Haily his wife. God Father Patrick Scanlon,
God Mother Mary Ross.
Mr Garstang[27]

35. 1782, July 21, Anne Waterson, born July 14, the daughter of

[25] Entry in Pembridge's hand on behalf of William Coombs, or Coombes, for
whom see *C.R.S.*, 65, note 341 to Introduction. For "Foscott" see note 12.

[26] Ex-Jesuit; cf. Foley, VII, p. 657; Kirk, p. 200. "Ingsbach" at the end of this
entry is Englishbatch (see note 18).

[27] In Pembridge's hand. For Dom William Garstang O.S.B. see Birt, p. 129; also
C.R.S., 65, pp. 182-3. (undated letter from him to Fr. Naylor in Bath).

Michael Waterson and Dorothy Waterson his Wife. God Father Patrick Duggin.

M. Pembridge

36. 1782, Augst 11. Baptized Elizabeth Hartland, born Augst 5, the Daughter of Joseph Hartland and Elizabeth Hartland his Wife. God Father James Fanran, God Mother Celia Fanran.

M. Pembridge

37. 1782, August 25. Baptized Laetitia Church, born 24 Augst, the Daughter of William Church and Anne Church his Wife. God Father James Slade, God Mother Mary Mills. + Died Oct. 7. 1782.

M. Pembridge

38. 1782, Septber 26. Baptized Francis White, born 8th Septber, the Son of John White and of Laetitia White his Wife. God Father [blank], God Mother Mrs Dun.

M. Pembridge

39. 1782, 29 Sept. Baptized Augustine John Quintus, born 28 Augst, the Son of Dominic Anthony Quintus and of Mary Quintus his Wife. God Father Thomas More, God Mother Sarah Hagarty.

M. Pembridge

40. 1782, 30 Septber. Baptized John Joseph Smith, born 27 Sept., the Son of Anthony Smith and Martha Smith alias Burn his Wife. God Father Mr James White of Bristol, God Mother Mrs Mary Dowling by proxy of Mary Hughes.

M. Pembridge

41. 1782, Novber. 5. Baptized George Dowden, born Nov. 1, the Son of John Dowden and Martha Dowden his Wife. God Mother Mrs Anne Nadall, Bath.

M. Pembridge

42. 1782, Dec. 25. Baptized John Lions, born 4 Dec., the Son of James Lions and Elizabeth Lions alias Philips. God Mother Celia Dunn. +

M. Pembridge

43. 1782, Dec. 2 [probably another figure should follow this]. John Clare, born 5 Dec., the Son of John Clare and Elizabeth Clare alias Tobin. God Mother Mrs Sarah Cox.

M. Pembridge

1783 Mortuary List.

Jany.	11	Lucy Stone	Aged [blank]	Bath, R. in P.
	11	Silvester Macavoy	58 Ir.	Bath, R in P.
	12	Eleanor Donelly	32 Ir.	Bath, R. in P.
	25	Elizabeth Fitzmorris	70 Ir.	Bath, R. in P.
March	30	Mary Fry		Bath, R. in P.
June	16	Catharine Quigley	48 Ir.	Bath, R. in P.
July	25	Winefrede Kendal	66	Bath, R. in P.
Oct.	1	John Porter Esqr.		Wellington, R. in P.
Nov.	25	[blank] Riley, Ir.[28]		Stranger, Bath, R. in P.

[28] Buried in Bath Abbey, 28 Nov., "Mr Michael Reilly. Under Mr Orpwood's stone" (R.B.A., p. 469).

Nov.   26   Theobald Burke Esqr.[29]   62   Ir.   Ditto, R. in P.

1783 Status Animarum as 1782.
Additional Resident Families:-
    Mrs Throckmorton
    Miss Throckmorton
    Mr George Throckmorton   1784.
Servants:-   Dec. 4, Jane Dunn, Bath.
    John Haines and Wife   *This is probably a death-entry,*
    Mrs Pen   *perhaps inserted here because*
    Cook maid Anne Buet   *there was no room for it at*
    Groom   *the foot of the page, after the*
                                    final (Oct. 13) entry in the
    Mrs Brockholes   *1784 Mortuary list, below. It*
    Maid   *has no counterpart in the*
    Man Servant   *Abbey Register.*

    Miss Hide
    Miss Mary Hide
    John Mills, Servt.

                    1784 Mortuary.
1784, Jany.   30 Mrs Mary Nagle,[30]   Ir. Aged 64 Bath, R. in P.
       March   31 Thomas Arundell Esqr.,[31]   Aged 66 Bath, R. in P.
       April   15 Mary Bertrand,[32]   Ir. Aged 55 Bath, R. in P.
       April   22 Charles Kelly,   Ir. Aged 25 Bath, R. in P.
       May   5 Mrs Frances Woulfe, Stranger,
                                               Ir. aged 40 Bath, R. in P.
       May   9 Elizabeth Green,   aged 30 Bath, R. in P.
       May   17 Richard Carlas,   aged [blank] Bath, R. in P.
       July   19 Frances Key,   aged 17 Bath, R. in P.
       July   30 Anne Price, suddenly,   aged 82 Bath, R. in P.
       July   31 Catharine Hay,   Ir. aged [blank] Bath, R. in P.
       Augst.   12 Thomas Butt, suddenly   aged 65 Bath, R. in P.
       Sept.   14 Mrs Bridget Leyster,[33] Stranger, Ir., aged 52, Bath, R. in P.
       Oct.   4 Mrs Mary Donavan,[34] unexpectedly, Stranger, Ir., aged 38,
                                                   Bath, R. in P.

---

[29]   Buried in Bath Abbey, 1 Dec., as Bourke (*ibid.*)

[30]   Buried in Bath Abbey, 6 Feb., as Neagle (*R.B.A.*, p. 470). See also note 1.

[31]   Or Harran; natural son of Thomas, second son of the 5th Lord Arundell of Wardour; cf. *Notes on the Family History by the 12th Lord Arundell* (ed. E. Doran Webb, 1916) p. 74, note.

[32]   Buried in Bath Abbey, 20 April, "Under Dr Wall's monument" (*R.B.A., loc. cit.*)

[33]   Buried in Bath Abbey, 17 Sept., as Lester (*ibid.*)

[34]   Buried in Bath Abbey, 7 Oct., as Miss Maria Donovan (*ibid.*)

Oct.   9 Elizabeth Smith,   aged 43 Bath, R in P.
Oct.   13 James Kendall,   aged 23 Bath, R. in P.
*To the next page is affixed a sheet of paper containing, in a different
hand, the following rough notes and a baptismal entry later copied into
the Register by Pembridge as no.51, infra., p. 20. (Not in Taunton
transcript).*

S. [?] I. Arathoar [?] and Anne Weare Lambe.
Permission to grant Fac: to Confreres.
Confirmation.
Cemetery — Consecration of Count Eyre's Chapel and ground.
Priviledged altar.

Nov 3, 1783, Baptized Thomas Day, born Nov. 2, the son of Thomas
Day and Mary Day alias Fleming his wife. God Father Mr Thomas Day
of Ingsbach, God Mother Miss Susan Day of Ditto.
                                         pr. Mr. Willm Coombs.
Entries henceforth in Pembridge's hand (until p. 22).

Status Baptizatorum 1783.
44.   1783, Jany. 19. Baptized John English, born 6th Jany., the Son
      of Edmund English and Margt. English his wife. God Father
      Cornelius Hughes, God Mother Catharine Randal.
                                         M. Pembridge.
45   1783, Feb. 19. Baptized Mary Martin, born 26 August, the
      Daughter of Thomas Martin and Anne Martin his Wife. God
      Father Samuel Dillon, God Mother Mary Wade [? Wate].
                                         M. Pembridge.
46.   1783, March 18. Baptized Anne Fox, born 10 March, the Daughter
      of N. Fox and Anne Fox his Wife. God Father Master Charles
      White by proxy of Thos Brown, God Mother Mrs Mary Ready.
                                         M. Pembridge.
47.   March 23 + Baptized Andrew Forsayth, born 17 Feby., the Son
      of Richard Forsayth and Margaret Forsayth his Wife. God Father
      John Kegan, God Mother Catharine Sheagan. Died May 8 1784.
                                         M. Pembridge.

1783 Status Baptizatorum.
48.   April 27. Baptized Mary Casey, born 12 April, the Daughter of
      John Casey and Elizabeth Casey his wife. God Father John Kegan,
      God Mother Elizabeth Hall.
                                         M. Pembridge.
49.   July 27. Baptized John James Payne, born 17 July, the Son of
      Edward Payne and Mary Payne his Wife. God Father Edmund
      English, God Mother Mrs Catharine Randall.
                                         M. Pembridge.
50.   Oct. 9, 1783. Baptized privately in danger of Death, Mary Anne
      Jackson, born the 2d Oct. Supplied etc. Oct. 19; the Daughter of

John Jackson and Anne Jackson his Wife. God Father Henry
Wheland, God Mother Mary Ready.

M. Pembridge.

51. Nov. 3, 1783. Forscote, Baptized Thomas Day, born Nov. 2,
     Forscote, the Son of Thomas Day and Mary Day alias Fleming
     his Wife. God Father Mr Thomas Day of Ingsbach, God Mother
     Miss Susan Day of Ditto.

pr Mr Willm Coombs.[35]

52. Nov. 23, 1783. Baptized Anne Denie,[36] born Nov. 19, Bath, the
     Daughter of John Baptist Denie and of Anne Denie alias Dean his
     Wife. God Father Michael Haney, God Mother Mary Deane.

pr Mich. Pembridge.

53. Dec. 14, 1783. Baptized Charles Billington, born 10 Augst, the
     Son of John Billington and [blank] Billington his Wife. God
     Father Thos Short, God Mother Mary Prosser.

M. Pembridge.

54. 1783, Dec. 21. Baptized Thomas Moore, born 18 Dec., the Son of
     Thomas Moore and Mary Moore his Wife. God Father Charles
     Purnell, God Mother Anne Davies.

pr. M. Pembridge.

1784.

55. Feb 8. Baptized Isabella Denvir — born 17 Jany the Daughter of
     John Denvir and Elizabeth Denvir. God Father Thomas Barret,
     God Mother Mary Short.

pr M. Pembridge.

56. March 7, 1784. Baptized Ambrose Jakes, born 4 March, the Son
     of Robert Jakes and of Elizabeth Jakes alias Bird his lawful Wife.
     God Father William Hopkins, God Mother Dorothy Haynes.

pr. M. Pembridge.

57. March 17, 1784. Baptized (in danger of death) Thomas Anthony
     Smith, born March 16, the Son of Anthony Smith and of Martha
     Smith alias Burn. Supplied the rest April 1. God Father Mr Thos
     Smith by proxy of Mr Dowling, God Mother Mrs Eleanor White
     of Bristol.

M. Pembridge.

Baptizatorum 1784.

58. 1784, April 1. Baptized Sophia Miles, born March 1, the Daughter
     of Charles Miles and Anne Miles his Wife. God Mother Sarah
     Madan.

M. Pembridge.

59. 1784, April 4. Baptized Thomas Lovat, born 26 March, the Son
     of Thomas Lovat and Mary Lovat his Wife. God Father Thomas
     Barret, God Mother Mary Collins.

pr. M. Pembridge.

[35] Copy of entry on p. 19.

[36] Entered the Bar Convent, York, 1793; cf. H. J. Coleridge, St Mary's Convent,
Micklegate Bar, York (1887) p. 396.

60. 1784, April 6. Baptized Robert Mican, born 1 April, the Son of
+ James Mican and of Esther Mican his Wife. God Father James
Donelly, God Mother Elizabeth Russell.

pr M. Pembridge.

61. [*sic.*] 1784, 15 March. Greenhill, Wooton Basset, Baptizatus est
Gulielmus Cruse Filius Caroli et Mariae Cruse. Natus eadem die.
Patrini fuere Gulielmus Davey et Joanna Cruse.

pr. Thom Cottrell.[37]

62. 1784, June 18. Baptized Frances Ross, born 11 June, the Daughter
of William Ross and Mary Ross his wife. God Father James
Donelly.

M. Pembridge.

62. [*sic*]. 1784, July 11. Baptized Mary Baker, born 18 June, the
Daughter of William and Hannah Baker his wife, God Father Thos
Short, God Mother Mary Hughes.

pr. M. Pembridge.

63. 1784, July 19. Baptized Mary Anne Payn, born July 5, the
Daughter of Edward Payn and Mary Payn his Wife. God Father
Christopher Lieb, God Mother Sarah Hagarty.

M. Pembridge.

64. 1784, July 22. Baptized Thomas Dowding (born on the same day)
+ in danger of death — the Son of John Dowding and Martha
Dowding his Wife. Supplied the rest.

65. 1784, Oct. 29. Baptized John Ryan, born Oct. 26, the Son of
Daniel Ryan and Bridget Ryan alias Cockran his wife. God Father
Mr James Murphy, God Mother Eleanor Ryan.

pr. M. Pembridge.

66. Nov. 13, 1784. Baptized by Giles Hall, John Pearce the Son of
+ N. Pearce and N. Pearce his Wife, in danger of death, born 30 Oct.
Supplied the rest Nov 13. God Father Giles Hall and God Mother
N. Hall.

pr. M. Pembridge.

67. Nov. 14, 1784. Baptized Sarah English, born 28 Oct., the Daughter
of Edmund English and Margaret English his wife. God Father
Nicholas Dowling, God Mother Catharine Randall.

pr M. Pembridge.

No. 68. 1784, Novber. 28. Baptized Mary Anne Nonnett, born Sept. 9.
the daughter of Philip Nonnett and Elizabeth Nonnett his wife.
God Father Laurence Cagahan, God Mother Anne Jackson.

pr M. Pembridge.

No. 69. 1784, Dec. 13. Baptized Elizabeth Lucy Grace, born Nov 28, the
daughter of William Grace and Judith Grace his Wife. God Father
Thomas Brown and [*sic.*] Mary Cloreng.

pr. Mr Simpson[38].

[37] Franciscan; see Fr. Thaddeus, *The Franciscans in England* (1898) *passim.* For
the Cruse family and their house "Greenhill", Wootton Bassett, Wilts., see
C.R.S. Monograph 1, pp. 236-7.

[38] John Cuthbert Simpson O.S.B. He died in the following year; see end of
1785 mortuary list, overleaf.

70.   1785.
      1785, March 21 [erased].

Mortuary List 1785.

Jany.	10	Christopher Lieb	Aged 54	Bath, R. in P.
	15	John Waren	55	Bath, R. in P.
	24	[Anne *deleted*] Elizabeth Magennis	52	Bradford, R. in P.
	31	N. Duff, Stranger	45	Bath, R. in P.
Feb.	4	Mrs Mary Hickson,[39] suddenly	60	Bath, R. in P.
	2	Thos Gallowaye, Stranger, Do.	43	Bath, R. in P.
	19	Joseph Edwards, Found dead		Bath, R. in P.
	26	Mary Prosser	46	Bath, R. in P.
March	20	Mr James Henesey	91	Bath, R. in P.
April	7	James Keyse	20	Bath, R. in P.
April	20	Philip Short	32	Bath, R. in P.
May	5	Margaret Carpenter	34	Bath, R. in P.
July	8	John Dowding	41	Bath, R. in P.
July	22	Robert Dalton Esqr.	73	Bath, R. in P.
Oct.	7	Mr Edward Canning	34	Bath, R. in P.
Nov.	1.	John Simpson, Priest[40]		Bath, R. in P.

[*Above entry in a different hand; otherwise in Pembridge's hand until p. 25.*]

p.45   Status Animarum Sept. 1, 1784.
      Quibus Subjungitur X Confitentur apud alios.

David Nagle Esqr.		X
Mrs Harold		Robt. Dalton Esqr.
John Stonor		Mrs Dalton
Mrs Smythe		Miss Dalton
Mrs Bathoe		Miss Constantia Dalton
Mrs Plunkett		Thos. Metcalf Esqr.
Mrs Southcote		Willm. Vaughan Esqr.
Dr Niheel		Mrs Vaughan
Miss Porter	40	Walter Smythe Esqr.
Lady Mannock	10	Miss Smythe
Lady Palmer		Miss Plowden
Mrs Blake		Miss Mary Plowden
Maurice Blake Esqr.		Mrs Fitzherbert[41]
James Weldon Esqr.		Miss Teresia Fitzherbert
Miss Weldon		Mrs Throckmorton
Miss N. Weldon		Mr George Throckmorton

[39] Buried in Bath Abbey, 6 Feb., "Under Mr Meyrell's" (? Meynell's) "stone, south aisle" (*R.B.A.*, p.470).

[40] Aged 60 (Birt, p. 114); buried in Bath Abbey, 5 Nov., "By Mrs Malon's monument" (*R.B.A.*, p. 471).

[41] Not *the* Mrs Fitzherbert; she was abroad at this time; cf. Sir S. Leslie, *Mrs Fitzherbert* (1939) pp. 22-43.

Dr Stack		Mr Edward Canning	
Miss Hyde		Willm Dicconson Esqr.	
Miss Anne Hyde	50	Mrs Dicconson	
Miss Mary Hyde	20	Miss Fleming	
Mrs Martin		Miss Cath. Fleming	
Miss Procter		Mrs Stack	
Mr Robinson		Miss Stack	
Mrs Robinson		Mrs Chetwynde	
Miss Robinson		Mrs Yates	
Willm Robinson		Eliz. Davies	
Mrs Day Rob. [*sic.*]		Amelia Hellier	
Mr Day	60	Thos. Slade	
Mrs Day		Mary Jellamy	
Miss Day	30	Anne Williams	
Mr Thos. Day		Mary Merrick	
Mrs Thos. Day		Mrs Charlotte Duval	

p.46   X

	Mr English		Mr Haney		Mrs Pen
	Mrs English	100	Honora Henelly		John Haines
	Peggy Do.		Marg. [? Mary] Welch		Thos. Giles
	Betsy Do.		Mary Dean		Mr Lowndes
	Mr Ryan		Mrs Denis	140	Thos. Dawber
70	Mrs Ryan		Mary Dean [*sic*]		Mrs Amesbury
	Mr Murphy		Mr Keagan		Anne Cliff
	Mrs Murphy		Mr Lynch		Willm. Baker
	Miss Murphy		Mr Farrill		Dr Niheel's Servant
	Thos. Murphy		Andrew Fitzgerald		Mr Dicconson's butler
	Mr Dowling		Farrill Junr.		
	Mrs Dowling	110	Sam. Dillon		
	Mr Butler		Mrs Lowndes		
	Mrs Butler		Mrs Church		
	Mr Hughes		Anne Church		
80	Mrs Hughes		Henriett Church		
	Mrs Randall		Lucy Waring		
	Mary Servt		Anne Buet		
	James Dowding		Mrs Mills		
	Martha Dowding		Martha Bulbeck		
	John Dowding		Anne Wood		
	Mrs Foresayth	120	Sarah Stringfellow		
	James Donelly		Cath. Bannister		
	Donelly Mcavoy		Mary Langdale		
	Nath. Quin		Hannah Baker		
90	Mrs Knowles		Sarah Baker		
	Sally Madan		Mary Birt		
	Mr Love		Alice McDermont		
	Mrs Love		John McDermont		
	Mr Kendall		Mr Obyrne		
	Mrs Butt		Mrs Singpower		
	Mrs Pettingall	130	Mary Hawkins		
			Mrs Trayner		

Mr Smith[42]
Mrs Smith[42]

Mrs Mathews
Mrs Nadall
Mr Lieb
Louisa Lieb

p.47   1784 Status Animarum.

Mr Norris		Mr Gale		George Nash	
Mrs Norris		Ross Magennis		Mrs Burn	210
Henry Wheland		Ditto Wife	180	Mrs Smith burn[43]	
Mrs Leech		Mr Fryer		Mr Smith	
Mr Leonard	150	Mrs Hugo		Eliz. Camplin	
Mrs Leonard		Mary Hugo		Cath. Camplin	
Thos. Lewis		Ginev [?] Hugo		Mrs Thornton	
Mary Prosser		Richd. Ryan		Mary Ross	
Fanny Prosser		Michael Brian		John Ross	
Thos. Moore		John Quigley		Anne Aston	
Cath. Moore		Thos Short		Mary Aston	
Cath. Moore [sic.]		Mrs Short		Anne Branna [?]	220
Barb. Moore		John Short	190	Mary Branen [?][44]	
Eliz. Boxall		Jos. Short		John Roberts	
Willm. Wogan	160	Miss Dale		John Jakes	
John Mills		Eliz. Berwick		Anne Jakes	
Mr Hall		Richd. Maddox		John Laytham	
Mrs Hall		Ditto Wife		Ditto Wife	
Sally Hall		Marg. [? Mary] Wall		Charles Francis	
Thos. Brown		Mrs Welch		Cath. Dowdell	
Jane Robinson		Mary Darling		Helena Donelly	
Penelope Price		Willm. Darling		John Lovat	230
John Roper		Godwin Darling	200	Jerem. Lions	
Charles Purnell		Marg. Magrar		Ditto Wife	
Mr Quigley	170	Hannah Hughes		Anne Pearce	
Cath. Connor		Mr Coombs		Eliz. Peddel	
Mary Jenkins		Eliz. Cottell		Richd. Hubbenton [?]	
Thos. Jenkins		Winefride Albert		Joseph Edwards	
Mr Faneran		Anne Miles		Henry Bags	
Mrs Faneran		Flora Coombs		Thos. Clark	
Francis Curly		Mrs Gray		Mary Murphy	
Mr Amesbury				Celia Dun	240

[p.48]   1784 Status Animarum.

Mrs Deaves
John Warren   Matrimoniorum.
Cath. Potter   1784, Nov. 23, Married Mr

[42]   These two entries are each followed by a hieroglyphic resembling a capital "B" (not in Taunton transcript). The surname "Smith burn" occurs later in this list (entry no. 211) and as no. 18 in the 1785 *Status Animarum* list (*infra.*, p. 28) where no. 239 is Mr John Smithburn (*infra*, p. 31). The surname Smithbarne is found in a recusant context in Elizabethan York; see *C.R.S. Monograph* 2, pp. 212-27, *passim*. But see also note 19.

[43]   See previous note.

[44]   In the Ms. this and the preceding surname have indeterminate endings; possibly Brannan is intended (as in Taunton transcript and in other register-entries). See also note 10 & Index.

Anne Giles
Thos. Dutten
Cath. Dutton
Mr Brickman
Mrs Cosgrove
Mary Dennough
Charlotte Flyn 250
Mr Souliard
Miss Smythe's Maid
Mrs Payne
Cath. Hagarty
Mrs Carpenter
Martha Blake
Mary Baldwin
Anne Davies
Patrick Magrar
Mary Hughes 260
Mary Wade
Mr Vivier
Mr Molland
Mrs Molland
Mrs O Neal
Amy Castel

Richard Croutch[45] of Warminster,
Miss Frances Raw, Cornwall,
Witness Mr John Kendall,
pr. M. Pembridge.

1785 Status Baptizatorum.

Next two entries in Simpson's hand; thereafter in Pembridge's.

No.70. January 2d 1785. This day was baptised in this Chapel, John Baptist Joseph, born 29 Dec. 1781, son of John Baptist Denie and Ann his Wife. Sponsors Joseph Saleur and Mary Matthews. Witness Jno. Simpson O.S.B.

No.71. January 31st 1785. This Day was baptised in this Chapel, Michael, born 27th inst., Son of Michael Hoghin and Elizabeth his Wife. Godfather Richd. Ryan, Godmother Mary Ann Hugo. Witness Jno. Simpson O.S.B.

No.72. Feby 28. Baptized Francis Foresayeth, born 9 Feby., the Son of Richard Foresayeth and Margaret his Wife. God Father James Donelly, God Mother Ann Zingerbouer alias Singpower.
pr. Mich Pembridge O.S.B.

No.73. March 21. Baptized in this Chapel, Mary Nash, the Daughter of George Nash and Catharine Nash his Wife, born 9th March. God Father James Murphy, God Mother Eleanor Dooling.
pr. Mich. Pembridge — O.S.B.

1785, April 2. Baptized in this Chapel, Anna Maria Plunket Edgecumbe, born March 4, the Daughter of Captain John Edgecumbe Esqr. and Anna Maria Edgecumbe Plunket his Wife. God Father Mr Nicholas Molland, God Mother Mrs Dorothy Molland.
pr. Mich Pembridge.

---

[45] For this family see *C.R.S. Monograph 1*, p. 230 & note 347. If this was Richard Crowch, apothecary and surgeon, of Warminster, Wilts., this would appear to be his second marriage. See also death-entry, 11 Sept. 1806, *infra*, p. 127.

July 9. Baptized by Mr Simpson, George Claire, born 3d Feby., the Son of John Claire and Elizabeth his wife. God Mother Mary Parsons.

Ita testor M. Pembridge.

July 17th. Baptized by Mr Simpson, Mary Donnevan, born 12 of March, the Daughter of Cornelius Donnevan and of Mary his Wife. God Mother Mary Jenkins.

Ita testor M. Pembridge.

Augst 21. Baptized Willm. Lions, born 13 July, the Son of James Lions and Elizabeth his wife (alias Philips). God Father William Grady, God Mother Bridget Murphy.

M. Pembridge.

Status Baptizatorum [*heading and 17 entries in Digby's hand*].

1785   See below [*i.e. entry dated 16 Nov., 1785; infra, p. 27*].

Dec. 4, 1785, was baptized Ann Denvir, daughter of John and Elizabeth Denvir, born on the 4th of November 1785. Godmother Mary Ross.

Wm. Digby.

Dec. 4, 1785, was baptised Louise Laurent daughter of John Claudius and Mary Laurent, born on the 27 of November. Godfather John Claudius Hubert.

Wm. Digby.

Dec. 11, 1785, was baptised Catharine Baptist, daughter of Joseph and Catharine Baptist, born on the 22 of November 1785. Godfather Stephen Ryley, Godmother Elizabeth Raffertin.

Wm. Digby.

Dec. 14, 1785, was baptized Frances Harriette Welch, daughter of Nathanael and Mary Welsh, born on the 14 of December 1785. Godmother Mary Ross.

Wm. Digby.

Dec. 26, 1785, was baptised Stephen Jeremiah Daly, son of Denis and Mary Daly, born on the 17th of December 1785. Godfather Jeremiah Murphy, Godmother Elizabeth Murphy.

Wm. Digby.

Status Baptizatorum 1786.

Jan. 9, 1786, was baptised without solemnity, Mary West, daughter of Jacob and Anna West, born on the 10th of December 1785. The ceremonies were supplied at chapel on the 15th of January 1786. Godmother Martha Dowding.

Wm. Digby.

See below [*i.e. entry dated 7 Feb. 1786; infra., p. 27*].

March 21, 1786, was baptised without solemnity, Mary Leech, daughter of John and Mary Leech, born on the 2d of March 1786. Godfather James Feneran, Godmother Celia Feneran. Ceremonies to be supplied.

Wm. Digby.

April 2d, 1786, was baptised, Thomas Denie, Son of John and Ann

Denie, born on the 27 of March 1786. Godfather William Robinson, Godmother Mary Dean.

Wm. Digby.

The above entry is crossed-out, with the note: 1791 June 10 M.P. + [*see p. 49.*]

See below [*i.e. entry dated 6 April 1786 at foot of page.*]

May 29, 1786, was baptised James Ryley, Son of Stephen and Jane Ryley, born on the 14 of May 1786. Godfather James McCormack, Godmother Jane Perral.

Wm. Digby.

Status Baptizatorum 1786.

June 5, 1786, was baptised Sarah Maria Perry, daughter of Henry and Sarah Perry, born on the 12 of May 1786. Godfather Dominic Quintas, Godmother Bridget Heagarty.

Wm. Digby.

Aug. 21, 1786, was baptised Winefrida Dowding, daughter of James and Mary Dowding, born on the 7th of Aug. 1786. Godmother, Mary Dean.

Wm. Digby.

Aug. 28, 1786, was baptised without solemnity, William Egan, son of William and Ann Egan, born on the 28 of Aug. 1786. Ceremonies to be supplied.

Wm. Digby.

Sept. 12, 1786, were baptised without solemnity Anastasia and Bridget Ryan, daughters of Daniel and Bridget Ryan, born on the 11 of Sept. 1786. Ceremonies to be supplied.

Wm. Digby.

Status Baptizatorum 1786.

Sept. 17, 1786, was baptised Thomas English, Son of Edmund and Margaret English, born on the 14 of September 1786. Godfather, Michael Butler, Godmother Ann Amesbury.

Wm. Digby.

N.B.

On the 16 of November 1785, was baptised by Mr Garstang, Mary Lane, daughter of Timothy and Elizabeth Lane, born on the 15 of November 1785. Godmother Eleanor Donoghue.

Feb. 7, 1786, was baptised without solemnity, Thomas Fullam, Son of Thomas and Sarah Fullam, born on the 28 of January 1786. Godfather Matthew Kelly. The ceremonies were supplied on the 12 of Feb. 1786.

Wm. Digby.

April 6, 1786, was baptised Joseph Frances, Son of James Friar and Martha Frances, born out of wedlock on the 19 of March 1786. Godmother Mary Friar.

Wm. Digby.

[*Three further 1786 baptisms occur on p. 34 and one on p. 37.*]

Henceforth in Pembridge's hand, until p.34.

Status Animarum Confitentium, Paschate An. Doi. 1785. Lit. P. denotat Pembridge, S. Simpson, A. Alibi,[46] Ir. Irish, St. Stranger.

Name		Mark	Name	Mark	No.
Winefride Albert		P	Mrs Chetwynd	A	
Miss Sus. Day Senr.		P	Mrs Yates, Servt. Do.	A	Coombs
Mr Nicholas Dowling	Ir.	P	Elizabeth Davies, Do.	A	
Mrs Jane Dowling		P	Amelia Hellier, Do.	A	
Thomas Venis		S	Willm. Dicconson Esqr.	A	
N. Strange Esqr.	Ir. St.	S	Mrs Diccenson	A	
John Dowding		S			30
Mr Daniel Ryan	Ir.	P	Mr Tomlinson, Servt. Do.	A	
Lady Mannock		P	Thos. Dauober [?] Do.	A	
Mrs Mills, Servt. Do.		P	Mrs Throckmorton Senr.	A	
	10		Mr George Throckmorton	A	
Mr Thos. Day, Forscote[47]		P	Mrs Penn, Servt. Mrs Do.	A	
Mrs Burn		P	Mr John Haines, Servt. Do.	A	
Mrs Randall		P	John Giles, Servt. Do.	A	
Miss Langdale		P	Walter Smythe Esqr.	A	
Lucy Waringe		P	Miss Smythe	A	
Sarah Stringfellow		P	Mrs Fitzherbert	A	
Miss Porter		P			40
Mrs Smith burn		P	Miss Fitzherbert	A	
Teresia Price	St.	S	Miss Teresia Fitzherbert	A	
Mr Langdale	Str	S.	Mrs Duval, Servt. Mrs Do.	A	
	20		Robt. Dalton Esqr.	A	
Mrs Smythe		P	Mrs Dalton	A	
Mrs Robinson		P	Thos. Metcalf Esqr.	A	
Mary Flynn		P	Miss Dalton	A	
Mrs Butt		P			

1785

Name		Mark	Name	Mark	No.
Mr Peter Smith		P	Miss Constantia Dalton	A	
Timothy MacDermont	Ir.	P	Mrs Saltmarsh	A	
John Mills		P	Mrs Amesbury	A	
	50		Anne Cliff	A	
Anne Davies		P	Miss Plowden	A	
Mrs Norris		P			80
Dr Nihell		P	Miss Mary Plowden	A	
Jane Robinson		P	Willm. Vaughan Esqr.	A	
Monsr. Saleur		S	Thos. Slade, Servt. Do.	A	
Honora Henelly	Ir.	P	Mary Williams, Do.	A	
John Stoner Esqr.		P	Anne Jellamy, Do.	A	
			Mary Merrick, Do.	A	
Martha Robinson	children	P	Mrs Vaughan	A	
Willm. Robinson			Mr Henry Smythe	A	
Henry Robinson	Do	S	John Throckmorton Esqr.	A	

[46] Presumably persons who claimed to be penitents of some other priest than Frs. Pembridge and Simpson, e.g. the Rev. William Coombs, named in two entries and known to have acted as Mrs Chetwynd's chaplain (see *C.R.S.*, 65, p. 74).

[47] For this place-name, see note 12.

	60	
Miss Proctor		P
Miss O'Neil	Ir.	P
Michael Bryan	Ir.	P
Mrs Knowles		P
Sarah Madan		P
Thos. Brown		P
John Rosser		P
Mrs Howel	St.	P
Edward Howel	St.	P
Mrs Eliz. Hall		P
	70	
Sarah Hall		P
Richd. Abbot	Str.	S
John Menzies	St.	S
Peter Foster		S
John Orrell	St.	S

1785. Joseph Love Junr.		S
N. French Esqr.	Ir. St.	S
Willm. Jakes		S
Mrs Darell		P
Miss Darell		S
Mrs Martin		S
Mr Kendall		P
	110	
Miss Plunket	Ir.	P
Miss Woulfe	Ir.	P
Mrs Matthew	Ir.	P
Jane Porter		P
Miss Weldon	Ir.	P
[John deleted] Robert Mican	Ir.	P
Mr Gale		P
Cath. Cole		P
Mary Camplin		P
Mrs Macauliff	Ir.	P
	120	
Cath. Camplin		S
Barbara Moore		P
Francis Curly	Ir.	P
Anne Pit		P
Mary Magrar	Ir.	P
Anne Wood		P
Mrs Haines		P
Hannah Baker		P
Martha Bulbeck		P
Mr James Donelly	Ir.	P
	130	
Emma Barbara Dutton		P

Mrs Throckmorton		A
	90	
Mr Willm. Dalton		A
Miss Fitzgerald		A
Mr Edwd Canning		A
Mrs Deaves		A
Charlotte Duval		A
Mrs Stack	Ir.	A
Miss Stack	Ir.	A
Miss [Eliz. deleted] Barb. Darell		A
Henry, Mr Stonor's Servt.	Ir.	A
Mr Saltmarsh	St.	A
	100	
Anne Hagarty		A
Dr Stack	Ir.	A
Mrs Saltmarsh's Maid		A

Thomas Moore	Ir.	P
Cath. Potter		P
Thos. Dutton		P
Eliz. Cottle		P
David Nagle Esqr.	Ir.	P
Lady Palmer	Ir.	P
Ross Magennis	Ir.	P
Anne Buet		P
[Peter Foster S deleted]		
Agnes [?] Legate, Miss Smythe's Maid		S
	140	
N.N. Stranger Man St. Ir.[48]		S
James Macauliff	Ir.	S
James Weldon Esqr.	Ir.	S
Miss [Mary deleted] Jane Weldon Ir.		S
Mrs Strange	St. Ir.	S
Miss Strange	St. Ir.	S
Miss Webb	St.	S
Margt. Curwin	Ir.	S
Anne Marr	Ir.	S
Gentleman	St. Ir.	S
One Ditto		S
	150 [sic]	
4 Others		S
Mrs Southcote		S
Mrs Lowndes		S
Giles Hall		P
Mrs Ryan		P
Mrs Church		P
Mr Short		P
	160	
Eleanor Dennough	Ir.	P

[48] Heavily smudged: possibly an accidental blot, or perhaps an erasure of "Ir".

1785				Celia Dunn	Ir. P
Louisa Lieb		P		Mary Wade	Ir. P
Elizabeth Giles		P		Miss Margt. Hide	P
Mrs Moore	Ir.	P		Miss Anne Hide	P
Mary Hughes		P		Mr Mich. Butler	Ir. P
Mary Chopping		P		Thos. Waring	P
Mrs Harold	Ir.	P		Lady Mostyn	St. P
Mary Welch	Ir	P		Miss Cath. Fleming	P
Mary Birt		P		Miss Stoker	P
Mary Dory		P		Mrs Pettingal	S
	170				200
Mr Edwd. Canning		A		Catharine Moore	Ir. P
James Slade		S		Sam. Dillon	Ir. P
Anne Bannister		P		Miss Day Junr.	P
James Collins		P		Sarah Cox	S
Joseph Gatti, Ital. Str.	Mr Smyth[49]			John Crook	Ir. S
John Bap. Mezeno	Do.			Thos. Hindes	Ir. S
Joseph Brena	Do.			Rebeca Kelly	Ir. S
Francis Bretti				Mr Robinson	P
Ant. Mandali, Ital.	Mr Smyth[49]			Penelope Price	P
Francis Lettino [?]				Mrs Walsh	Ir. P
	180				210
Mrs Short		S		Martha Dowden	P
Miss Fitzgerald		A		Miss Mathews	P
[Mr Michael Blount, St. S deleted]				Alice Macdermick	Ir. P
Mr Menzies	St.	S		Mrs Throckmorton's Junr. Maid	A
Sarah Hicky	Ir.	S		Mary Cloring	Ir. S
Anne Hill		S		Mrs Colgrove	Ir. P
2 Women Servts.	Ir.	S		Mary Murphy	Ir. P
Joseph Nagle	St. Ir.	P		Mary Baldwin	P
Mrs Nagle	St. Ir.	P			
Mary Jenkins		P			
	190				

1785. Frances Prosser		P		Maurice Blake Esqr.	Ir. S
Mrs Helen Thornton		P		Sr. Walter Vavasour	St. S
	220			Catharine Dowdell	P
Mrs Butler, Ir. Bennet Street		P		Rachel Baker	P
Elizabeth Boxall		P		Willm. Baker	Smyth[49]
N. Mitchell Esqr.	St.	S		Willm. Hopkins	S
Mr Michael Haney	Ir.	P			250
Thos. Clark		P		Mr George Amesbury	P
Mrs Denie		P		N.N. Woman	St. S
Margt. Wall	Ir.	S		2 Others	S
Mr Lowndes		S		Here ended the Term.	
Anne [Emmaneul deleted] Samuel		S			
Mrs Mary Robinson[50]		S		Extras:	
	230			Mr Edmund English	Ir. [P deleted]

[49] Perhaps the secular priest John Smith (or Smyth), mentioned in *C.R.S.*, 56, p. 172, note 4; *C.R.S.*, 65, p. 65.

[50] The name "Mary" is written heavily over what looks like "Danby" and "Robinson" is written in place of "Maid".

Richd. Ryan	Ir.	S	Mrs English		P
Michael Smith	Ir.	S	Mr Molland		
Mr Love		P	Mrs Molland		
Mrs Love		P	Mrs Neal	Ir.	
Mary Dean Senr.		P	Miss Dale		
Andrew Fitzgerald	Ir.	P		260	
Mary Hugo		P	Miss Fleming		A
Helen Hugo		P	Anne Aston Junr.		P
Mr John Smithburn		P	Mary Aston		
Mrs Traynor	Ir.	P	Bridget Brannan		
	240		Richd. Hubberston[?]		
Anne Miles		P	Nathanl. Quin	Ir.	P
James Dowden		P	Mr Day, Ingsbatch, Sick		P
Charles Purnell		P	Mrs Day		P
Anne Ross		P	Martha Blake Sick		P
			Mr Murphy	Ir.	
				270	
			Mrs Murphy		P
Cath. Murphy			Mary Grays		
Henry Wheland	Ir.		Mr Hughes	Ir.	
Mary Parsons			Mrs Hughes		
Hannah Hughes	Ir.	P	Mr Lynch	Ir.	
Mary Hawkings		P	Mary Daniel		
Mrs Payne			Jeremiah Lyons		
Sarah [?] Hagarty[51]			Ditto Wife		
Mrs Carpenter		P	Thos. Prosser		
Mrs Foresayeth	Ir.		Richd. Maddox	Ir.	
	280		Ditto Wife		
Mr Keagan				310	
Baron Newman			Frances Carlis		
Thos. Gregory	Ir.		Ditto Daughter		
Emy [?] Castle		P	Mrs Nadall		
Willm. Norris		P	Mr Keasberry		
Patric Durie			Ditto 2 Daughters		
Michael Brannan			Mr Malachy Obyrne	Ir.	
James Farrill Senr.	Ir.		Thos. Perry	Ir.	
Ditto Son			Eliz. Peddell		
	290 [sic]		Mrs Brown		
James Faneran	Ir.			320	
Ditto Wife			Richd. Dean		
Mrs Edgecumb Plunket	Ir.		John Hagler		
Thos. Murphy			Ditto Daughter		
John Quigley			Henry Baggs		
Elizabeth Jakes		P	Mr Leonard		
Robt. Laytham			Mrs Leonard		
Ditto Wife			Mr George Nash		
John Fryer			Ditto Wife		
Mrs Hugo			Thos. Lovat		
	300		Ditto Wife	330	

[51] The Christian name is written over another, now indecipherable.

1785. Willm. Wogan	Ir.
Cath. Connor	Ir.
Cath. Coffee	Ir.
Willm. Darling	Not Com.[52]
Godwin Darling	Not Com.
Thos. Jenkins	Not Com.
Monsr. Vivier	
Mich. Micmurtery	
Ditto Wife	
John Connor	Ir.
	340
Connor and Wife	St. Ir.
Eliz. Berwick	Not Com.
Anne Church	Not Com.
Henrietta Church	Not Com.
Mr Brickman	
Anne Pearce	
Charles Francis	P
John Roberts	
Thos. Lewis	Ir.
	350
Mrs Singpower	Ir. S
Anne Donelly	Ir.
Mary Twigg	Ir.
Mary Harland	Ir.
John Franaran	Ir.
John Casey	Ir.
Jos. Jackson	Ir.
George Jackson[53]	Ir.

Muffin Man	Ir.
Bartholomew Coffill	Ir.
	360
Diana James	St.
Mrs Bathoe	
Ditto Maid Hopperkin	
Mrs Havering	Ir.
Mrs Colhoon	
Ditto Sister	
Dr Stack's Man	
Frances Keyse	
[James Lennoll *deleted*]	
James Church	
Mr Jolli	
	370
Elizabeth Green	Ir.
Mrs Leech	Ir.
Mrs Brian	Ir.
Mary Dean Junr., Sick	P
Monsr. Denie	
Mrs Jackson	Ir.
Mr Macpherson	
Richd. Keen	Ir.
Perreali, Italian Man	
German Clock-Man	
	380
Mrs Blake	Ir. S
Anne Richardson	
[Catharine Cosgrove Ir. P *deleted*]	

Mrs Day, Forscote	Mr Coombs
Mr Coombs Senr.[54]	
Mr Hart	
Mrs Hart	
Cath. Yates	
Cath. Campbell	Ir. S
Jedoull, French Man	
Philip Short	S
	390
Cath. Hickson, Child	Ir. P
Juliana Holland	Ir.
John Maguire	Ir.
John Ryan	Ir.

Children 1785	Age
Martha Robinson	13
Willm. Robinson	
Anne Church, 1 Com. Augst 21	14
Henrietta Church	12
Elizabeth Barrick	
Teresia Haines	12

[*The next two names appear to be part of
the adults'* Status Animarum *list.*

Frances Prosser	P
Mary Mican	P

---

[52] ? Abbreviation of "Communion".

[53] Christian name written over another, now indecipherable.

[54] Perhaps the father of the Rev. William Coombs: "the blacksmith, tooth-drawer, inoculator, beer-seller and Catholic priest-maker" who went by the name of "Doctor" Coombes, of whom there is an account in J. Skinner, *Journal of a Somerset Rector, 1803-34* (ed. H. & P. Coombs, Bath, 1971) pp. 281-2.

				£ s d
Bridget Ryan	Ir.		Collections made at the Chapel for the	
Eleanor Dooling	Ir.		Poor of the Congregation:-	
Michael Hoghin	Ir.			
Elizabeth Hoghin	Ir.	1781	May 16	16 3 6¾
Willm. Grace	Ir.	1782	Jan. 6	30 1 0
Judith Grace	Ir.	1782	May 5	14 2 3
	400	1783	Jan. 5	26 11 5
Philip Nennett		1783	May 17	19 3 2¼
Lawrence Cahagan	Ir.	1783	Dec. 22	19 19 10
John Denvir	Ir.	1784	May 2	14 7 6½
Elizabeth Denvir	Ir.	1784	Dec. 25	21 2 1
John Billington	Ir.	1785	May 22	13 13 3½
Mr Coppinger	St. S		Bell-tree Chapel pr. M.P.	

Confirmatorum.

In Capella Bathoniae, Bell Tree House, ab Illustrissimo D. Carolo Walmesley, Ramatensi, Die 20 Maii 1785:-

Virorum et Puerorum.
Antonius Gale[55]
Thomas Dutton
Georgius Ainsbury
Joannes Mills
John Orrell
Peter Foster
Puerorum.
Willm.Robinson: Andrew, 1 Com.
Henry Robinson: Luke
John Short
Joseph Short
Edward Wogan
William Darling
Joseph Dowding
John Dowding
Robert Jenkins

Feminarum et Puellarum.
Mary Proctor
Margaret English : Mary Magdalen[56]
Jane Robinson : Mary Magd.
Barbara Dutton : Mary Magd.
Mary Darling
Martha Dowding
Elizabeth Green
Catharine Moore
Barbara Moore : Lucy, 1 Com.
Puellarum.
Mary Hugo
Helen Genevieve Hugo
Catharine Camplin : Mary
Sarah Hall : Mary
Martha Robinson : Mary, 1 Com.
Elizabeth Barrick : Catharine
Anne Church : Teresia
Henrietta Church : Elizabeth
Margaret English : Anne
Teresia Hains : Mary
Mary Anne Donelly
Mary Anne Moore
Anne Ross   Lucy Dowding
Elizabeth Ross
Feminarum.
Anne Pit
Catharine Potter

[55] In October 1791 Anthony Gale, clothworker, of Bradford-on-Avon, Wilts., made his mark with a cross when taking the oath laid down by the Catholic Relief Act of that year (*C.R.S. Monograph 1*, p. 249).
[56] Confirmation-names.

1785 Marriages

Oct. 3, 1785. John Mansfield Esqr. and Miss Elizabeth Woulfe were married at this Chapel. Witness N. Woulfe Esqr., Father to the Lady, N. White Esqr. and Mrs Mathew, Aunt to the Lady.

M. Pembridge.

Next three entries in Digby's hand.
Feb. 27, 1786. Lawrence Coombes and Sarah Coombes received the sacrament of marriage in this chapel. Witnesses George Harney and Joseph Love.

Wm. Digby.

1786 Deaths[57].

Mrs Harold	Mary Welsh
Mary Hawkins	James Friar
Mary N.	J. Billington
Henry Bags	
John Stonor	
Constantia Dalton	

1786 Status Baptizatorum.

Oct. 4, 1786, was baptised James Guy, Son of Samuel and Mary Guy, born on the 29 of April 1786.

Wm. Digby.

The next two entries, in Wilks's hand, have a diagonal line through them.
Baptized, November 2d 1786, Mary Anne Foresight [*"aythe" written above the last 4 letters*], daughter of Richard and Margaret Foresight. Godfather James Donnelly and Godmother Mary Donnelly.

Joseph Wilks.

Baptized November 3d 1786, Margaret Tainty, daughter of James and Mary Tainty. Godfather Patrick Hickey and Godmother Catharine Foresight.

Joseph Wilks.

The following, in Pembridge's hand, is presumably a list of his penitents; Fr. Heatley's (apparently) are listed separately, on pp. 36-7.
1792, Confitentium – Paschali Tempore.

P			
	Mrs Hussey	Ir.	St James's Square
	Mrs Butler	Ir.	Bennet Street No. 20
	Miss Butler	Ir.	Ditto
	Miss Cavenagh	Ir.	Ditto
	Mrs Connor, Maid	Ir.	Ditto
	Placid Duquen, Fr. Footman		Ditto

[57] The approximate dates of three of these deaths can be ascertained from the following burial-entries in *R.B.A.*, p. 471: Mrs Harold, 2 Jan. 1786; John Stonor, 26 April, "By Mr. William Smith's stone"; "Miss Constantia Dalton. Under Mrs Maloon's monument", 19 May.

	Monsr. Le Maire, Fr. Dentist ⎫ Ditto 2 Sons ⎭		left Bath	
10	Mrs Susan Day ⎫ Mr Day Surgeon ⎭		Westgate Buildings	
	Miss Day		Inglisbatch	
	Mrs Duval		St John's Court	
	Mr Allen	Ir.	School Master	Stall Street
	Mary English ⎫ Elizabeth English ⎭		Ap. 20 1st Communion	Broad Street
	Mrs O'Drisgal	Ir. Lady	Mrs French's Family	
	Mr Rian	Taylor[58] Ir.	Broad Street	
	Catharine		Mr Crowtch's Maid	
20	Mr Mich. Butler	Ir.	Lodgings, Bennet Street	
	Anne Austen Junr		Avon Street	
	Mr Norris	⎫		
	Mrs Norris	⎬	James's Street	
	Catharine Norris	⎭	1st Communion, April 13	
1792.	Martha Fangre	Ir.	Mrs Blake's Maid	
	Mary Anne Connor		Hon. Petre's Maid	left Bath
	Mich. Brien	Ir.	Taylor[58] Stall Street	
	John O'Brien	Ir.	Carpenter Corn Street	
	Lucy Waring			
30	Mrs Delasson		St Andrew's Parade	
	Mrs Hussey	Ir.	Baron Ditto's Lady	left Bath
	Marg. Reynolds		Murford Street	
	N. Macarty	Ir.	Taylor[58]	
	Clement		Spaniard Passenger	
	N. Bourk	Ir.		
	Miss Talbot		Westgate Buildings	
	John Orrell		New Vauxhall	
	John Doyer	Ir.	Sick man Viner's Court	
	Mrs Matthews		Russell Street[59]	
40	Mr Giles Hall		Margaret Hill[59]	
	Matthew Micmerty		Murford Street	
	Winefride Albert		Maid Servt Circus No.17	
	Celia Dunn	Ir.	Chandos Passage	
	Mrs Anne Kensy	Ir.	Ir. Stranger Pierpoint Street	
	Michael Mackay	Ir.	Taylor[58] under Mr Denie	
	Miss French	Ir.	No.9 Oxford Row	
	Mrs Short		Corn Street Chapel	
	Mary Coffee		Bell Tree Lane	
1792.	N. Kennedy	Ir.	Mr Butler's No.20 Bennt.[60]	
+	Edward [blank] Irish travelling Packman May 4			
50	Mrs [blank] Ir. at Mr Tobin's, No.7 St Ja. Parade			
	Mrs Canning Ap.5 Church Street, Crescent, No.4			
	Mich. Brian 6 Ir., Stall Street			
	Mrs French's Maid Ir., No.9 Oxford Row Penny Tuell[61]			

---

[58] i.e. tailor.

[59] Street-name: Margaret's Hill

[60] i.e. Bennet St. See second entry in this list.

[61] Presumably the maid's name; see five lines lower (overleaf).

Mary Ellis-Brown   Scotch Passenger
Mr Lowndes
Mr Walsh's Man-Servant   No.9 Marlborough Buildings
May 12 Simon Hensy   Crooked Row
May 16 Penny Tewell
Miss Talbot [and Maid *deleted*]

The above list ends halfway down a page, the remainder of which is blank; the following entries only are written on the reverse side. It is not clear whether they are part of the 1792 list.

N. Walsh Esqr.
2 Daughters
N. Howard Esqr.
3 or 4 Servants
Mr and Mrs Coroutch[62]
David Nagle Esqr.
2 Servants
Mr and Mrs Hughes
Mrs Randall [*heavily smudged*]

Marriages [*heading and entry in Digby's hand*] .

Oct. 5, 1786, were married Henry Poole and Mary Robinson. Witnesses Peter Smith and Augusta Towls.

The following list, apparently including Dom Hugh Heatley's penitents, and concluding with a note of his death, is in Pembridge's hand.

Confitentium Paschali Tempore 1792. D Heatley.

Miss Carney – Stranger		Henry Williams	
Mary Ashton		Miss Keasberry	
Mr and Mrs Dowling		Miss Cath. Fleming	
Mrs Martha Smith		Thos. Short	
Mr Brian		Mrs French	
Mrs Butt		Miss N. French	
Mr Peter Smith		Richd. Hubberston [?]	
Miss N. Walsh		Miss More	
10 Miss Talbot and Maid		N. Hawkins – Maid	30
Mrs Randall		Mrs Burn	
Willm. Hansey		Mr Delasson	
Mary Blackwell		Mr Gale	
Mrs Clark		Mr Moore	
Mrs Canning		Mary Burt	
Mr Day Senr.		Miss N. French	
Mrs FitzWilliams		Miss Mary Kirk	
Miss Plunkett		Mrs Martin	
Mrs Gartside	20	Anne Hughes	Belltree
2 Misses Weldon		Miss Walsh	40
		Mary Madden	
		Miss Macharty	

[62]   ? Crowch; see note 45.

Barbara Meaher [?]
Mrs Malachy O'Byrn
Mrs Lowndes
Miss Antoinette Vandegarde
Anne Church
> Ditto Daughter
> > *[end of page; continued below]*

1792.	Miss La Porte
D⁰ Heatley	John Strawbridge
Mrs Blake	50
Anne Pitt	
Eliz. Pitt	
Mrs Walsh	
Mrs Hynes	
Thos. Dutton	
Mrs Bassett	
Anne Hyde	57

Aprilis Die 9 Consummavit Opus Missionis D.H. aet 33 — et Die 28 Vitam finivit obiitq in Dno. R. in P.[63]

In Wilks's hand:

Register

beginning Oct. 3, 1786, when I came to n.13 on S. James' Parade, Bath.

Joseph Wilks.

In Pembridge's hand:

Obituary 1792.

June 4 Joanna Moore Age 14

In Wilks's hand:

1786 Baptized.

November 26. Baptized Charles James Jadoul, Son of James and Bridgett Jadoul. Godfather Charles Troubelle and Godmother Mary Maggee

Joseph Wilks

1787.

January 24. Baptized Mary Frances Trussell, daughter of Charles and Marianne Trussell. Godfather James Jadoul and Godmother Bridget Jadoul for Mary Frances Voertz.

Joseph Wilks.

January 25. Baptized privately without ceremonies — O'Hara and died before they were supplied.

Joseph Wilks.

January 27. Baptized Mary Daniel, daughter of John and Mary Daniel. Godfather Thomas Moore and Godmother Catharine Moore.

Dead [*underlined*] .

Jerome Heatley.

---

[63] For entry of Fr. Heatley's death and burial, see *infra*, p. 120; also p. 52.

1787

February 17. Baptized James Moylan, Son of Simon and Julia Moylan. Godfather Timothy Macdermot and Godmother Mary MacDonnell.

Joseph Wilks.

Next entry in a different hand, presumably Smyth's:
March 9th 1787. Baptized John Pierce Walsh Porter, son of Pierce and [*blank*] Walsh Porter. Godfather Pierce Walsh, Godmother Mary Porter.

John Smyth.[64]

Next four entries in Wilks's hand, except that the words italicised in the second entry were inserted by Heatley:

Baptized

Patrick Hickey
Godfather Edward Holland and Godmother Mary Tanty.

Jerome Heatley.

Baptized at Ingsbatch *John Miles, Son* of *Charles* and *Ann Miles. Born April 1st 1787.* Godfather *James* Ruddock and Godmother Martha Blake.

Jerome Heatley.

April 19. Baptized Mary Diana[65] and James, Negroes adult in the service of Mistress and Governor Levett.

Joseph Wilks.

May 4. Two children baptized by Jerome Heatley, and both died: one at Dunkerton mills; the other at Maidgate.[66]

June 26. Baptized Elizabeth Bligh, daughter of Patrick and – Bligh, Godfather – Donnelly and Godmother Mary Donnelly.

Joseph Wilks.

Next two entries in Heatley's hand (repeated on p. 93):
1787.
May 4. Baptized Anna Monica Coombes, Daughter of Lawrence and Sarah Coombes. God Father Joseph Love, God Mother Lucy Coombes.

by Hugh Heatley.

May 4. Baptized John George Perry, Son of John and Jane Perry. God Father George Harvey, God Mother Eliz. Gill.

by Hugh Heatley.

In Wilks's hand:
1786.   Marriages
October 15. Were married Thomas Hornyhole[67] Esq. and Teresa Fitzherbert; witnesses [*blank*] Fitzherbert and Lucy Fitzherbert.

Joseph Wilks.

[64] See note 49.

[65] There is no comma between these names; it is not clear whether they represent one person or two.

[66] Meadgate in the parish of Camerton. See Heatley's two May 4th entries.

[67] Hornyhold or Hornyold.

1786
January 27. Were married John Menzies and Mary Yates.
                                        Joseph Wilks.
1788, April. Were married Patrick Bligh and Jane Jacobs.
                                        Joseph Wilks.
May 3. Were married William Clarke and Mary Goodson.
                                        Joseph Wilks.
May 26. Were Married Thomas Bawden and Martha Dowden.
                                        Joseph Wilks.

November 1786. [*Mortuary list by Wilks and Heatley.*]
Died Nov. 1, George Jackson, aged about 30.
Nov. 4, Ann Knowles, aged 86
Nov. 24, Philip Lynch
1787.

February	7,	Mary Wade, aged 65.
	10,	Frances Clarke, aged 28.
March.		Mark Louis, aged 54.
		Samuel Hubard, aged 25.
		Hannah Hughes, aged about 70.
April	9,	[*blank*] Amesbury, aged 48.
	19,	[*blank*] O'Hara, aged about 28.
May		Elizabeth Murphy
		Oliver Martin[68]
		– Macdowel
		Mary Proctor
September 3d,		Robert Jakes, aged 33.
1787, Oct. 5.		Died Mary Daniel
Oct.	9,	– O'Neal[69]
Oct.	24,	Richard William Stack M.D.
–		James Fanneran
Nov.	5,	Edward Quin, aged 103.
Dec.	15,	William Latham, aged 42.
Dec.	19,	Martha Reynolds
		Thomas Waving[70]
Dec.	24,	Catharine Stuart
1788.		
Jan.	1,	Alicia Southcote, aged 68.[71]
	14,	Walter Smythe, aged 63.[72]
	28,	Marguerite Wall, aged 53.
March 5,		Mary Bowden

[68] He probably died in June; he was buried in Bath Abbey on the 11th of that month "Under Mr Meynell's stone" (*R.B.A.*, p. 472).

[69] "Mary Oneill" buried in Bath Abbey, 13 Oct. (*ibid.*)

[70] Buried in Bath Abbey, 21 Dec., "Under Mr Berrisford's stone" (*R.B.A.*, p. 473).

[71] "Mrs Alicia Southcoates. Under Mr Kelley's monument" (*ibid.*, 7 Jan 1788).

[72] Buried in Bath Abbey, 20 Jan., "Own stone" (*ibid.*).

May 11,   James Clement Ratclyffe,[73] aged 61.
              Alicia McDermot   Sept. 20, Lucy Sims
Aug.   6,   Jane Hugo, aged [blank]   25, John Fitzpatrick
                                                 Oct.   — Shaw
                                                 Nov. 30, Mary Moore

In Heatley's hand:
1787.
July 23d 1787. Baptized Thomas Holland, son of Edward and Jane Holland. Godfather Patrick Hickey, Godmother Catharine Foreseyth.
                                                         Hugh Heatley.

Two entries in Wilks's hand:
August 12. Baptized Mary Denie, Daughter of John and Ann Denie. Godfather [blank] Butler, Godmother Mary Deane.
                                                         Joseph Wilks.
September 9. Supplied the ceremonies of baptism to Ann White, Daughter of Joseph and Emma [Elizabeth *deleted*] Barbara White, baptized in appearance of danger some days before. God Father John Short and God Mother Mary Norris.
                                                         Joseph Wilks.

1787 [*date and entry by ex-Jesuit Fr. Thomas More*].
Sepr. 16th, 1787. Baptised Richard Fitzgerald, the Son of Sir James and his Wife Lady Fitzgerald. God Father Thos. More and God Mother Mrs. Dalton, Mother of the said Lady Fitzgerald.
                                                         Thos. More.

In Heatley's hand:
Octob. 3d. Baptized Elizabeth Cicely Perry, daughter of Thomas and Sarah Perry. Godfather Dominic Quintas and Godmother Mary Payne.
                                                         Hugh Heatley.
Oct. Baptized [blank] Roy [*in Wilks's hand; subsequent entries in his or Heatley's hand, as signed*].
Nov. 7. Baptized Ann, Daughter of James and Marguerite Sullivan, Godfather John Shanley and Godmother Mary Murphy.
                                                         Joseph Wilks.
Dec. 22. Baptized Dorothy William George, daughter of [*father's names omitted*] and Elizabeth George. Godfather William Mawhood[74] and Godmother [blank].
                                                         Joseph Wilks.
Dec. 30. Baptized William Bligh, Son of Michael and Marguerite Bligh. Godfather Patrick Dugan and Godmother Mary Fransel.
                                                         Joseph Wilks.
1788.
Feb. 3. Baptized William Macpherson, Son of William and Ann

---

[73] "Honble James Clement Radclyffe. Under Leonard Thompson's stone" (*ibid.*, 16 May).

[74] The diarist; he was not present at this baptism of his granddaughter but was in London at the time. The father's Christian name, as well as his surname, was George; the mother was Mawhood's daughter Elizabeth ("Betsey"). The couple lived at Frome. See *C.R.S.*, 50 (*The Mawhood Diary*, ed. E. E. Reynolds) *passim.*

Macpherson. Godfather Joseph Saleur and Godmother Sarah Randal.

Joseph Wilks.

1788.

Feb. 3. Baptized Jemina Catharine Dowden, Daughter of Thomas and Mary Dowden. Godfather Thomas Nevill and Godmother Marguerite Donnellan.

Joseph Wilks.

March 9. Baptized Robert Denver, Son of John and Mary Denver. Godfather James Dowden, Godmother Celia Feneran.

Hugh Heatley.

1788.

March 30. Baptized Matilda Nonnet, Daughter of Philip and Elizabeth Nonnet. Godfather James Jadoul and Godmother Brigit Jadoul.

Joseph Wilks.

March 23. Baptized Joseph Orrell, Son of John and Mary Orrell. Godfather John Swarbrick, Godmother Ann Orrell — Mary Hughes proxy for Ann Orrell.

Hugh Heatley.

April 7. Baptized John Edward Slevin, Son of John and Elizabeth Slevin. Godfather Thomas Moore for Daniel Slevin.

Hugh Heatley.

1788.

April 16. Baptized Elizabeth Frier, Daughter of James and Martha Frier. Godfather John Short for John Frier, Godmother Ann Mary Frier.

Hugh Heatley.

April 20. Baptized James English, Son of Edmund and Mary English. Godfather John Kendal and Godmother Cath. Butts.

Joseph Wilks.

Baptized May 1 [blank] Robins, Daughter of [blank] Robins. Godfather Edward Wogan and Godmother Frances Forsar.

Joseph Wilks.

X 12 May. Baptized Walter Mansfield, Son of John and Elizabeth Mansfield. Godfathers David Nagle and Edward Power, Godmother Mrs Matthews.

Joseph Wilks.

X May 4. Baptized [blank] Perry [blank] of John and Jane Perry. Godfather Matthew Gill and Godmother Elizabeth Gill.

Joseph Wilks.

1788.

June 28. Baptized Ann Esther Miles, Daughter of Wm. and Susanna Miles. Godfather Michael MacArthey.

Hugh Heatley.

Same day. Baptized John Carr, Son of Michael and Sarah Carr. Godfather John Cameron, Godmother Elizabeth Cameron.

Hugh Heatley.

July 12. Baptized Mary Ann Jadoul, Daughter of James and Brigit Jadoul. Godfather Martin Stalraff, Godmother Mary Payne.

Hugh Heatley.

Next entry (apart from date and first word) in Ainsworth's hand:
July 27. Baptized William O'Brien, Son of Andrew and Esther O'Brien, born the 12 of July. Sponsors William Matthews and Catherine Reiley.

Joseph Wilks.

July 30. Baptized [*blank*] Foresaythe [*in Wilks's hand; subsequent entries in his and Heatley's hands, as signed*].
1788.
Aug. 13. Baptized Ann West, Daughter of Jacob and Rachel West. Godfather Jacob West junior.

Hugh Heatley.

Aug. 17. Baptized Barbarina Jane Denie, Daughter of John Baptist Denie and Ann Denie, his wife. Godfather James Smith and Godmother Jane Elston.

Joseph Wilks.

1788.
Dec. 13. Baptized at Dunkerton-mill, Mary Lucy Coombes, Daughter of Lawrence and Sarah Coombes. Godfather Joseph Love and Godmother Lucy Coombes.

Hugh Heatley.

Dec. 20. Baptized James Hickey, son of Patrick and Elizabeth Hickey. Godfather Michael O'Brian and Godmother Hannah Hickey.

Hugh Heatley.

1789
Feby. 8. Baptized without solemnity, Harriott Heffermam, Daughter of [*blank*] and [*blank*] Heffermam. She died before ceremonies were supplied.

Hugh Heatley.

Feby. 17. Baptized Elizabeth Guy, Daughter of Samuel and Mary Guy. Godfather Jacob West.

Hugh Heatley.

1789.
April 14. Baptized Hellen Magragh, Daughter of James and Allice Magragh, born the 25th March. Godfather Wm. Hopkins.

Hugh Heatley.

April 23. Baptized James Carrell, Son of John and Ann Carrell, born April 9. Godfather William Donoghue, Godmother Allice Hikey.

Hugh Heatley.

1789 [*the next three entries are in Wilks's hand.*]
June 22. Baptized Martha Miles, Daughter of Charles and Ann Miles. Godfather James Ruddock and Godmother Martha Blake.

Baptized Barbara Sullivan, Daughter of Philip and Eleonora Sullivan. Godfather William Demizong,[75] Godmother Barbara Summerfield.

Hazard twins.

---

[75] For this name, in connection with two marriages in Bath Abbey, see *R.B.A.*, pp. 312, 313: marriage of William Dermizong, 31 Aug. 1788; W. Dennizong witness to a marriage, 10 Feb. 1789.

Following the above entry, the transcript in the Somerset County Record Office continues: "(on a loose slip of paper) Winefrid Denie born October 9th 1789 on Friday. Christened the Sunday following October 11 by Mr Wilks, Godfather James Murphy, Godmother Mary Matthews." This slip of paper is now missing but the baptism was, in any case, entered in the register; see foot of page.

1788 Deaths. [*List and 5 Baptisms in Heatley's hand.*]
Dec. 22 Died Susanna Miles.
1789, Sept. 11 Died Mary Tanty
    Sept. 12 Mary Lenhard, aged 58.
    Sept. 14 Thos. Rice of London, Aged 49
    Sept. 16 John Kendal, Grocer.
    Novr. 25 Ann Ryan
          Lady Mannock.[76]
1790, Jany. 31 Wm. Fitz-Patrick, a Stranger

1789.
July 24. Baptised Catharine Magrath, Daughter of Edward and Catharine Magrath. Godfather Peter McMurtry and Godmother Catharine Collingridge.

                                          Hugh Heatley.
1789.
August 3d was born, and on the 4th of the same month was Baptized Ann Coughlin, Daughter of Michael and his wife Margaret Coughlin. Godfather Jacob West and Godmother Mary Burt.

                                 by me Hugh Heatley O.S.B.
June the 19 was born, and September 10 was Baptized Mary Ann Holland, Daughter of Edward and his wife Jane Holland. Godfather John Kelly and Godmother Ann Carroll.

                                 by me Hugh Heatley O.S.B.
1789
September 17th was born, and on the 20th of the same month was baptized Thomas Connell, Son of Philip and Margaret Connell. Godfather Michael O'Brian and Godmother Eleanor Dunovan.

                                 by me Hugh Heatley O.S.B.
September [*blank*] was born, and on the 25 of the same month was Baptized privately in appearance of danger Mary White, Daughter of Joseph and Emma Barbara White. Godmother Catharine Collingridge. Ceremonies were supplied on the 27th of the same month.

                                 by me Hugh Heatley O.S.B.
The next entry (see top of page) is in Ainsworth's hand.
October 11th 1789 was baptized Winefrid Denie born the 9th of the same month, Daughter of John Baptist Denie and Anne Denie his lawful

[76] Elizabeth Mary (*née* Stonor), wife of Sir Francis Mannock, died October 1789, aged 75, at Gay Street, Bath; buried at Winchester (*C.R.S.*, 12, p. 34; *C.R.S.*, 42, p. 166).

wife. Godfather James Murphy, Godmother Mary Matthews.

Joseph Wilks.

1790 [*Date and next eight entries in Heatley's hand.*]
Decr. 11, 1789 was born, and Jany. 1, 1790 was Baptized John Collins, Son of James and Elizabeth Collins. Godfather John Thomase and Godmother Mary Thomase.

by me Hugh Heatley

Jany. 20 was born, and on the 25 of the same month was baptized without Solemnity Catharine Sullivan, Daughter of Timothy and Margaret Sullivan. She died before the Ceremonies were supplied.

by me Hugh Heatley.

Jany. 11th was born, and Feby. 3d was Baptized John Morris, Son of John Morris, a Protestant, and Mary Morris. Godmother Mary More.

by me Hugh Heatley.

Feby. 8th 1790 was born, and on the same day was baptized Stephen Tempest, Son of Stephen Tempest Esqr. and Elizabeth Tempest. God-father Henry Blundel Esqr. by proxy of Thomas Hornyhole Esqr. and Godmother Mrs Frances Olivia Tempest by proxy of Miss Frances Plowden.

by me Hugh Heatley.

Feby. 20th was born, and on the 23d of the same month was Bap-tized Elizabeth West, Daughter of Jacob and Rachel West. Godfather John Mac'Arthey and Godmother Ann Hopkins.

by me Hugh Heatley.

1790
March 27 was born, and March 28 was Baptized Simon Moylan, Son of Simon and Julia Moylan. Godfather Thomas Hogan and Godmother Elizabeth Moore.

by me Hugh Heatley.

April 24 was born, and May 1st was baptized Margaret Gawley, Daughter of Hannah Gawley. Godfather John Thomase and Godmother Mary Thomase.

by me Hugh Heatley.

1790
May 8th was born, and May 23d was Baptized James Corf, Son of James and Elizabeth Corf. Godfather Ross MacGinnis and Godmother [*blank*].

by me Hugh Heatley.

Wilks's hand:
June 20, 1790. Baptized by me, James, Son of Patrick and Mary Bisset. Godfather John Wall and Godmother Mary Murphy.

Joseph Wilks.

Heatley's hand:
June 30th 1790, died Eliz. Corlays, aged 58 years.
October 30th 1790, died Mary Dowding, aged 39 years.
November 18th 1790, died George Hughes.
November 22nd 1790, died Henry Wheland.
April 14th 1791, died Mary Coffe, aged 38 yrs.

July 4th 1790. Baptized James Flannegan, born June 21,1790, Son of John and Mary Flannegan. Godfather Bartholomew Hays and God-mother [*blank*] MacArthey.

by me Hugh Heatley.

July 20th 1790. Baptized privately Lewis Philip Nonnet, in danger, born July 19. Son of Philip and Elizabeth Nonnet. Godfather Charles Grilliett.

by me Hugh Heatley.

1790.

August 26th. Baptized Mary Heffermam, Daughter of [*blank*] and [*blank*] Heffermam, born Aug. 21. 1790. Godfather Michael Mekan and Godmother [*blank*] Ross.

by me Hugh Heatley.

In Birdsall's hand:

1806.

1806, Augt. 23rd. Was received at Bath a letter from Mr Thos. H. F. Whitgreave dated Moseley, Augt. 21st, 1806, including the baptismal, Register of those who were baptized at the Catholic Chapel at Horton in the House of the late Clement Paston Esqr. as follows:

Baptized Anno Dni	By whom	God Fathers and God Mothers
April 20th 1772 Joseph Clem. Scates	J. Waters[77] O.S.B.	Cl. Paston Esqr. Mrs Paston.
1774 March 22d James Gordon	J. Smyth E.R.S.	Cl.Paston Esqr. Mrs Paston
1775 Decr. 27th Thos. Gordon	P. Westby[78] E.R.S.	{ James Walmesley Mary Smallwood
1776 November 6th John Scates	J. Smyth	{ James Walmsley Mary Smallwood
1774 Augt. 10th Ann Scates	J. Jenison[79]	{ James Walmesley Mary Smallwood
1774 Augt. 10th Francis Wimbow	J. Jenison	{ Charles Boyanl [*sic.*] Mary Smallwood
1776. June 24th Catharine Whimbow	P. Westby	{ James Walmesley Constantia Brockshaw.
1777. Novr. 7th Mary Vaughan	D.Young[80] O.S.B. Thornbury Castle Gloucestershire	Mr Vaughan of Thornbury castle and Mrs Vaughan of Milbury Heath Lodge.

Turn over.

---

[77] Dom James Placid Duviviers, or Waters (Birt, p. 127). For the next priest, "Smyth", see note 49.

[78] Perhaps an ex-Jesuit, Peter Westby, or Walker, for whom see Foley, VII, pp. 828-9; Mrs B. Stapleton, *Oxfordshire Post-Reformation Catholic Missions* (1906) p. 209.

[79] Probably the ex-Jesuit James Jenison, mentioned in *C.R.S.,* 65, p. 73.

[80] Dom Daniel Bernard Young for whom see Birt, p. 123; Stapleton, *op. cit.,* p. 208.

Baptized An. Dni	By whom	God Fathers and God Mothers
1777. Augt. Mary Harris	D. Young O.S.B.	James Walmesley, Mary Smallwood proxies for Cl. and Mrs Mary Paston.
1778. Jany. 27th. Elizabeth Whimbow	D. Young	Char. and Eliz. Green
1779. March 14th Hester Scates	D. Young	James Walmesley Hester Alden
1781 Novr. 11th was born, and baptized 1782. Jany. 15th Wm. Vaughan	Wm. Combes in Thornbury castle Gloucestershire	Samuel Challoner and Mary Vaughan of Thornbury Castle
1787 Ann Whimbow	J. Smyth	Charles Green, Mary Jorden

NB. The above is a correct copy of the Register of Horton as sent to Bath Augt. 23rd. Signed Thos. H.F. Whitgreave and dated Moseley (near Wolverhampton, Staffordshire) Augt. 21st, 1806.

John Birdsall.

The above copy occupies the first two of six pages in the Register between a series of pages devoted to 1790 and was perhaps misplaced when the Register was re-bound. The other four pages (ending with the 1781 marriage-entry, printed infra., pp. 47-8) are in Pembridge's hand, except for five converts entered by Wilks.

25.[81] 1781, Dec. 16. Baptized Thomas Foresight (born the 29 Novbr.) the Son of Richard Foresight a Prot. and Margaret Foresight his lawful Wife, a Cath. God Father John Halfpenny by proxy of Andrew Fitzgerald, God Mother Eleanor Donelly.

M. Pembridge.

21.[82]   Mortuary List — 1781.

Died

1781 Feb.	23.	Walter Carey		R.P.
1781 April	24.	William Broderic	Ir.	R.P.
1781 July	16.	Mary St. George	Ir.	R.P.
1781 Sptber.	1.	George Burt		R.P.
1781 Sept.	17.	Isaac West, drowned		R.P. Bradford[83]
1781 Oct.	4.	Joanna Dean		R.P. Bath
1781 Oct.	23.	Margaret McAuliff	Ir.	R.P. Bath
1781 Oct.	30.	Charles Stonor Esqr.		R.P. Rouen
1781 Nov.	21.	Rd. Mr More, Priest		R.P. 53 Bath[84]
1781 Dec.	14.	Esther Whitlock		R.P. 73 Box aet 72[85]

(the "Feb., April, July" rows' "Bath" appears bracketed as a group)

[81] For the preceding entries, numbered 3 to 24, see pp. 10-12 and, for nos. 26 to 73, see pp. 16-25.

[82] Perhaps a page-number, if this leaf was originally bound earlier in the register.

[83] Bradford-on-Avon, Wilts.

[84] Christopher More, ex-Jesuit (see *C.R.S.*, 65, p. 73). Buried in Bath Abbey 25 Nov., "Under Mr Chapman's monument, north aisle" (*R.B.A.*, p. 468).

[85] The "73" in this entry and "53" in the previous one appear to have been inserted later, so this, rather than the original 72, may be the correct age. Mrs Esther, or Hester, Whitlock (*née* West), a poor widow of Box, Wilts., is mentioned in *C.R.S. Monograph 1*, p. 235.

The 1782 Mortuary list, below, is a copy of part of the list printed on page 15.

1782 Jany.	5.	Hannah Haney, Ag.58	R.P.	Bath
1782 Jany.	16.	Jean Daman, Frenchman	R.P.	Bath
1782 Feby.	23.	Margaret Kelly alias Rian,[86] 28	R.P.	Bath
1782 Feby.	26.	Mary Lynch, Ag. 54	R.P.	Bath
1782 March	16.	Bridget Martin, Aged 61,	R.P.	Bath
1782 April	12.	Elizabeth East, aged 86,	R.P.	Bath
1782 April	15.	Elizabeth Crabb, aged 92,	R.P.	Philips Norton
1782 May	18.	Mrs Margaret Riley, aged 32	R.P.	Littleton[87]
1782 May	19.	Mrs Anne Pool, aged 77,	R.P.	Weston[88]
1782 June	21.	Mrs Catharine Malpas, aged 73	R.P.	Bath
1782 June	26.	Mr Anthony MacHugo, aged 54,	R.P.	Bath

Converts of this Congregation at different times:—

Mrs Knowles	*[5 names below in Wilks's hand]*
Mrs Chetwynd	West and Wife
Mr Day Senr.	Ruddock
Mrs Day	White
Miss Sus. Day	Wade
Mrs Randall	
Mrs Hughes	
Mrs Charlote Smith	
Mr Anthony Gale	
Giles Hall 10	
Mrs English	
Mrs Norris	
Charles Francis	
Mr Coombs Senr.	
Mr Love	
Mrs Love	
Martha Blake	
Miss Procter	
Miss Dale	
Jane Robinson 20	
John Mills	
Mary Darling	
Mrs Dowling	
Thos. Dutton	
Mr Norris	
Cath. Dutton	
Mr Short	
Mrs Short	

Matrimony.

June 20, 1781 were married Anthony Smith, County York, and Martha

---

[86] Surnames reversed (see *supra,* p. 15).

[87] See p. 15, note 21.

[88] Now in Bath.

Burn,[89] North., in the presence of Nicholas Dowling and Jane Dowling and Martha White — by Michael Pembridge.

October 4, 1790 [*Date and entry in Wilks's hand.*]
Baptized by me Mary Desmond, daughter of Cavan Desmond and Marcella Desmond. Michael M'cann and Catharine Hannan, Godfather and God Mother.

Joseph Wilks.

1790 [*Date and seven entries in Heatley's hand.*]
October 24. Baptized Isabella Foresaythe, born October 15th 1790, Daughter of Richard Foresaythe and Margaret Foresaythe. Godfather Joseph Norton by proxy of Andrew Fitz-Gerald, and Godmother Catharine Hill.

by me Hugh Heatley.

October 29, 1790. Baptized Mary Williams, born Octobr. 27, 1790, Daughter of Henry and Margaret Williams. Godfather James Smith and Godmother Mary Marsh.

by me Hugh Heatley.

1790
November 16th 1790. Baptized Julia Culbert, born half a year before, Daughter of John Culbert and Eleanor Culbert. Godfather Andrew Fitz-Gerald and Godmother Margaret Foresaythe.

Hugh Heatley.

November 20th. Baptized Mary Ann Rassenno, born on the 15th. of the same month, Daughter of Dominic and [*blank*] Rassenno. Godfather Ambrose Puzoli and Godmother Mary Rose Ashton.

Hugh Heatley.

1790 [*Entry in Heatley's hand, but signed by Wilks.*]
November 28th 1790. Baptized George English, born November 4th 1790, Son of Edmund and Margaret English. Godfather William Robinson and Godmother Catharine Burn.

Joseph Wilks.

February 6th 1791, was baptized Teresa Mary Metcalfe,[90] Daughter of Thomas and Teresa Metcalfe, born on the same day. Godfather Mr George Throckmorton and Godmother Mrs Dalton.

Hugh Heatley.

Novembr. 28, 1789, was born and on the same day was baptized Mary, Daughter of Sir James FitzGerald Bart. and of Birgit his wife. Godfather Thos. Peter Metcalfe Esqr. and Godmother Elizabeth Trafford by proxy of Miss Cliffe.

Wm. Coombs.

Wilks's hand:
February 25, 1791, was baptized John Henry Dillon, Son of Henry and

---

[89]   See notes 19 & 42.

[90]   She married Charles Eyston in 1814 (second register, *infra*, p. 192). Mrs Bridget Dalton, *née* More, was her grandmother (see *C.R.S.*, 65, p. 73).

Frances Dillon. Godfather Charles Clifford vice John Dillon and [*sic.*]
Lady Mary Eyre vice Lady Dillon.

Joseph Wilks.

Henceforth in Heatley's or Pembridge's hand, as signed:
1791.[91]
April 10th 1791, was baptized Peter Gallargh, born March 29th 1791,
Son of John and Catharine Gallargh. Godfather Daniel Sullivan and
Godmother Catharine Flynn.

Hugh Heatley.

May 22d 1791, was baptized Joseph Moore born May 2d 1791, Son of
John and Mary Moore. Godfather Patrick Slevin and Godmother
Catharine Keeff.

Hugh Heatley.

May 29th 1791, was baptized Mary Ann Murphy, born May 8th 1791,
Daughter of Dennis and Mary Murphy. Godfather John Murter and
Godmother Margaret Madders.

Hugh Heatley.

June 10, 1791 + born Thomas Denie, Son of John and Ann Denie,
baptized (Domi) in periculo Mortis by Mary Ann Deane (re manente
dubia); rebaptized (etiam Domi). God Father William Robinson (by
proxy), God Mother Mary Ann Deane.

June 11. [*See also earlier entry, supra., pp. 26-7.*]

pr. Michael Pembridge.

1791.
June 19, 1791. Baptized Philip Sullivan, born June 11, 1791, Son of
Philip and Eleanor Sullivan. Godfather Patrick Pissett and Godmother
Catharine Knowels.

Hugh Heatley.

Same day. Baptized Mary (born on the same day out of wedlock)
daughter of Wm. Connelly and Mary Henritt. Godfather Nicholas Taaffe
and Godmother Catharine Weare.

Hugh Heatley.

June 29, 1791. Baptized Teresa Hughes, born on the 26th of the same
month, daughter of John and [*blank*] Hughes. Godfather James
Dowding and Godmother Martha Sanger.

Hugh Heatley.

1791.
June 14, born Mary Robins, Daughter of Charles and Mary Robins (als.
Gridlin). Baptized + July 3. God Father Jacob West Senr., Godmother
Elizabeth Prosser.

+ pr. Michael Pembridge.

1791.
July 10, 1791, was baptized William Trodden, born July 4th 1791, Son

---

[91] Dom Samuel Bede Day O.S.B. is said by Birt, p. 161, to have been born at
Wellow in 1791; no baptismal entry occurs in this register.

of William and Ann Trodden. Godfather James Allen and Godmother
Rose Cosgrove.

Hugh Heatley.

July 31st 1791, was baptized James, born July 25, 1791. Son of Thomas
and Elizabeth Moore. Godfather Michael Bryan and Godmother Martha
Sanger.

Hugh Heatley.

1791.
August 23, 1791. Baptized James FitzGerald, born August 22, 1791,
Son of Sir James and his wife Lady FitzGerald. Godfather John
Trafford Esqr. by proxy of Philip Howard Esqr. and Godmother Mrs
Teresa Metcalfe by proxy of Mrs Dalton, mother of the said Lady
FitzGerald.

Hugh Heatley.

September 1, 1791. Baptized Francis Odber, born August 28, 1791, son
of Martin and Margaret Odber. Godfather John Short and Godmother
Phebe Roberts.

Hugh Heatley.

1791.
September 6, 1791. Baptized John William Bryan, born August 31st
1791, Son of John and Alice Bryan. Godfather —Long and Godmother
Joanna Crowley.

Hugh Heatley.

Same day. Baptized without solemnity John Tery in immediate danger;
born April 30, 1791, son of Wm. and [blank] Tery. Dead.

Hugh Heatley.

November [blank] 1791, was baptized Michael Benjamin, born August
29th 1791, Son of Michael and his wife Mary MacArthey. Godfather
Benjamin Heether, Godmother Hannah MacManus.

Hugh Heatley.

Deaths.
Octobr. 20, 1791, died Mrs Mary Throckmorton. [In Heatley's hand.]

1791.
November 18th 1791. Baptized William Joseph, born October 30th
1791, Son of Joseph and Emma Barbara White. Godfather William
Hopkins and Godmother Mary Short.

Hugh Heatley.

November 28th 1791, was baptized Harriot Mathews, born on the 13th
of the same month, daughter of Mathew and Mary Mathews. Godfather
Mathew Mathews, junior.

Hugh Heatley.

1791.
December 13th 1791, was baptised Elisabeth, born November 7th
1791, daughter of Timothy and Eleanor Sullivan. Godfather James
White.

Hugh Heatley.

1792.
Jany. 9th 1792, was baptized Mary Catharine born Jany. 8th 1792,
daughter of Alexius and Catharine Delangre. Godfather George Petre
and Godmother Mary Petre.

Hugh Heatley.

1792.
Jany. 15. Baptized Francis English, born son of Edmund and Margaret
English. God Father Peter Smith, Godmother Martha Smith.

pr. Michael Pembridge.

Jany. 15th 1792. Baptized Michael, born December 31st 1791, Son of
John and Elizabeth Maher. Godfather Robt. Fitz-gerald and Godmother
Catharine Murphy.

Hugh Heatley.

Jany. 23, 1792. Baptized Ann, Daughter of Jacob and Rachel West,
born Jany. 19, 1792. Godfather Jacob West Junior and Godmother
Rachel West junior.

Hugh Heatley.

Jany. 24, 1792. Baptized Philip William, born on the same day, son of
the Honle. George Petre and of Mrs Mary Petre his Wife. Godfather
Wm. Witham Esqr. by proxy of Phil. Howard Esqr. and Godmother
Lady Juliana Petre, by proxy of Mrs Catharine Garthside.

Hugh Heatley.

1792.
Feby. 6th 1792, was born and on the 10th of the same month was
baptized Catharine, ,daughter of Michael and Elizabeth Smith. Godfather Edmund English by proxy of John Mills, Godmother Martha
Smith.

Hugh Heatley.

Feby 28, 1792. Baptized John, born [blank] son of John Hill [blank]
and Catharine Hill, Godmother [blank] Hughes. Dead.

Hugh Heatley.

1792. [Unsigned, but in Heatley's hand.]
Feby. 29. Baptized Richard, born Feby. 25th 1792, Son of James and
Mary MacDonnelly. Godfather John Maher and Godmother —Burn.

March 12th 1792. Baptized Eliza, born the day before, daughter of
Garret and Ellen Barry. Godfather James Donnelly.

Hugh Heatley.

March 18th 1792. Baptized William, born the day before, son of
Thomas and Catharine Brown. Godfather Thos. Collingridge Junior by
proxy of Thos. Collingridge Senr., Godmother Mary Collingridge by
proxy of Ann Collingridge.

Hugh Heatley.

1792, April 15. Baptized Mary Sidnel, born 19 March, Daughter of
George and Mary Sidnel of Pickwick[92]. God Father James Branning by

---

[92]   Near Corsham, Wilts., a few miles from Bath.

proxy of N. Kerly, God Mother Mary Hendrick.

In the Chapel at Bath, pr. Mich. Pembridge.
1792, May 7. Baptized George Bisset, born 24 April, the son of Patrick Bisset and Mary Bisset. God Father Bartholomew Hayes, God Mother Rose Grant.

In the Chapel at Bath Corn Street,[93] pr. Michael Pembridge.
1792, May 20. Baptized Mary Gorth, born 29 April, the daughter of James and Elizabeth Gorth. God Father James White, God Mother Mary Webb.

In the Chapel at Bath, pr. Michael Pembridge.
1792, April 8. Baptized George Williams, born 5th April, the Son of Henry and Margaret Williams. Godfather Nicholas Dowling, Godmother Mary Kirk.

Hugh Heatley.
Pembridge's hand: Ultimum hoc suae missionis opus 9 April Putrida correptus febri. Obiit in Domino, 28 Aprilis AD.1792, aet. 33, R. in P.[94]

1792, Baptizatorum. [*In Pembridge's and Ainsworth's hands, as signed.*]
June 16. Baptized Mary Frances Dillon, born June 15, Daughter of Honble. Henry and Frances Dillon. God Father Rt. Honble. Lord Dillon by proxy of George Butler Esqr., God Mother Lady Dillon by proxy of Mrs George Butler.

Michael Pembridge.
June 24. Baptized Mary Anne Hazard, born June 23, Daughter of John and Eleanor Hazard. God Father Edward Hazard, God Mother Elizabeth Brufy

Michael Pembridge.
June 25, 1792. Baptized in the Chapel at Bath John Baptist Kennedy, born 19 June, Son of Roger and Mary Kennedy. God Father Francis Allen, God Mother Elizabeth Hodginson.

Michael Pembridge.
1792, Aug. 26, was baptized Dennis Mahony, born Aug. 16, Son of Dennis and Catharine Mahony. God Father Patric Sullivan, God Mother Catharine Moren.

by me Mich. Pembridge.
1792 + Sept. 14. Baptized William Doyle, born 3 Sept., Son of Patric and Eleanor Doyle. God Father Francis Curley, God Mother Arabella O'Byrn.

by me Mich. Pembridge.
1792 + Sept. 16. Supplied the Ceremonies omitted on James Bryen, baptized by the Curate of St Michael's Church, the Rd. Mr Wake. James Bryen was born 31 July, Son of James and Rebecca Bryen. God Father Patric Doyle, God Mother Mary Doyle.

by Michael Pembridge;

[93]   The chapel which had replaced the Bell-tree in 1786 (see *C.R.S.*, 65, p. 71).

[94]   For entry of Fr. Heatley's death and burial, see *infra,* p. 120; also end of 1792 *Status Animarum* list (printed *supra,* p. 37).

1792, Baptizatorum, Bath.
Sept. 23. Baptized Mary Henrietta Church, born 8 Sept., Daughter of G. and Anne Church. God Father John Mills, God Mother Henrietta Church by proxy of Anne Church, Grand-Mother.

Bath R.C. Chapel, Michael Pembridge.
Sept. 24th. Baptized Catherine Rassenno, born on the 23d of the same month, Daughter of Dominic and [blank] Rassenno. Godmother Mary Rose Ashton.

Ralph Ainsworth.
1792, October 4. Baptized Mary Anne Metcalf, born the same day, Daughter of Thomas and Teresia Metcalf. God Father Rd. Mr More[95] by proxy of N.Tempest Esqr., God Mother Lady Throckmorton by proxy of Mrs Dalton.+

Michael Pembridge.
1792, October 5th. Baptized John Connelly, Son of William and Mary Connelly. Godfather William Riordon, Godmother Jane Riordon.

Ralph Ainsworth.
1792, October 11th. Baptized James Magrath, born the 7th of the same month, Son of John and Helena Magrath. Godfather William Nayle, Godmother Margaret Linch.

Ralph Ainsworth.
1792, Oct. 14. Baptized John Keeffe, born Oct 4, Son of James and Mary Keeffe. God Father Daniel Keeffe, God Mother Anne Magrath.

Michael Pembridge.
1792, Nov. 18th. Baptized John Baptist Francis Donegany, born Nov. 9th, Son of Joseph and Mary Donehgani. Godfather John Baptist Vecchio, Godmother Catherine Moore.

Ralph Ainsworth.

1792, Baptizatorum. [*In Ainsworth's and Lawson's hands, as signed.*]
Nov. 19th. Baptized Margaret Desmond, born the 17th of the same month, Daughter of Caven and Marcella Desmond. Godfather Francis Curley, Godmother Frances Hughs.

Ralph Ainsworth.
1792, Nov. 21st. Supplied the ceremonies omitted on John Bigerty baptized the day before by Bartholomew Hayes. John Bigerty was born October 26th, son of Patrick and Sarah Bigerty. Godfather Timothy Crowley, Godmother Mary Bissett.

Ralph Ainsworth.
Dec. 6th 1792. Baptized Thomas Reynolds born the day before, Son of James and Teresa Reynolds, Godfather James Barnes, Godmother [blank] Sweet, by proxy of Elizabeth Warrington.

Ralph Ainsworth.

[95] Doubtless Thomas More, ex-Jesuit Superior, at that time living in London, who died at Bath in 1795 (Foley, VII, p. 520; *C.R.S.,* 65, p. 73). Mrs Metcalf (like Lady Fitzgerald, *supra,* p. 40) was a daughter of his sister, Mrs Dalton (*C.R.S.,* 65, *loc. cit.*; Davey, p. 71).

Dec. 28th 1792. Baptized Anna Coffee daughter of Jeremiah and Mary Coffee, she was born December the 6th. Godmother Margaret Macdonald.

Ralph Ainsworth.

1793, Baptizatorum, 1793.

Jan. 6th 1793. Baptized Philip Francis Pique, born Dec. 8th 1792, Son of John and Marianna Pique, Godfather Philip Nonnett.

Ralph Ainsworth.

March 10th 1793. Baptized James Cooper, born January 15th, Son of Richard and Margaret Cooper.

Ralph Ainsworth.

March 21st 1793. Baptized Anna Carr, born the same day, daughter of of [blank] and [blank] Carr.

Ralph Ainsworth.

March 31st 1793. Baptized Anne Brenan, born the 18th of the same month, daughter of John and Anne Brenan. Godfather Nicolas McDonnell, Godmother Anne Thomas.

Ralph Ainsworth.

April 10th 1793. Baptized Teresa Dorey, daughter of Joseph and Teresa Dorey, born April 1st 1793.

Ralph Ainsowrth.

1793, Baptizatorum.

May 4th. Baptized Elisa Friar, born the 2d of the same month, daughter of John and Elisa Friar. Godfather Charles Friar, Godmother Mary Wright.

Ralph Ainsworth.

May 4th. Baptized sub conditione William Jones, aged 17 years, Son of [blank] and [blank] Jones.

Ralph Ainsworth.

June 14th. Baptized Mary Fenerty, daughter of Thomas and Frances Fenerty. Godfather Timothy Bean by proxy of Richard Mills, Godmother Mary Roche by proxy of Barbara Mondaire.

Ralph Ainsworth.

1793, June 23. Supplied the Ceremonies omitted on Michel Maher, Son of John and Elizabeth Maher, baptized by Surgeon Day the 11th of May; the Godfather was called Franc Allen and Godmother Frances Mary Hynde.

H. Lawson.

1793, June 24. Baptized James Bourke, born the same day, the son of [blank] Bourke; the Godfather Richard Caghlan, P. Toole the Godmother.

H. Lawson.

1793, June 25. Winifrida English baptised, born the 24th, the Daughter of Mr Edmund and Mrs Margaret English. The Godfather James Murphew, God Mother Mrs Dorothy Moland.

H. Lawson.

1793, July 21. Baptized James Dowding,[96] born the 2d of July, the Son of James and Mary Dowding. Godfather Patrick Doyle, Godmother Mary Mathews.

H. Lawson.

1793, July 9th. Baptised John Henry MacCann, born the 16 of June, the Son of Michael and Dorothy MacCann. The Godfather Calogan O'Neil, Godmothers Margaret Necket and Margaret Musterson.

H. Lawson.

July 28th. Supplied the ceremonies omitted on Edward Allen, Son of Francis and Jane Allen, born June 19th. Godfather Roger Kenedy, Godmother Mary Kennedy.

Ralph Ainsworth.

N.B. Aug. 4th. See the following page [*i.e. the next entry but two*].

1793, Aug. 14th. Baptised John Heffernan, the Son of John and Sarah Heffernan. The Godfather Laughlin Larkin.

H. Lawson.

1793, Aug. 21. Baptised John Keiffe, born the 31 of March, the Son of John and Ellen Kieffe. No Godfather or God Mother.

H. Lawson.

1793, Aug. 4th. Baptized Jane Carroll, born July the 15th, daughter of John and Anne Carroll. Godfather Simon Hencey, Godmother Elizabeth Shears.

Ralph Ainsworth.

1793, Oct. 24th. Baptized Elizabeth Williams, born the 21st of the same month, daughter of Henry and Margaret Williams, Godfather Michael Butler, Godmother Mary Matthews.

Ralph Ainsworth.

1793, Nov. 13th. Baptized Elisa Smythe, born October the 7th, daughter of Michael and Elisabeth Smythe. Godfather John Robinson.

Ralph Ainsworth.

1793, Dec. 1st. Baptized Denis Sullivan, Son of John and Helen Sullivan and born Nov. 28th. Godfathers Michael Quinlan and John Burke, Godmother Helen Barrow.

Ralph Ainsworth.

1793, Dec. 4th. Baptized Anne Drine, born the 24th of November, daughter of David and Brigit Drine. Godfather John Ranedin, Godmother Elizabeth Molyneux.

Ralph Ainsworth.

1794, Jan. 21. Baptized Frances Mary Nanno Nagle, born Jan. 16th, daughter of Richard and Catherine Nagle. Godfather Joseph Nagle by proxy of David Nagle, Godmother Catherine Mapas [?] Talbot by proxy of Margaret Trant.

Ralph Ainsworth.

1794, Jan. 22 [? 24] Baptized Anne Perry, daughter of William and

[96] Later a Benedictine (Birt, p. 156).

Susanna Perry, born the 4th of the same month. Godfather Laurence Gahigan, Godmother Cecilia Taffe.

Ralph Ainsworth.

1794, Feb. 6th. Baptized Philip Wright, son of Philip and Mary Wright, born Feb. 4th. Godfather Charles Friars, Godmother [*blank*] Hugo.

Ralph Ainsworth.

1794, Feb. 9th. Baptized William Brown, son of Thomas and Catherine Brown, born Feb. 8th. Godfather Thomas Canning, Godmother Mary Canning.

Ralph Ainsworth.

1794, March 16th. Baptized Brigit Monk, daughter of James and Mary Monk, born March 7th 1794. Godfather Laughlan Larcon, Brigit Neville [*sic.*].

Ralph Ainsworth.

See 22 leaves farther [*i.e. the point in the Register at which the baptismal entries for 1794 are resumed; infra, p. 72*].

Status Animarum sive Congregationis. [*List in Pembridge's hand.*]
Julii 1, 1792.

David Nagle Esqr.	No. 1 Circus
Mr Harold Nephew	
Mrs Honora Harogan	Housekeeper
Mary Dean	Cook

| Miss Plunkett | No. 3 Circus |

John Walsh Esqr.	No. 9 Marlborough Buildings
Mrs Walsh	
Miss Walsh and 2 Sisters	
Man-Servant	

| Mr Dalton | Brock Street |

| Mr Thos. Canning and Mrs Canning | No. 4 Church Street |
| Man and 2 Maid Servants | |

| Thos. Metcalf Esqr. and Mrs | Rivers Street No. 9 |
| Man and 2 Maid Servants 20 | |

Mrs Hussey	St James's Square
Mr and Mrs Dowling	Belvidere No. 10
Mrs French	No. 9 Oxford Row
Mrs Drisgill	
3 Daughters – Man and Maid Servant	
Mr and Mrs Butler	No. 1 Bennet Street

179 [*presumably* 1792] Status Animarum.
George Butler Esqr. and Lady   No. 23 Bennett Street
Miss Butler – Miss Cavenagh – Mr Kennedy, Butler
Miss Hawkins, Maid. Monsr. Duquen, Servant 40

Mr and Mrs Hughes		Russell Street
Miss Matthews		Ditto
Mrs Randall		Ditto
Mr Weldon, 2 Nieces		Alfred Street
Mr and Mrs Smith and Mrs Burn		No. 4 Fountain Pl. [?]
Mrs Clark		No. 4 Vineyard
Mr and Mrs Crowtch — Edmund Collingridge and Maid		
		Walcot Parade
Mr and Mrs Hall		Margaret Hill[97]
Mrs Leech		
Mr and Mrs Rian	60	Broad Street
Mr Kirly		
Mr and Mrs English, 5 Sons, 4 Daughters.		Broad St.
Mr and Mrs Molland		Milsom Street
Miss Fleming and Sister Catharine		John Street[98]
Mrs Payne		Ditto
Mrs Chetwynd and 3 Maids	80	Gay Street
Mr and Mrs Lowndes and Mrs Church		Barton Street
Mr and Mrs Robinson, 2 Sons, 1 Daughter		
Mrs Susanna Day		Westgate Buildings
Mr Willm. Day, Surgeon		
Honble Miss Talbot and Mary Ball		Westgate Buildings
Mrs Martin, Mrs Hugo, Miss Hugo, Mrs		
Thornton		St James's Parade
N. Tobin Esqr. and Mrs		Ditto
John Mills, Mary Blackwell	100	Ditto
Mrs Burk		Ditto
Miss Dale and Miss Bernick		Ditto
Willm. Hopkin and Wife		Corn Street
Thos. Short and Wife and Son		Ditto
Jacob West and Wife and Son and		
Daughter		Back Street Ditto
Thos. Brown and Wife		Horse Street
John Meares and Wife		Peter Street[98] and Mary Moore
Thos. Moore and Wife and Daughter	120	
Anne Hughes		Bell Tree House
John Odber and Wife and Son and Daughter		
Mary Coffee and Son		
John Allen Stall Street Mich. Brien		Ditto
Anne Cosgrove Do		
Anne Pearce, 2 Daughters		
Robins and Wife		
James Murphy and Wife and Daughter		Bridewell Lane
Elizabeth Hodginson		Westgate Street
German Clock Maker	140	Ditto
Mr Denie and Wife, Son and Daughter		Norgate[99]

---

[97] Street-name: Margaret's Hill.

[98] Street-name.

[99] i.e. Northgate Street.

Mary Deane	Ditto
John Morrison	Walcot Street
Anne Collingridge James N.	Bishop's Servant
Dr Mahagan	No. 4 Lower Charles Street
2 Misses Hyde	No. 27 New King's Street
Francis Allen	
Willm. Norris, Wife and Daughter	James Street
Anne Aston and Daughter 160	
John Carroll – Rosano and Wife	Avon Street
John James, Son and Daughter	Ditto
Mrs Duval	John's Court
Mr Williams and Wife[100]	No. 1 Northumberland Buildings
James Dowden Sen., 3 Daughters	
James Reynolds and Wife	Morford Street
William Reynolds	Ditto
John and James Hensy	Ditto
Lucy Waring	
Mr and Mrs Love and Son 180	
Elizabeth Russell	
Daniel Castle and Wife	Parsonage Lane
Mr Keasebery, Son and 2 Daughters	
John Mcpherson	
Margaret Lyons	
Sarah Maden	
Eliz. Dennohough	
Mary Darling	
Mary Cliff	
John Clark	
Mr and Mrs Day and Daughter	Inglisbach
Anthony Gale	Bradford[101]
Mr Thos. Day and Wife 200	Lady Mead[102]
Mr Peter Smith	Lady Mead[102]
Mr Michael Smith	Bladud Buildings
John Dutton	Twirton
Barbara White	Holliway
Richd. Hubberston[?]	Walcot Work House
Mrs Edgecumb Plunket	Walcot Street
Mrs Butt	
Mr Doyle	Walcot
Honble. Mr Dillon, Lady, Mrs Trant	Gay Street
Miss [Dell *deleted*] Trant and Miss Kirk	– Maid
Mr and Mrs Howard Pulteney Street	N. Cotes, Servant
Mrs Garthside	Laura Place[102]

[100] Kirk, p. 2, prints information about an eighteenth-century priest, Sir William Anderson, derived from an old breviary "at Mrs Williams', Northumberland Buildings, Bath".

[101] Bradford-on-Avon (see note 55).

[102] Location, not personal name.

John Wright		Market Place
John and Eleanor Hazard	220	
Edward Hazard		
Roger and Mary Kennedy		
James and Elizabeth Gorth		
James White		
Mary Webb		
John Brickman		
George and Mary Sidnell		
James Branning		
Philip Nonnet and Wife		Margaret Buildings
John Pike and Wife		St Andrew's Terrace
Mary Martyn		
Mary Ashton		
Mrs Doyle		
Mr Heffernam		
John McCan	240	
MacMirty, Wife and 2 Sons		
Mary Bowden and Son		
Anne Hughes, 2 Sons		Guinea Lane
John Wogan and Son		
Patric Carroll		
Mich. Brannan		
Mr Jadoul		
Mr Perry		
Jane Russell		
Mrs Pettingall		
Mary Laytham and Daughter		
John Imetto and Daughter		
Mrs O'Byrn		
Mrs Celia Dunn and Niece		
Bartholomew[103]	260	
Mr Hayes and Wife		
Mrs Pool		
Abigail Murphy		
Margaret Keif		
Catharine Leonard		
Julia Hynde		
Patrick and Mary Bisset		
Rose Grant		
Patric Macarty		
Mr and Mrs Delassons		St Andrew's Terrace
Mathew and Anne Trodden		
Garret Farrell and Son	280	

[103] Possibly the Christian name of "Mr Hayes" below. Bartholomew Hayes occurs several times in this Register as a parent and godparent, and as administering the sacrament of baptism, presumably in an emergency (see index for references to him).

Mrs Feneran
Anne and Eliz. Pitts
John Leonard
Mary and Anne Samuel
Mr and Mrs Howell
Stephen Read
Thomas Hill
Joseph Cook
Mich. McDonald
Mrs Veltam
Willm. and Catharine Odber
Martha Sanger
Mrs Shean
Mr and Mrs Vivier   Brock Street
Timothy and Eleanor Sullivan   300
Mr Bezani and Wife
Mr Borrachini [?] and Wife
Samuel Dillon   Crooked Row
Mrs Seaford
   Cum multis aliis.

1792 Status Animarum.
Patric Sullivan
Dennis Mahony
Catharine Mahony
Catharine Moren   310
N. Seaford
Doctor Meaghane[104]   lower Charles Street
Mrs Bishop   Ditto
Mrs Biddulph
Mrs Jaddoul
John Barry
James Flynn
Mrs Hutchinson
Willm. and Mary Connelly   320
Willm. Riordon
Jane Riorden
John and Helena Magrath
Willm. Neal
Margaret Lynch
Joseph and Mary Doneghan
John Baptist Vecchio
Catharine More   330
1792. Caven and Marcella Delmond [? Desmond]
Frances Hughes
Mrs Jadoul
John Gibbins
Patric Bigerty
Timothy Crowley

[104] Dr Meagher, of 1 Claverton Buildings, occurs in *Robbins's Bath Directory* (Bath, 1800) p. 75. He died 10 Feb. 1801 (*infra*, p. 124).

Matrimoniorum. [*In Pembridge's hand.*]

Wilks's hand:
1788.
June 2d.
Were married in the Catholic Chapel of Corn Street at Bath, The most noble Charles Alexander de Calonne, Lord and Count of Hannonville in the Kingdom of France, but of the parish of Saint Mary Le Bone in the County of Middlesex, a widower, and Dame Anne Rose Joseph de Nettine (widow of the Chevalier Joseph Micault d'Harselay, Counsellor of State, Lord and Count of Clussy and Serres and of the Barony of Torcy in the Kingdom of France) of the city of Bath, by me Witnesses [*no signatures*].

Joseph Wilks.

Pembridge's hand (3 entries):
1792.
Feby. 16, were married, Richard Nagle Esqr. of the County of [Cork *deleted*] Westmeath, and Miss Catharine Fitzgerald. Witnesses: the Rd. Mr Heatley, David Nagle Esqr. and Miss French.

pr Michael Pembridge.
1792.
August. 14, were married John Meare and Elizabeth Norman. Witnesses: Martin O'Brien, Mary Short and Mary Wilcock.

by me Mich. Pembridge.

Matrimoniorum.
1792.
Augst. 20, were married in this Chapel, Simon Hensy and Mary Wedcock by me. Witnesses: Martin O'Brien, Caroline Prichard.

M. Pembridge.

Heatley's hand:
November 26th 1791, were married Samuel Odber of the County of [*blank*][105] and Mary Jenkins of the County of [*blank*]. Witnesses: Theresa Shepherd, and Catharine Brown.

Hugh Heatley.

Ainsworth's hand:
1793.
April 18th,[106] were married Philip Wright and Mary Anne Hugo. Witnesses: the Rev. Mr. Lawson, Charles Friar, Mary Anne Dale and Mary Friar.

Ralph Ainsworth.

Lawson's hand (2 entries):
1793.
July 14, were married Thomas Smith and Anne Brannan. Witnesses: Ellen Rose and Jacob West.

H. Lawson.

[105] Perhaps Wiltshire; see *Registers of Stourton* (ed. Ellis) *passim*.
[106] Also in *R.B.A.*, p. 318 (same date).

1793, July 31, were married Robert Scot and Maercy Elston. Witnesses: Henry Williams and Martha Smith.

Henry Lawson.

Words italicised in Ainsworth's hand; others in different hands:
1794, Jan. 7th, were married Jean Cottin et Catherine Scholastique Vendercruice.[107] Witnesses: Jaques Gouget et Madelaine Avril Gouget.

Ralph Ainsworth.

In Ainsworth's hand, with witnesses' names in a different hand:
1794, Jan. 7th, were married Richard Phaolon and Elizabeth Edwards. Witnesses: Henry Hubbert, Charlotte Merrick.

Ralph Ainsworth.

In Lawson's hand, apart from witness's name:
1794, October 14, were married Thomas Rundel and Elizabeth Biley. Witness: Mary Brown.

H. Lawson

Lawson's hand (2 entries):
1795, January the 11, were married by me Edward Howel and Elizabeth Taylor. Witness: John Martyn and N.

H. Lawson.

1795, January,[108] were married Julien Havez and Anne Bailey. Witnesses: Anne Love and Jacob West.

Henry Lawson.

Next 4 entries in hands of officiating priests, with various witnesses' signatures:
July 1st 1795, were married Thomas Jones and Mary Jeanne Bruno.
[*signed*] Thos. Jones.   Mar. Jeanne Bruno.
Witnesses: Picquenot.[109]   Justine Ride.

Ralph Ainsworth.

1795, Sep. 7th, were married in the Catholic Chapel in Corn Street at Bath François Pascal le Roux and Catherine Renée Radener. By me

Ralph Ainsworth.[110]

Witnesses: Feray, Curé de Mirbel.
François Pascale le Roux.
Eugene Kerouartz.   Clara Stuart.   Catherine Reine Radener.
Elizabeth Farewell.   Guillaume Schoere.
Louis l'Herminier.   Rene le Goff.   Lecorre.

---

[107] Also in *R.B.A.*, p. 319 (same date) but with the wife's maiden name spelt "Vander Cruyce" and with witnesses given as "Jaques Youget, Madeline Avril, Jamme Youget, Marie Piette".

[108] Dated 3 Jan. in *R.B.A.*, p. 320, with the husband's surname spelt Havee and Jacob West omitted.

[109] French priest; see next page (1796 entry); also p. 75 (baptism).

[110] In the original, Ainsworth's signature comes after those of the witnesses; presumably he intended to sign under the words "By me" but the Abbé Feray got in first.

L'an mil-sept cent quatre-vingt-quinze, le mardy quinze Septembre, toutes les formalités à ce requires deuement observées, nous soussignés, Curé de Mirbel, avons, avec la permission de Monsieur Ainsworth, Chapelain de la Chapelle Catholique de Bath, reçu le mutuel consente- ment de mariage de Louis-Joseph-Eloy l'Herminier et de Marie-Jeanne Champion; le dit l'Herminier fils majeur de Pierre l'Herminier et de feue Marguerite Carbonnier, et la dite Champion fille majeure de feu François Champion et de feue Jeanne le Camp, tous deux françois d'origine et demeurants depuis plus d'un an en la susdite ville de Bath, et leur avons donné la bénédiction nuptiale avec les cérémonies prescrites par la sainte église catholique, apostolique et romaine, en présence des témoins avec Monsieur Ainsworth et nous soussignés, à Bath le dit jour et an que ci dessus.

Feray, Curé de Mirbel.

Louis Joseph Eloy l'Herminier.

Marie Jeanne Champion.   J. Gouget.

Felix Rolland.   R. Gavel,   François le Broun.

Ralph Ainsworth.

1796

L'an mil-sept cent quatre-vingt-seize, le cinq Janvier, aprés la dispense de la publication des bans obtenue conformément aux lois, nous Curé de Mirbel, Diocése de Lizieux, avons fait la célébration du mariage d'entre Michel Roussel, fils majeur de feu Pierre Roussel et de Marie Cappelle de la paroisse d'Irf, Diocése de Seez, d'une part, et entre Catherine Beauregard, fille majeure de feu Claude Beauregard et de Catherine André de la paroisse de Lacoult, Diocése de Nancy, tous deux demeurant depuis plusieurs années dans cette ville, sans qu'il se soit trouvé aucune opposition civile ny canonique, en recevant des parties leur consente- ment mutuel par parole de présent suivant les cérémonies de l'église catholique, en présence de Mr Decastellas,[111] Doyen des comtes de Lions et de Mr Picquenot, Curé de Neuville et Doyen d'Ivry, Diocése d'Evreux, qui ont signé avec les parties et nous le présent acte.

Catherine Beauregard.   Michel Roussel.

l'abbé de Castellas, Doyen comte de Lyon.

Picquenot. Boulanger. J. Gouget.

Feray, C. de M. [i.e. Curé de Mirbel]
R. Ainsworth.

The following entries appear, from the ink, the handwriting (Pembridge's) and the totals, to be a continuation of the Status Animarum list of 1782 (supra., pp. 7-8). When the register was earlier copied (cf. p. viii, note 4) this leaf was differently located (between the marriage-entry of 20 June 1781, printed on pp. 47-8 and the list headed "Easter 1782" starting on

[111] cf. F. X. Plasse, *Le Clergé Francais Refugié en Angleterre* (Paris, 1886), p. 433, where, however, he is said to have died in 1795, in London.

p. 12). Evidently, like others, it was misplaced when the Register was given its present binding.

Richd. Maddox
Anne Hughes
Hannah Hughes
Amy Castle
Mr and Mrs Ryan
George Jackson
Helena[?] Casey
Mrs Sheward
Richd. Hubberston[?]
Celia Dun
Mrs Dun
Miss Plunket   Circus
Mr and Mrs Dowling
Mr and Mrs Day   Forscot
Mr Day Senr and Junr.
and Miss Day   Ingsbach
Mrs Martin
Hannah and Rachl[112] Baker
Lydia Bird
Eliz. Jakes
Jane Magra
Catharine Dowdel
Thomas More, Wife and
3 Daughters
Lady Palmer
Bartholomew Coffill
Mary Ashton
Anne Ashton
Eliz. Ashton   137

Willm. Norris and Wife
James Collins
Mrs Thornton
Mrs Crabb
Mrs Neal and Mrs Molland
Mr Gale
Mary Dory
Ross Magennis and Wife
Catharine Conner
James Keys
Dorothy Tracey
Andrew Fitzgerald
Margaret Foresight
George Hughes and Wife Mary
Mr and Mrs Short
Eliz. Boxal
Mrs Ready
Eliz. Burt
Julietta Laytham
Eliz. Harris
Flora Coombe
Mr Welden and Miss Welden
Anne Hareland
Mary Ross
Mary Jenkins
Mrs Church
Jane Robinson
Penelope Price
Thos. Brown
Martha Blake
Betty Green   174

Miss Dale
Mrs Randal
Mrs Hawkins
Mr O'Burn
Mary Murphy, beggar
Betty Peddell
Eleanor Dennohaugh
Anne Miles
Sarah Hagarty
Thomas Dutton
Jeremiah Lions
John Dowding
Mary Dowding
Mr and Mrs Keagan
Frances Carlas
Mrs Frances
Mrs Saunderson

Mrs Middleton
Eliz. Trappil
Mary Long
Alice McDermont
Betty Cottell
Mary Parsons
Edward Quin
Eliz. Macavoy
Mrs Vaughan
Mrs Cox
Mary Jellamy
James Dean
Bridget Martin
John Brian
Mrs O'Bryan
Mary Cotton   208

[112] *sic.*; overwritten upon "Sarah".

Entries in hands of officiating clergy and various witnesses:

Le Jeudy seize Février mil-sept cent quatre-vingt-dix-sept, toutes les formalités préalablement observées, nous soussigné, Missionnaire de la ville de Bath, avons reçu le mutuel consentement de mariage de Pierre Marie François, Comte de la Pasture, fils de Pierre Antoine François de la Pasture, Marquis de Verchocq, et de Marie Catherine Agathe d'Acary, Marquise de Verchocq, d'une part, et d'autre part d'Elysabeth Foulkes, veuve de Archibald Hamilton Foulkes, fille de Gerard Gustavus Coltée du Carel et d'Elysabeth Coltée du Carel, et leur avons donné la bénédiction nuptiale avec les cérémonies de l'eglise catholique en presence des soussignés avec nous le dit jour et an que dessus. Un mot raturé nul[113] — Feray, prêtre.

Pierre Marie Francois, Comte De la Pasture
Elizabeth Ducarel.
Pierre Antoine Francois De la Pasture, Marquis De Verchocq.
Marie Catherine Agathe, M'ise de Verchocq.

R. Ainsworth.

1798, April 21[?] were married Patrick Cahall [*and*] Ruthe Meguay. Witnesses: John Kelly and Ruthe Lithmon, by me   H. Lawson.
Bath.

Le lundi quatre Février mil-sept cents quatre-vingt-dix-neuf, toutes les formalités préalablement observées, nous soussigné Curé de Mirbel, Diocéze de Lisieux, avec la permission de Monsieur Ainsworth, Missionnaire de la Chapelle Catholique de Bath, avons reçu le mutuel consentemente de mariage de Louis François le Mée, fils majeur de defunt François le Mée et de defunte Christine Lamon [? hamon] d'une part, et d'autre part de Renée le Goff, veuve de François Bertrand, fille de defunct Jean le Goff et de defunte Françoise le Lane, tous deux françois d'origine et demeurans depuis plusieurs années en la ville de Bath, et leur avons donné la bénédiction nuptiale avec les cérémonies prescrites par la ste. église en presence des témoins avec Mr Ainsworth et nous soussignés à Bath le dit jour et an que ci dessus. L'époux, ne sachant signer, a fait sa marque; trois mots raturés nuls.[114]

Renée le Goff.

+ marque de Louis François le Mée.
Eugene de Kerouartz, fils de Mr de Kerouartz.
Christian Wilhelm Schoere.
George Bertrand, C. de Frise.
Feray, C. de Mirbel.

R. Ainsworth.

---

[113]   a reference to the word "fille", deleted.

[114]   i.e. three words deleted ("René le goff", originally written in the wrong place).

1799, September 24th, were married John Short and Mary Pit. Present, Mary Short, by me

H. Lawson.

1800, June 26th, were married Noah Howard and Rosina Downes. Present [*blank*] Doyle

R. Ainsworth.

1800, Aug. 23d, were married in the Catholic Chapel at Bath (juxta ritum Ecclesiae Catholicae) John Bisani and Frances Etoile. Present as witness [*sic.*] Helen Rose and Mary Hencey.

R. Ainsworth.

June 11th 1801, were married in the Catholic Chapel at Bath, Thomas Neale and Catherine Burke. Present as witnesses James Haggerty, John Molloy, James Dobbin, Honora Haggerty, Mary Kennedy and Mary O'Brien.

R. Ainsworth.

June 15th 1801, were married at their lodgings, Dr Walter Kennedy Craufuird and Miss Emilie O'Connor, daughter of Sir Patrick O'Connor, Present as witnesses, her aunt and her maid servant.

R. Ainsworth.

Next five entries in Calderbank's hand:

1801, September 28th, were married in the Catholic Chapel at Bath, Henry Beaumont and Mary Anne Archer. Present as Witnesses, Mrs Cohoun and Mr Burke, by me

Jas. Calderbank.

1801, October 25th, were married in the Catholic Chapel at Bath, Mr Thos. King and Miss Margaret English. Present as Witnesses, her Father, Mr Edmund English and her Sister, Mary English, by

Ralph Ainsworth.

1802, February 22nd, were married in the Catholic Chapel at Bath, Mr. Edmund English and Miss Mary Eliza Evans. Present as Witnesses, Miss Mary English and Mr John English, by me

Jas. Calderbank.

1802, July 11th, were married in the Catholic Chapel at Bath, Patrick Curly and Sarah Leigh. Present as Witnesses, Rose Cosgrove and Michael O'Brien, by me

Jas. Calderbank.

1803, April 19th, were married in the Catholic Chapel at Bath (Juxta ritum S. Ecclesiae Catholicae), Bernard Cox and Jane Smith. Present as Witnesses, Mr G [?] Gouget and Mrs Chapin, by me

Jas. Calderbank.

Confirmatorum. [Ainsworth's hand.]

In Capella C. Bathoniae ab Illustrissimo D. Carolo Walmesley, Ramatensi, die 5 Maii 1793:—

Cornelius Hughes	Maria West
Joannes West	Maria Magd. Burne
Antonius Wright	Maria Moore
Michael Osmond	Agnes Rose

Michael West
Edmundus Collingridge
Joannes Bapt. Odber
Edmundus English
Josephus Smith
Gulielmus Jones
Josephus Robinson

Maria Perry
Elizabetha Dale
Martha Smith
Maria Anna Cortis
Maria Teresia Stych
Winefrida West
Anna English
Maria Magd. English
Elizabetha Trant
Maria Odber
Maria Norris
Anna Hughes
Maria Day

Confirmat: [*Ainsworth's hand.*]

In Capella C. Bath. ab Illus. D. Car. Walmesley, Ramat., die 29 Aprilis 1796:—

Maria Mackey
Anna Hencey
Catharina Phelon

Maria Magd. Moore
Maria Smith
Anna Merrick
Maria Paulina Magd. De L'Eguile

Confirmat: [*Ainsworth's hand.*]

In Capella C. Bath. ab Illus. D. Carolo Walmesley, Ep. Ramat., die 24. Septem. 1796:—

Anna Pitt
Maria Pitt
Elizabetha Pitt

Confirmatorum. [*Lawson's hand.*]

In Capella Catholica Bathoniae ab Illustrissimo DD. Gregorio Sharrock, Telmess., die 22 Augusti, Anni 1800:—

Frances Mary[115] Batty
W. Thomas Batchelor
James Francis Cunningham
Rebecca Mary Dunning
John Cornelius Denie

Anne Monica Denie
Anne Mary Dayly
Eliz. Mary Heal
Nancy Sarah Hughes
Eliz. Mary Howell
[*blank*] Mary James

Left-hand column, below, in Lawson's hand; right-hand in Ainsworth's:

Arrabella Mary Kelly
Eliz. Anne Keen
Effingam Thomas Lindsay
Peggy Mary Lanan
Mary Anne Mulligan
John Mathew Muttry
Bridget Mary Prior
Catherine Elizabeth Pope
Anne Mary Pope

Winefrid Mary Jellyman
Elizabeth Anne Brown
Mary Mary Seifreid
Martha Mary Hughes
Barbara Joanna Agnes Denie
Winefrid Cecilia Denie
Mary Elizabeth Parker
Richard Joseph Goodman
Sarah Catherine Rourk

---

[115] Unlike that for 1808, printed on p. 69, these earlier lists give little indication of confirmation-names.

Anne Mary Mag. Purnall
James Edward Maguire
Anne Sarah Maguire
Thom. Anthony Smith
John Joseph Taylor
Eliz. Catherine Whimble
John Thomas Wogan
Anne Mary White
Mary Anne West

Sarah Mary Meagher
Mary Anne Hughes
Eliz. Catherine Weston
Anne Mary Rowe
James George Rowe
Vincent Gabriel de Bois Boissel
Carolina Aloysia Geach
Eliz. Lucy Davis
Eleanora Catherine Hayden
Eleanora Mary Anne Butler

Calderbank's hand:
Confirmati in Capella Catholica Bathoniae ab Illustrissimo et Reverendissimo D.D. Gregorio Gulielmo Sharrock, Episcopo Telmess., die Maii tertia, Anni 1801:—

Susa. Winefride Day   –   Sponsor Miss [*blank*] Day
Jo.[116] Charles Day   –   Sponsor Mr [*blank*] Day
            Elisabeth Ketcherside

Calderbank's hand:
Ab eodem Illustrissimo et Reverendissimo D.D.G.G. Sharrock, Episcopo Telmessem, die Maii quarta, Anni 1802, confirmati fuere:—

Elisabeth Teresa Wright
  –   Clare Irwin
Victoire Louisa Julienne
Elisabeth Mary Yarmouth
Charlotte Mary Brooks
Eliza Mary McDonald
Jane Mary Wilmot
Catharine Connor

Judith Leaven
Mary Bridget Nugent
Margt. Anne Hind
John Joseph Martin
Winefride Morgan
Jas. Joseph Davies
Anne Price

Calderbank's hand (asterisks indicate damage to page):
Ab eodem illus. et. Revdissimo D.D.G.G. Sharrock, Ep. Telmess., die 14a Novembris 1803, confirma*us fuit Anthonius Holloran in articulo *tis [*no doubt the damaged words are "confirmatus" and "mortis".]*

Ainsworth's hand:
Confirmat. in Capella Catholica Bathoniae ab Illusmo. et Revmo. D.D. Gregorio Gulielmo Sharrock, Episcopo Telmessen. die 30, mensis Maii, anni 1806:—

Louisa Maria, Magdalena Browne
Catharina, Maria Cecilia Browne
Maria Louisa Gildemeester
Clara Christiana Maria Irwin

Sarah, Anna English
Joanna, Maria Read
Rebecca Ketcherside
Francisca, Birgitta Nagle

Maria, Martina Nagle

Ainsworth's hand:
1807, April the 27th, was confirmed by the Rt. Revd. G. W. Sharrock,

---

[116] This and the name above, both written in the margin in lighter ink, are doubtless confirmation-names.

Bishop of Telmessum, Matthew Costello, an infant in danger of death.

Birdsall's hand:
1807, May the [*blank*] was confirmed by the Rt. Rev. G. W. Sharrock, Bishop of Telmessum, Catharine Maguíre, aged 41, in articulo Mortis.

1807, Augt. 26th, was confirmed by the Rt. Revd. G. W. Sharrock, Henry Michael Carrol; and Decr. 7th, Ann Lewis: both infants in danger of death.

1808, Jany. 29, John Howgate and Mary Barrington — item.

Birdsall's hand:
1808, Augt. 8th, Were confirmed in the Catholic Chapel at Bath by Rt. Revd. Dr Collingridge, Episcop. Thespiens:—

Ann Shewring by the name of Maria		Sophia Jinks	Mary
Irene Maguire	Mary	Henrietta Church	Ann
Mary Ann Frere	Margaret	William Penny	
Frances Boyce	Mary	Matthew Halpen	
Laetitia Smallman	Mary Magd.	Eliz. Gibbs	
Grace Fisher	Mary	Ann Rosanna	
Eliz. West	Mary Mag.	John Wall	
Nicolas Paillet	Antony	James Quin	
Eliz. Dutton		Ann Lauler	
Sarah Callan		Mary White	Eliz.
Patrick Mulloy		Eliz. White	Mary
Elizabeth Mulloy		Mary Ann Martin.	
Mary Browne		Jane Moger.	
Ann Thornman	Mary	Eliz. Abbot.	
Edwd. Galespy		Ann Keene	
Eliz. Browne		John Carrol	
Mary Browne	Mary	Thos. James	Joseph
Martha Browne	Ellen	Ann West	Mary
Ann Winbow		Mary Kingston	
Cornelius Dowding		James Groves	
Mary Williams		Catharine Knapp	
Eliz. Williams			

Next 2 pages blank, then follow entries in Calderbank's, Ainsworth's and Birdsall's hands, as signed:
1803, July 12th, were married in the Catholic Chapel at Bath, Nicholas Paillet and Margaret White; present as Witnesses, Edward Roach and Elenora Hall, by me

Jas. Calderbank.
1803, Novr. 10th, were married according to the rite of the H. Catholic Church Jacob West and Margaret Callers; present as Witnesses, James Doyle and Rachele West, by me

Jas. Calderbank.

1804, Jan. 10th, were married in the Catholic Chapel at Bath, Thomas Jordan and Sarah England; present as witnesses, John and Catherine Gogin.

R. Ainsworth.

1804, Jan. 15, were married George Lewis and Catherine Randal; present as witnesses, Mr and Mrs Clarke and Sarah Randal.

R. Ainsworth.

1804, July 30th, were married in the Catholic Chapel at Bath, George Hade and Frances Batty; present as Witnesses, Anne Dove and many of the Congregation, by me

Jas. Calderbank.

1805, Feby. 3rd, were married in the Catholic Chapel at Bath, Charles Gerish and Elisabeth Griffin; present Catharine Sullivan, Miss B. Ketcherside – by me

Jas. Calderbank.

1805, April 14th, were married in the Catholic Chapel at Bath, George Viner and Martha Hughes; present as Witnesses, Mrs Rochefort and her servant maid.

R. Ainsworth.

1805, Sep. 22d, were married in the Catholic Chapel at Bath, William Stiles and Elizabeth Yarmouth; present as witnesses, Henry Williams and Dorothy Lees.

R. Ainsworth.

1805, Dec. 20th, were married in the Catholic Chapel at Bath, John Peneston and Sarah Harris. Present as witnesses, James Harris and Elizabeth Hale.

R. Ainsworth.

1806, July 29th, were married in the Catholic Chapel at Bath, James Joseph Boulnois, de l'Evêché de Laon dans la Picardie en France, and Marianne Nunnes of the parish of Mangots-field,[117] by me

John Birdsall.

Present as Witnesses, Revd. Michael Pembridge and Hellen Rose.

1806, Nov. 27th, were married in the Catholic Chapel at Bath, John Day and Winefrid Morgan. Present as Witnesses, Edward Calley and – Lalor.

R. Ainsworth.

Next nine entries in Birdsall's hand:

1807, Jany. 7th, were married at Horton, ritu catholico, William Rodway and Elizabeth Winbow, both of that place. Witnesses, Elizabeth Winbow Senr. and Ann Winbow.

by John Birdsall.

1807, Jany. 26th, were married in the Catholic Chapel at Bath, William Hopson and Catharine Byrne. Present as Witness, Mary Hensey.

by John Birdsall.

---

[117] Mangotsfield, Glos., near Bristol.

1807, Nov. 25th, were married in the Catholic Chapel at Bath, Thos. Prince and Jane Reed of the Parish of Witcombe.[118] Present Henry Williams.

Ralph Ainsworth.

1808, May 30th, were married in the Catholic Chapel at Bath, John Driscol and Mary Burke of Bristol. Witnesses, Mrs. Burke her Mother, and John Wall.

John Birdsall.

1809, March 18th, were married in the Catholic Chapel at Bath, John Harris Arnold and Jane Sutton; present as Witnesses, Margaret Sutton, Matthew Darcy Talbot, and Lucy Gibbon.

Ralph Ainsworth.

1809, April 16th, were married in the Catholic Chapel at Bath, Charles Goldfinch, and Rachel West; present as Witnesses, Mary and Ann West.

by Ralph Ainsworth.

1809, July 16th, were married (ritu catholico) at Bath, Thomas Fitz-herbert Esqr. and Mary Ann Chichester; present as Witnesses, the Grand-mother of the latter, Mrs Chichester, Mr Thos. Clifford and Mrs Clifford.

by Wm. Coombes.

1809, July 19th, were married in the Catholic Chapel at Bath, Thos. Tunstall Esqr. and Miss Mary Trapps; present as Witnesses, Miss Talbot, Timothy O'Brien Esqr. and others.

by John Birdsall.

1809, Sepr. 11th, were married in the Catholic Chapel at Bath, Pierre Gerard and Euphrosine Hussenot; present as witnesses, Charles L'Acoste and Victoire Julien

by John Birdsall.

Ainsworth's hand:

1813, Dec. 26th, were married (ritu Catholico) Matthieu Paul Louis Anne Prigny De Quérieux, Capitaine de Vaisseau dans la marine Im-periale, Chevalier de la Légion D'honneur and Miss Sarah Marshall. Present as witnesses, le Contre-Amiral Durand De Linois, Comte de l'Empire, Commandant de la Légion D'honneur, and Francoise Sachery De Beaurepaire.

by me Ralph Ainsworth.

Heatley's hand:
1788.[119]

June 15, were married Mr Cosmas Nevill and Miss Maria Anna Bella Gardener. Witnesses, Thomas Moore and Catharine Collingridge.

Hugh Heatley.

---

[118]   Presumably Widcombe, Bath.

[119]   This entry also occurs in *R.B.A.*, p. 312, dated 16 June, suggesting that the Catholic ceremony preceded the Anglican, in contravention of Hardwicke's Act (26 Geo. II, cap. 33). The entry in the Abbey Register describes the bridegroom as "of Holt, co. Leicester" and the bride as of Bath. The two witnesses at the ceremony in the Abbey were William Roberts and John Gardiner. For the Nevills see Mr B. Elliott's article in *R.H.*, 7, pp. 249-62. See also note 60 to second register (*infra*, p. 193).

The next entry, in Heatley's hand, is crossed-out and marked "Null".
1791, James Donnelly and Flora Falkener (alias Cole) were married.
Witnesses, a stranger and [*blank*] Burn.

Hugh Heatley.

Ainsworth's hand:
1802, May the 1st: married Andrew Monk and Mary Rogers.

R. Ainsworth.

In Ainsworth's and Lawson's hands, as signed (see supra., p. 56):
1794. Baptized March the 16th Elizabeth Strode, Child to Byflet and
Eliz. Strode. Godfather Mr Otburn, Godmother Anne Nagle.

H. Lawson.

March 17th. Baptized William Macdonald, born the 13th, the Son of
[*names omitted*]. The Godmother Mrs Hopkings.

H. Lawson.

1794, April 25th. Baptized Thomas Peter Metcalf, son of Thomas and
Teresa Metcalf, born the same day. Godfather Sir John Throckmorton,
Godmother Lady Fitzgerald.

Ralph Ainsworth.

1794, May 16th. Baptized Raymond Thomas Hugo Arundel, son of
Raymond and [*blank*] Arundel,[120] born the same day. Godfather
[*blank*] by proxy of Hugo Smythe, Godmother Lady Smythe.

Ralph Ainsworth.

1794. Baptizatorum.

1794, June 10th. Baptized Eleanor Doyle, daughter of Patrick and
Eleanor Doyle, born May 14th. Godfather John Mears, Godmother
Martha Smith.

Ralph Ainsworth.

1794, June 22d. Baptized Thomas Maguire, son of Patrick and Catherine
Maguire, born May 29th. Godfather Laughlan Dignum, Godmother
Anne Garrety.

Ralph Ainsworth.

1794, June 4th. Baptized John Martin, Son of John and [*blank*] Martin,
born the same day.

Ralph Ainsworth.

1794, July 8th, was baptized Isabella Mary Burrough, daughter of Joseph
and Mary Burrough, born July 5th. Godfather Philip Wright, Godmother
[*blank*].

by Ralph Ainsworth.

1794, July 25th. Baptized Mary Wogan, Daughter of Edward and
Frances Wogan, born July 22d. Godfather Dominiq Rezano, Godmother
Anna Rezano.

Henry Lawson.

[120] The mother was Mary Anne Elizabeth (only daughter of Sir Edward Smythe,
4th Bart., of Acton Burnell) who in 1792 had married Thomas Raymund Arundell,
third son of James Everard Arundell of Ashcombe, Wilts., and grandson of the
6th Lord Arundell of Wardour; cf. E. Doran Webb (ed.) *Notes by the 12th Lord
Arundell of Wardour on the Family History* (1916), genealogical table facing p. 84;
Kirk, p. 214; *C.R.S. Monograph 1*, pp. 166, 168, 207, 217-8. This, their first
child, died in infancy (see *infra*, p. 121).

1794, August 17th. Baptized Joanna Ferrer, daughter of John and Mary Ferrer, born July 29th. Godfather Michael Pheilan, Godmother Joanna Glasson.

Ralph Ainsworth.

1794, August 24th. Baptized John Birt, son of Charles and [*blank*] Birt, born August 14th. Godfather Dominick Rosano, Godmother Anne Rosano.

Ralph Ainsworth.

August, 24th 1794. Baptized Richard Phelan, son of Richard and Elizabeth Phelan, born August 23d. Godfather William Hopkins, Godmother Margaret Downing, by proxy of Margaret Sumpsion.

Ralph Ainsworth.

1794, September 17th. Baptized Aegidius (Giles) Hall, Son of Giles and Christian Hall, born September 15th. Godfather Martin Obrien, Godmother Mary Norris.

Ralph Ainsworth.

1794, September 21. Baptized Henrietta Barry, daughter of Garrett and Helen Barry, born Aguust 20th. Godfather Simon Hencey, Godmother Frances Mary Hynde.

Ralph Ainsworth.

1794, September 24. Baptized Thomas Buck, son of Stephen and Frances Buck, born the same day. Godfather Thomas Hughes by proxy of William Hopkins, Godmother Mary Matthews by proxy of Winefrid Felton.

Ralph Ainsworth.

1794, October 14th. Baptized Anne Mary Rose Rosano, daughter of Dominick and Anne Rosano, born the 13th of the same month. Godfather John Vecchio, Godmother Anne Mary Rose Ashton.

Ralph Ainsworth.

1794, December 4th. Baptized M. Bony, daughter of Patrick and Catherine Bony, born the last month. Godfather Francis Curley, Godmother Elizabeth Halsy.

Ralph Ainsworth.

1795, January the 20. Baptized Eliza Mahony, Daughter of Denis and Eliza Mahony. Godfather Michel Quinlan, God Mother Eliz. Butler.

H. Lawson.

Next entry in Ainsworth's hand, with witnesses' signatures:
L'an mil-sept cent quatre-vingt-quinze, le huit Janvier, Jacques Louis Marie George Owen, né de ce jour à Bath du légitime mariage de très haut et très puissant Seigneur Jacques Louis François Marie Toussaint, chef des noms et armes, chevalier, Marquis de Kerouartz, Comte de Penlivet, colonel de cavalerie; et de très haute et très puissante Dame Marie Joseph Reine de Cleuz Dugage, été baptisé par nous, Recteur de Neuville, Doyen D'Ivry, Diocese d'Evreux en France, soussigné. Le parain très haut et très puissant Seigneur Francois Marie Louis, chevalier, Comte de Kerouartz, officer au regiment d'infanterie de Roy de France; la maraine très haute et très puissante Dame Ellen Owen, Dame de

Porkington,[121] representée par très haute et très puissante Dame Jeanne Jacquette de Roquefeuil, Marquise du Gage, en vertu de la procuration de la ditte Dame Owen faite à Londres le quatre Décembre de l'année dernière qui nous a été représentée.

J. Cte de Kerouartz.   Le M'is de Kerouartz.

J.J.Roquefeuil, Marquise du Gage.   Picquenot.

Henceforth in the hands of Ainsworth, Lawson, Picquenot and Feray, as signed:
Feb. 2, 1795. Baptized Winefrid Moore aged 52.
See next page   Ralph Ainsworth.

The above reference to the next page is because it starts with an entry for February (the 13th) misplaced between two March entries.
Feb. 12th 1795. Baptized Helen Ryley, daughter of Michael and Elisa Ryley, born the 6th of the same month. Godfather James Barry, Godmother Brigit Burke.
                                                     Ralph Ainsworth.
Feb. 15th 1795. Baptized John Coffe, son of John and Joanna Coffe, born the 10th of the same month. Godfather William Micnahertin, Godmother Anne Connel.
                                                     Ralph Ainsworth.
Feb. 18th 1795. Baptized Maria McNamara, daughter of Gabriel and Aloysia McNamara, born the 6th of the same month. Godfather Patrick Condell, Godmother Rosana Downes.
                                                     Ralph Ainsworth.
1795, March 8th. Baptized Brigit Magrath, daughter of Thomas and Margaret Magrath born the 1st of the same month. Godfather Andrew Foley, Godmother Catherine Rowman.
                                                     Ralph Ainsworth.
1795, February 13th. Baptized Mary Appolonia Nagle, daughter of Richard and Catherine Nagle, born the 9th of the same month. Godfather David Nagle, Godmother Mary Porter by proxy of Margaret Trant.
                                                     R. Ainsworth.
1795, March 25th. Baptised Susanna Clarke, the duaghter of John and Mary Clarke. Godfather John Brisco, Godmother Jane Buckley.
                                                     Henry Lawson.
April 2d 1795. Baptised William Ganly, 2 Months old, the son of Michel Ganly and Frances Ganly. Godmother Elizabeth Hutchinson.
                                                     H. Lawson.
April 26th 1795. Baptised Mary Cooper, 3 months old, the Daughter of James Cooper,and Margaret Cooper. No Godfather nor Godmother.
                                                     Henry Lawson.
April 27th 1795. Baptised Joanna Chaddock, daughter of James and Sarah Chaddock, born the 8th of the same month.
                                                     Ralph Ainsworth.

[121] ? Salop.

May 21st 1795. Baptised Maria Helen Brown, daughter of Thomas and Catherine Brown, born the 20th of the same month. Godfather Thomas Canning by proxy of Edmund Collingridge, Godmother Teresa Wilkes by proxy of Helen Rose.

Ralph Ainsworth.

L'an 1795, le vingt Juin, Marie Jeanne, née le treize de ce mois, fille de Marie Jeanne Bruno et de Thomas Jones qui a declaré en être le pére, a été baptisée par nous prêtre soussigné; le parain Louis May qui a declaré la scavoir signer; la maraine Justine Ride qui a signé.

Justine Ride.   Picquenot.

1795, July 3d. Baptized Henrietta Catherine Fryer, daughter of John and Eliza Fryer, born June 22d. Godfather Charles Fryer, Godmother Anne Mary Barrow.

Ralph Ainsworth.

1795, July 5th. Baptized Agnes Cooper, daughter of William and Sarah Cooper, born May the 27th. Godfather Nicolas Taffe, Godmother Elizabeth Moore.

Ralph Ainsworth.

1795, Aug. 24. Baptized Catherine Beard, Daughter of John and Mary Beard. Godfather John Ashton by proxy of Samuel Lyne, Godmother Mary Lyne.

Henry Lawson.

1795, September 14. Baptized Edward Hazard, the Son of Edward and Helena Hazard. Godfather Nicolas Taaffe, Godmother Catherine Were.

Henry Lawson.

1795, September 29. Baptized John McMahon, born the 29th of August 1795, Son of John and Mary McMahon.

H. Lawson.

1795, October 4th. Baptized Mary Anne Quin, daughter of James and Helena Quin.

H. Lawson.

1795, November 1st. Baptized James William Ledwidge, the son of James and Ruthe Ludwidge. Godfather Patrick Meguire, Godmother Margaret Ryan.

Henry Lawson.

1795, Novem. 16. Baptized Jane Nugent, born the 3d of April, Daughter of John and Jane Nugent.

Henry Lawson.

1795, December 3d. Baptized Joseph William Panzera, born 29th of October, son of Antonio and Mary Panzera. Godfather William Denney, Godmother Jane Denney.

H. Lawson.

1795, Decem. 5th. Baptized Michel Conolly, born 2d of December, Son of Michel and Elizabeth Conolly.

H. Lawson.

1795, December 9th. Baptized John Baker, son of John and Mary Baker, born Nov. 23d. Godfather William Connelly, Godmother Helen Hazard.

R: Ainsworth.

1795, December 13th. Baptized Frances Mary Hicks, daughter of Thomas and Mary Hicks, born Nov. 22d. Godmother Frances Matthews.

R. Ainsworth.

1795, December 19th. Baptized Anne Enright, daughter of Patrick and Mary Enright, born the 17 December. Godfather John Hasset, Godmother Elizabeth Prophey.

R: Ainsworth.

1795, December 28.Baptized Anne Love, daughter of Joseph and Sarah Love, born Dec. 27th. Godfather Lawrence Coombs. Godmother Sarah Coombs.

Ralph Ainsworth.

L'an mil-sept cent quatre-vingt-seize, le dimanche dix-sept Janvier, par nous soussigné, Curé de Mirbel, a été baptisé Philippe, fils de Philippe Pouteau et de Marie Nanorey, demeurant à Bath, né le quatre de ce mois. Il a eu pour parrain Augustin Melin, et pour marraine Catherine Charlut qui ont signé avec nous et le père de l'enfant.

Augustin Melin.   Catherine Charlut.
P. Pouteau.   Feray, C. de Mirbel.
                                           R. Ainsworth.

1795, December 29, Baptized John Williams,[122] born the 27th instant, the son of Henry and Margaret Williams, Godfather James Enright, Godmother Sara Sumner.

Henry Lawson.

1796, January 23. Baptised Mary Anne Heron, born the 12th instant, the Daughter of Hugh and Mary Heron. Godfathers John King, Thomas Fennel. Godmothers Elizabeth Nolles, Elizabeth Golahagh.

Henry Lawson.

1796, January 27. Baptised Elizabeth Howel, 5 weeks born, the daughter of Edward and Elizabeth Howel. No Godfather nor Godmother.

Henry Lawson.

1796, February 15. Baptised Anne Jane Lattin, born the third of January 1796, Daughter of Mr Patrick and Elizabeth Lattin. Godfather Robert Ferral by proxy of Charles N. Godmother Jane Fitzgerald by proxy of Anne Martainville.

Henry Lawson.

Entry in Lawson's hand; signature by Feray:
1796, Feb. 8th. Baptized John Burke, Son of John and Alice Burke, born the 3d of the same Month.

Feray, Curé de Mirbel.

Ainsworth's hand:
1796, May 14th. Baptized Dominic Alexander Charles Teighe, son of Dominick and Theresa Teighe, born the same day. Godfather Alexander Lilien, Godmother Anne Mary Teighe.

R. Ainsworth.

[122]   Later a priest and canon of Clifton diocese; cf. Oliver, pp. 438-9.

FIRST BATH REGISTER 77

Ainsworth's hand; Lawson's signature:
1796, March 2d. Baptized James Murphy, son of Daniel and Sarah Murphy. Born 2 weeks.

H. Lawson [R. Ainsworth *deleted*].
Henceforth in the hands of Lawson, Ainsworth and Feray, as signed:
1796, March 3d. Baptized Thomas Murphy, Son of Anne and Patrick Murphy. Godmother Mary McCarley.

H. Lawson.
1796, May the 15th. Baptized Anne Fearrir, born the 8th instant, Daughter of John and Mary Fearrir. Godfather Mr Swaltz [? Swalty], Godmother Mary Glason.

H. Lawson.
May 24, 1796, Baptised Cornelius McAllum, born at Bath the 14th instant, Son of John and Eleanor McAllum. Godfather Cornelius Hughes. No Godmother.

H. Lawson.

1796, May 22. Baptized Catherine Flynn, born May 7th, daughter of Andrew and Alice Flynn. Godfather Michael Toughey [?], Godmother Eleanor Redican [?].

P. Ralph Ainsworth.
June 4. Baptised Michel Ridmond, born the 21 of May 1796.

H. Lawson.
1796, June 8th. Baptized Elisa Clarke, born 4th of June, daughter of Thomas and Eleanor Clarke. Godfather Laughlin Larcon, Godmother Helen Briscoe.

R. Ainsworth.
1796, June 23d. Baptized Robert George Hazard, a foundling. God-mother [*blank*].

R. Ainsworth.
1796, July 5th. Baptized Elizabeth Catherine Phealon, daughter of Richard and Elizabeth Phelan, born the 3d of the same month. God-father James Enright, Godmother Charlotte Merrick.

R. Ainsworth.
1796, July 24th. Baptised Jane Strode, born the 16th of July, daughter of Byflet Strode and Eliz. Strode. Godfather Cornelius Daly, Eliz. Cavarly [*sic.*].

H. Lawson.
1796, July 28. Baptized Theophus Fryer, born the same day, the son of Langley Fryer and Elizabeth Fryer. Godfather Rev. William Victor Fryer,[123] Godmother Mary Anne Burrough.

H. Lawson.
+ 1796, August the 16th. Baptized Charles Victor [*Ainsworth's hand*].

[123] Secular priest (born Bath, 28 July 1768), nephew of Dr William Fryer, President of the English College, Lisbon; cf. W. Croft & J. Gillow, *Historical Account of Lisbon College* (1902) p. 199.

L'an mil-sept cent quatre-vingt-seize, le lundi vingt-deux Aoust, par nous
soussigné, prêtre, a été baptisée Magdeleine Jacqueline le Roux, née la
nuit dernière du légitime mariage de François Pascal le Roux et de
Catherine Radeneue.[124] Elle a pour parrain Jacques Gouget et pour
marraine Magdeleine Avril, avec nous soussignés. M. Avril. J. Gouget.
Feray, prêtre.

1796, August 21st. Baptized Christopher Irvine, born in Bath the 27th
of July 1796, son of Christopher William Irvine Esqr., inhabitant of
Tabago,[125] and of Jeanne Marianne Irvine. Present at the Baptism, Mlle.
Elizabeth Campbell. The Child held by Victoire Julien. Godfather
Walter Irvine Esq., Godmother Mde. Robert Young [sic].
R. Ainsworth.

Septem. 12, 1796. Baptized William Martin, born the 9th instant, son of
John and Helena Martin. Godfathers Thomas Fenerty and John, own
son.
H. Lawson.

Michael J. Smith. See next page [fifth entry below].

October 23, 1796. Baptized James Saw, born Octob. 14. Son of James
and Martha Saw. Godfather John Odber, Godmother Mary Brown.
H. Lawson.

November 6th 1796, Baptized Tate Sullivan, born the 5 instant, son of
Patrick and Norry Sullivan. Godfather Tate Carty, Godmother Matty
Carty.
H. Lawson.

L'an mil-sept cent quatre-vingt-seize, le vingt-trois Octobre, par nous
soussigné, Curé de Mirbel, Diocese de Lisieux en France, a été baptisée
Catherine Sophie Roussel, née le jour précédent à Bath du légitime
mariage de Michel Roussel et de Catherine Beauregard. Elle a pour
parrain Mr. Philippe Howard Esqr., représenté par Mr. Hugh Smythe
Esqr., et pour Marraine Noble Dame Catherine Gartside, avec nous
soussignés; à Bath le dit jour et an que dessus.
Catherine Gartside. Feray, Curé de Mirbel.
Hugh Smythe.

1796, Nov. 14th. Baptized Mary Anne Higgins daughter of Peter Higgins
and Susannah, born Aug. 22d. Godmother Elizabeth Moore.
R. Ainsworth.

1796, September 29th. Baptized Michael Joseph Smith, born the 24th
of the same month, son of Michael and Elizabeth Smith. Godfather
Peter Smith, Godmother Mary Mathews.
R. Ainsworth.

Next two entries in the hand of Picquenot, with various signatures:
L'an mil-sept cent quatre-vingt-seize, le vingt-quatre Novembre, Emile
Ange, né de ce jour du légitime mariage de Messire Leonard Hyacinthe

[124]　? Radener; see marriage-entry, 7 Sept. 1795 (supra, p. 62).
[125]　The island of Tobago. See also 9 June 1799 (infra, p. 86).

Thadée de la Monneraye, Ecuire, chevalier de l'ordre royal et militaire de St. Louis, Seigneur dufresne, capitaine au regiment d'infanterie de Mgr. le Duc d'Angoulême, et de Dame Marie Charlotte de la Monneraye, ses père et mère, demeurants en cette ville de Bath, a été baptisé par nous Jean Marie de Chateau Giron, prêtre du Diocèse de Rennes, prieur de St. Roch. Le parain Messire François Pierre Ange de la Monneraye, Ecuier, Seigneur de la Morinais, representé par Messire Pierre Bruno Jean de la Monneraye, Ecuier, chevalier de l'ordre de St. Louis, lieutenant des vaissaux de Sa Majesté le Roy de la France; la maraine Dame Françoise Geneviève de Conaic, Douairière de la Monneraye de Bourgneuf, grand-mère maternelle de l'enfant, qui ont signé le présent acte.

> Coniac de la Monneraye de Bourgneuf
> Pierre Bruno Jean de la Monneraye
> Léonard-Hyacinthe-Thadée de la Monneraye, Père.
> J.M. Dechasteaugiron, Ptre.

L'an mil-sept cent quatre-vingt-seize, le trois Décembre, Edouard François né d'hier du légitime mariage de Messire René Augustin de la Monneraye, Ecuier, Seigneur de Beaumer, chevalier de l'ordre royal et militaire de St. Louis, capitaine au régiment du Roy de France, infanterie, et de Dame Georgette Marie Françoise de Kerouartz, ses père et mère, demeurants dans cette ville de Bath, a été baptisé par nous Joseph Henry Picquenot, prêtre, Curé de Neuville, Doyen d'Ivry au Diocése d'Evreux en France. Le parain Messire François Marie Louis, Comte de Kerouartz, la maraine Dame Marie Charlotte de la Monneraye, épouse de Messire Leonard Hyacinthe Thadée de la Monneraye, chevalier de St. Louis, capitaine au regiment de Mgr. le Duc d'Angoulême, qui ont signé le présent acte avec nous et le père de l'enfant.

> Le comte F.L.M. de Kerouartz.
> M.C. de la Monneraye de la Monneraye
> René Augustin de la Monneraye.
> Picquenot.

Next two entries in Lawson's hand:
Nov. 20th 1796. Baptized Rosanno,[126] born 9th Nov., son of Dominick Rosanno and Anne Rosanno. Godfather John Bisani, Godmother Francesca Bisani.

> H. Lawson.

December 4th 1796. Baptized John Woodhead, born 17th of September. Father George Woodhead, Mother Helena Woodhead. No Godfather nor Godmother.

> H. Lawson.

Picquenot's hand, with witnesses' signatures:
1797. L'an mil-sept cent quatre-vingt-dix-sept, le vingt-deux Janvier, nous Joseph Henry Picquenot, Doyen d'Ivry et Recteur de Neuville au Diocese d'Evreux, avons supplées les cérémonies du baptême à Louis,

---

[126] *sic.* Christian name omitted.

né à Plimout le huit [*overwritten*] Juillet mil-sept cent quatre-vingt-onze du légitmie mariage de Messire Jean Dimar [?] de la Monneraye, Ecuier, Seigneur du Restineur [?], et de Dame Marie Charlotte Reine de Kerouartz, ses père et mère, ainsi qu'il nous a présentement été certifié par la mère de l'enfant, par Dame Francoise Geneviève de Coniac, Duairière de la Monneraye de Bourneuf, grandmère paternelle du dit enfant, et autres personnes dignes de foy ici présentes et soussignées, qui ont assisté à la naissance et baptême, ou en ont pleine connaissance. Le parain Messire Louis François Marie Toussaint, Ecuier, Marquis de Kerouartz; la Maraine Dame Marie Charlotte de la Monneraye, épouse de Messire de la Monneraye, capitaine d'infanterie et chevalier de St. Louis, qui ont signé le present acte.

Coniac de la Monneraye de Bourgneuf.
M.C.R. de Kerouartz de la Monneraye. Le M'is de Kerouartz.
R.A. Ch'en de la Monneraye. de la Monneraye. de la Monneraye.
Kerouartz De Kermel. Le M'is de Kermel. Le C'te de Kerouartz.
Reine de la Monneraye. L.H. Th: De la Monneraye.
P.B.T. de la Monneraye. de Roquefeuil, M'ise du Gage.
approuvés un mot raturé à la quatrième ligne, et le mot huit surchargé à la cinquième[127]

Picquenot.

Henceforth in Ainsworth's and Lawson's hands, as signed:
January 10th 1797. Baptized Thomas Ryan, son of Michael and Martha Ryan, born December the 19th 1796. Godfather Thomas Ryan, Godmother Mary Ryan.

R. Ainsworth.

Thomas Barry, born the 4th of January. Baptized by the father 22 of January, the son of Garret and Ellenor Barry. Godfather Mich O'Brian, Godmother Ellenor Selves; the ceremonies performed the 29 of January.

H. Lawson.

March 6th 1797. Baptized Anne Hurst, daughter of Josue and Anne Hurst, born February the 12th 1797.

R. Ainsworth.

March 7th 1797. Baptized Anne Wogan, daughter of Edward and Frances **Wogan**, born the 4th of the same month. Godfather Dominick Rosano.

R. Ainsworth.

1797, March 26th. Baptized Henry David Hopkins, born the 1st of March, Son of Michael and Honora Hopkins. Sponsors Michael Englsih and Mary Ferrer.

H. Lawson.

1797, May 25 [? 23]. Baptized William Prendiville, born the 18th instant, Son of William and Eliz. Prendiville. Godfather Michael Moony, Godmother Catharine Madan.

H. Lawson.

[127] The word deleted, near the beginning of the entry, is "Andrée" and the word "huit" is overwritten upon what looks more like "neuf" than "cinque" or "cinquième" as stated at the end of the register-entry. "Plimout" is doubtless Plymouth.

1797, May 11th. Baptized Mary Margaret Miles aged 33 years and 6 months.

R. Ainsworth.

1797, May 11th. Baptized Fitzgerald Geoghegan Columban Nagle, born May the 5th, son of Richard and Catherine Nagle. Godfather David Nagle, Godmothers Mary Hussey and Mary Clifford by proxy of Mrs Trant.

R. Ainsworth.

Piquenot's hand with various signatures:
L'an mil-sept cent quatre-vingt-dix-sept, le dix-neuf Avril, Amelie Felicité, née d'hier du légitime mariage de Messire Jean Baptiste Florian Jolly, Ecuier, Seigneur de Conteadeu [?] et de Dame Marie Ledet de Segrais, mariés à St. Malo en l'année 1790, a eté baptisée par nous Jean Marie Dechateau Giron, prêtre du Diocese de Rennes, et prieur de St Roch. Le parain Messire Amand Fiacre Salion, Seigneur de Chef Dubois, capitaine des vaisseaux du Roy de France; la Maraine Dame Felicité Meslé, Comtesse Douairière de la Noue Bogar, qui ont signé avec nous le present acte.
Meslé de la Noüe.   J.M. Dechasteaugiron, Ptre.
J.B. Florian Jolly de Conteadeu [?]

Next four entries in Lawson's hand:
July 2, 1797. Baptized Mary Sullivan. Father Patrick Sullivan, Mother Anne Sullivan. Godfather Michael Brian, Godmother Mary Heli.

H. Lawson.

1797, June 24. Baptised Catherine Herron, born the 6th of June. Daughter of Hugh Herron and Mary Heron. Godfathers N. Taffe, John Kenny and [*sic.*] Anne Kelly and Cath. Mealey.

H. Lawson.

Baptized William Howell, June the 24th.

H. Lawson.

July 10th 1797. Baptized [*blank*], born the 5th Instant. Father John Martin, Mother Bridget Martin. Godfather Hugh Herron, Godmother Lucy Anne Dowding.

H. Lawson.

Picquenot's hand, with witnesses' signatures:
L'an mil-sept cent quatre-vingt-dix-sept, le vingt-deux Juillet, une fille née d'hier du légitime mariage de Messire Joseph Marie de Querhoent,[128] Baron du dit lieu, chevalier de l'ordre royal et militaire de Saint Louis, capitaine d'infanterie, et de Dame Marie Jacquette Emilie de Benayé, les père et mère actuellement résidants en cette ville de Bath, et mariés dans celle de Dinant, Diocèse St. Malo en Bretagne, a été baptisée par nous Joseph Henry Picquenot, Doyen d'Ivry et Recteur de Neuville au Diocèse d'Evreux en France, en présence de Messr. Aimé Gabriel Fidel Dubois de St Gonant, chevalier de St. Louis, Mr. Sébastien, chevalier de

---

[128] Or Kerhoent; cf. De la Chenaye-Desbois et Badier, *Dictionnaire de la Noblesse* (Paris, 1863-76), XI, pp. 190-2; XVI, p. 604.

Querhoent, de Dame Henriette Ulalie Marie de Benayé Plancher, tante maternelle, cousin germain de la ditte enfant, approuvé le renvoy.

                          Benayé de Plancher.
Le B'on [?] De Querhoënt.   Le ch'er de Querhoent.
                          Dubois de St. Gonant,
                                          Picquenot.

Henceforth in Lawson's and Ainsworth's hands as signed:
1797, 27 June. Baptized Maria Francisca Rosa Havez, Daughter to Julien Havez and of Anne Havez, Godfather Mr Pouteau, Godmother Mrs Bisani.

                                          R. H. Lawson.
1797. Baptized August the 22, John Alexander Potteau, born August the 4th 1797, the Son of Philip Poteau and Mary Nanorey. Godfather John Kelly, Godmother Mary Charlotte Silvester.

                                          H. Lawson.
1797. Baptized Anne Osmond Aug. 8th, born July 26th, daughter of Noah and Elizabeth Osmond. Godfather Wm. Hopkins, Godmother Margaret Bessett.

                                          R. Ainsworth
1797, Sep. 6th. Baptized Henry Gooseberry born July 27th, son of Henry and Mary Gooseberry.

                                          R. Ainsworth.
1797, Sep. 27. Baptized Daniel Brien, son of Daniel and Mary Brien, born 26th of the same month. Godfather William Grady, Godmother Catherine Macnamara.

                                          R. Ainsworth.
1797, Oct. 11th. Baptized Catherine Howse Knapp,[129] daughter of John and Mary Knapp, born Sept. 1st. Godfather James Knapp by proxy of William Day, Godmother Catherine Hicks by proxy of Catherine Randal.

                                          R. Ainsworth.
1797, Oct. 15th. Baptized Elizabeth Cooper, daughter of John and Mary Cooper, born 28th of September. Godfather John Farrel, Godmother Jane Glasten.

                                          R. Ainsworth.
October 12, 1797. Baptized Charles Edward Shine, son of Charles and Elizabeth Shine, born the 30 of September. Godfather Thomas Brown, Godmother Mary Caverley.

                                          H. Lawson.
[The above entry, re-dated 19 October, is repeated four entries later.]

October 30th 1797. Baptized William Burrough, Son of Joseph and Anne Burrough, born the 12th of the same month and year. Godfather William Fryer, Godmother Eliz. Fisher.

                                          Henry Lawson.

---

[129] See *C.R.S.*, 56, p. 169. Her father is described as of Bath and Portsea, Hants. In May 1817 she married John Rowe of Marnhull, Dorset. She died in July 1818.

October 30th 1797. Baptized Ellinor Fryer, Daughter of John and Eliz. Fryer, born October 15, 1797. Godfather William Fryer.

H. Lawson.

1797, December 14. Baptized Eliz Reyley, Daughter of John and Anne Reyley, born the 14th of Nov. Godmother Mary Reyly.

H. Lawson.

January the 2d 1798. Baptized Anna Glyn, born the 26 of December 1797. Daughter of James Glyn and Mary Glyn. Godmother Mary Archer.

H. Lawson.

January 2d 1798. Baptized Catherine Monk, born 28th of December 1797, daughter of John and Anne Monk, Godfather Anthony Clavel.

R. Ainsworth.

February 18th 1798. Baptized Charles Dubois, born the 8th of the same month, son of Hubert and Honor Dubois. Godfather Joseph Mesger.

R. Ainsworth.

March 28th 1798. Baptized James Higgins, Son of Peter and Susanna Higgins, born January 28th, 1798. Godfather Thomas Fitzgerald, Godmother Elizabeth Concannon.

R. Ainsworth.

May 2d 1798. Baptized Thomas Brown, Son of Thos. and Catherine Brown, born the same day. Godfather Edmund Collingridge, Godmother Martha Collingridge.

R. Ainsworth.

May 2d 1798. Baptized Nicholas Barnewall son of Thos. and Maria Barnewall, born the 11th of April 1798. Godfather Nicholas Trimlestown, Godmother Alicia Trimelstown.

R. Ainsworth.

May 24th 1798. Baptized Christina Mary Elizabeth Arundel, daughter of Thos. Raymond Arundel and Elizabeth Mary Anne Arundel, born the same day. Godfather Sir Edward Smythe Bart., Godmother Lady Arundel.[130]

R. Ainsworth.

May 1st 1798. Baptized John Dealy, son of John and Esther Dealy, born the 20th of April. Godfather John Lyons, Godmother Julia Corbet.

R. Ainsworth.

X See next Page [*i.e. for July 1st entry, following that of Aug. 9th*].

1798, July 2d. Baptized Christina Ardenond, daughter of Peter and Mary Ardenond, born the 24th of June. Godfather Matheu Judie, Godmother Eliz. Howell.

H. Lawson.

1798, July 8th. Baptized Mary Anne Willis, born 1 of the said month. Daughter of Mr N. Willis and Mrs M. Willis. Godfather N., Godmother [*blank*].

H. Lawson.

[130] See note 120.

1798, August 9th. Baptized Mary Anne Veare, daughter of Richard and Mary Veare, born 19th of July. Godmother Helen Hall.

R. Ainsworth.

X July 1st 1798. Baptized George Phelan, son of Richard and Elizabeth Phelan, born the 30th of June 1798. Godfather Joseph Jamar, God-mother Miss Constansia Walsh.

Ralph Ainsworth.

1798, September 20. Baptized Catherine Kavenah, Daughter of Patrick and Elizabeth Kavenah. Godmother Honora Curren.

H. Lawson.

1798. Baptized George Wisdom Foster, born September the 19th, son of George and Eliz. Foster. Godfather H. Sandle by proxy for Francis Bolan. . [? Boland *or* Bolant] , God Mother Helena Brinby by proxy for Lucy Barrat.

H. Lawson.

1798, Oct. 8. Baptized Martha Newbol, born the 26th of March, daughter of William and Anne Neubowl. Godfathers Mic. Lator and William Brennar, Godmother Hon. Curren.

H. Lawson.

1798, October 8. Baptized Thomas Clarke, son of Thomas and Helena Clarke. Godfather Jeremiah Burgen, Godmother Joanna Hern.

H. Lawson.

1798, October 29. Baptized Eliz. Ferrers, born the 13th, Daughter of John and Mary Ferrers. Godfather Nicolas Taaffe, Godmother Mary Carter.

H. Lawson.

1798, October 29. Baptized Mary Anne Brookes, 5 years old, Daughter of Nancy Brookes, Godmother Hon. Miss Talbot.

H. Lawson.

XX *These crosses refer to the next entry but one, out of chronological order.*

1798, Nov. 26. Baptized Bernard Bun, 6 weeks old, Son of Bernard and Jane Bun. No Godfather nor Godmother.

H. Lawson.

XX

1798, Nov. 2d. Baptized Mary Knapp, daughter of John and Mary Knapp, born Oct. 1st. Godfather Joseph Knapp by proxy of William Day, Godmother Teresa Knapp by proxy of Catherine Randal.

R. Ainsworth.

Picquenot's hand (apart from names italicised) with witnesses' signatures:
L'an mil-sept cent quatre-vingt-dix-huit, le dix-huit Décembre, *Laure Julie* née de ce jour du légitime mariage de Mre. René Augustine de la Monneraye, Ecuier, chevalier de St. Louis, capitaine au régiment du Roy de France, infanterie, et de Dame Georgette Marie Francoise de Kerouartz, ses père et mère demeurants dans cette ville de Bath, a été baptisée par nous Joseph Henri Picquenot, Doyen d'Ivry et Curé de Neuville, Diocèse d'Evreux en France; le parain Mre. *Paul Jule,* Marquis

de Laporte, commandeur de l'ordre royal et militaire de St. Louis, chef d'escadres; la maraine Alexandrine Auguste Hortense Marie de Kerouartz, femme de Mr. le Marquis de Kermel, qui ont signé avec nous le présent acte.

De Kerouartz de Kermel.   De la Monneraye.

Laporte Nerin [? Nezin] .   Picquenot.

Next two entries in Ainsworth's hand:
1799.
1799, January the 15th. Baptized James Browne, Son of James and Elizabeth Browne, born the 7th of the same month.

R. Ainsworth.

1799, January the 15th. Baptized John Smith son of [*blank*].

Next three entries in Lawson's hand:
1799, January 24, born Helena Martin. Baptized the [*blank*], Daughter of John and Helen Martin. Godfather Richard Kenedy, Godmother Nancy Sullivan.

H. Lawson.

Feb. 9. Baptized Henry Holt, born 4 months, son of Henry and Mary Holt.

H. Lawson.

1799, March 9th. Baptized Joseph Mary White, born the 5th of February, son of Joseph and Barbara White. Godfather William Hopkins, Godmother Mary Short.

Henry Lawson.

Picquenot's hand, with witnesses' signatures:
L'an mil-sept cent quatre-vingt-dix-neuf, le vingt-cinq Mars, Claire Marie née d'hier du légitime mariage de Mssre. Jean Dymas [?] de la Monneraye, Ecuier, et de Marie Charlotte Reine de Kerouartz, ses père et mère, a été baptisée par nous soussigné. Le parain Mr. Pierre Bruno Jean de la Monneraye, Ecuier, la Maraine Alexandrine Auguste Marie Hortense de Kerouartz, épouse de Mr. le Marquis de Kermel, qui ont signé le present acte avec nous et le père de l'enfant

P.B.J. de la Monneraye.

J.D.De la Monneraye.   Picquenot.

Henceforth in Ainsworth's, Lawson's and Picquenot's hands, as signed:
1799, March 15th. Baptized Almande Mary Rice, daughter of John Anthony and Elizabeth Rice, born the 25th of February,

by J. Godelier.
R. Ainsworth.

1799, April 6. Baptized Michel Conor (born the 16th of October) son of Mic. and Mary Conor. Godfather James Maguerk, Godmother July Wall.

H. Lawson.

1799, March 25th. Baptized Richard Charles Dalton, son of (Count) Peter and Rosalia Dalton, born the 23d of the same month. Godfather

Charles Macartey by proxy of Thos. Barnwall, Godmother Aloysia Lady Trimleston.

R. Ainsworth.

See next page but one [*i.e. entry dated 22 May, between those for 6 June and 26 July*].

1799, June 28th. Baptized Henry Raymond Thomas Arundel,[131] son of Raymond Thos. and Elizabeth Arundel, born June 27th. Godfather Lord Arundel by proxy of William Charlton, Godmother Mary Smythe by proxy of Ernestine Jacques.

R. Ainsworth.

1799, June 9th. Baptized Marianne Irvine, daughter of Christopher William Irvine Esq. (inhabitant of the island of Tabago) and Jeanne Marianne Irvine, born the same day. Godfather Christopher Irvine Esq., Godmother Victoire Julien.

R. Ainsworth.

1799, July 10th. Baptized Edmond McDonough, Son of Miles & Susanna McDonough, born July 4th. Godfather James Brady, Godmother Elizabeth Vasey.

R. Ainsworth.

L'an mil-sept cent quatre-vingt-dix-neuf, le dix Juillet, Marie Julie Ambrosine née d'hier du légitime mariage de Mssre. Marie Joseph de Querhoent, Baron du dit lieu et chevalier de St. Louis, capte. d'infanterie, et de Dame Marie Jacquette Emilie de Benayé, ses père et mère de la province de Bretagne en France, a été baptisée par nous soussigné. Le parain Mssre. Ambroise Toussaint Marie, Comte de Parcevaux, la Maraine De. Marie Marquette Françoise Julie de la Boessière, Marquise de Lanascole, qui ont signé avec nous le présente acte.

Parcevaux.   Parens de l'enfant approuvé le renvoi.

Marie M.F.J. De La Boessière De Lanascol

Le Ch'er de Querhoent.   de Benayé de Plancher.

M'is de Lanascol.

Aline de Lanascol.   Dubois de St Gonant.

Querhoent.   Picquenot, C'e de Neuville, Doyen d'Ivry.

1799, April 28. Baptized Mary O'Quin, Daughter of James and Mary O'Quin, born 27th.

H. Lawson.

1799, June 2d. Baptized John Sullivan, Son of Patrick and Anne Sullivan. Godfather Patrick Doonan. Born May 11th.

H. Lawson.

1799, June 6. Baptized Eliz. Barbara Perugi, Daughter of Joseph and Jane Perugi, born May 24th. Godmother Anne Rosanno.

H. Lawson.

1799, May 22d. Baptized Eleanora Darell, daughter of Philip and Catherine Darell, born the 19th of the same month. Godfather Edward Hales Esqr., Godmother Eleanora Walsh.

Ralph Ainsworth.

[131] Eldest surviving son, died 1886. See note 120 & genealogy there cited.

1799, July. Baptized 26 of July, Peter Ardenand, born the 21 of July, son of Peter and Mary Ardenand. Godfather Henry Seine, God Mother Martha Saw by Proxy for Elizabeth Howell.

H. Lawson.

1799, August 29th. Baptized Richard Barry, Son of Patrick and Catherine Barry, born the 22d of August. Godfather Daniel Obrien by proxy of Jacob West, Godmother Eleanor Obrien.

R. Ainsworth.

1799, September 2d. Baptized Jane Keith, Daughter of William and Mary Keith, born the 18th of August. Godmother Jane Hickey.

R. Ainsworth.

1799, August 22. Baptized John Lawlor, born the 10th instant, son of Mic. and Mary Lawlor. Godfather James Doyle, Godmother Hester Fitzgerald and Cath. Reyley.

H. Lawson.

1799. Baptized the 2d of September [*Lawson's hand*].

1799, Sep. 3d [*possibly a figure 8, but more probably a 3 written over a 2*]: Supplied the ceremonies over John William Cowdey, son of Peter and Lucy Cowdey, born 11th of July 1799, batized [*sic*] the same day. Godfather James Dowding, Godmother Martha Bowden.

R. Ainsworth.

1799, Sep. 14th. Baptized Edward Martin, Son of John and Bridget Martin, born the 3d of September. Godfather Francis Curley, Godmother Mary Casey.

R. Ainsworth.

1799, Sep. 29th. Baptized William Cooper, Son of William and Sarah Cooper, born September 9th. Godfather Roger Kennedy, Godmother Honora Heagherty.

R. Ainsworth.

1799, December 24th. Baptized Edward Gannon, Son of Edw. and Laetitia Gannon. Godfather Michl. Rogers, Godmother Jane Denny.

[*Unsigned, but in Lawson's writing.*]

1800, January 2, was born Edward Wheland, the Son of John and Sarah Wheland. Baptized the 4th. Godfather O'Brian, Godmother Judith Glasson.

H. Lawson.

1800, January 9. Baptized Thomas Rosanno, born the 7th. Son of Dominick and Anne Rosanno.

H. Lawson.

1800, February 5th. Baptized James Brian, son of Dominick and Mary Brian, born the 2d of Feb. Godfather Cornelius Landers, Godmother Mary Lynch.

R. Ainsworth.

1800, Feb. 11th. Baptized — Whealend, son of Michael Whealend and Mary — born the 4th of February. Godfather John McGawley, Godmother Mary McGawley.

R. Ainsworth.

1800, March 14th. Baptized Thomas Shiles, son of Robert and Mary Shiles, born February 14th.

R. Ainsworth.

1800, May 4th. Baptized Mary Taffe, daughter of Nicholas and Anne Taffe, born the 28th of April 1800. Godfather John Gowe [?], Godmother Amelia Calaghan.

R. Ainsworth.

L'an 1800, le 29 Juin, nous soussigné Joseph Henry Picquenot, Curé de Neuville, Doyen d'Ivry, Diocèse d'Evreux, avons supplées les cérémonies de baptême à un garcon né à Jersey le 19 Novembre 1793 du légitime mariage de Mre. René Augustin de la Monneraye, capitaine au service de France, et de Dame Georgette Marie Françoise de Kerouartz, ses pére et mère. Son parain Me. Pierre Bruno Jean de la Monneraye, qui l'a nommé Hypolite Bruno; la maraine Marie Charlotte Reine de Kerouartz.

Picquenot.

1800. Henry Maguire, born the 6th of March. Baptized the 23d of March son of Patrick and Catherine Maguire. Godfather Jeremiah Bergen, Godmother Margaret English.

H. Lawson.

1800, July 28th. Baptized Martha Henrietta Barnwall, daughter of Thomas and Maria Therese Barnwall. Godfathers Nicolas Lord Trimlestown and Richard Kirwan by proxy of Henry Count de Brederode, Godmothers Elizabeth Hill and Antoinette Kirwan by proxy of Rosalia Dalton.

R. Ainsworth.

1800, August 13th 1800. Baptized John Alfred Knapp, son of John and Mary Knapp, born [blank]. Godfather Dr. Birket, Godmother Catherine Randal.

R. Ainsworth.

August 15th 1800. Baptized Richard Owen Nagle, Son of Richard and Mary Bridget Nagle, born the 12th of the same month. Godfather Edmund Nugent by proxy of the Honble. Thomas Barnwall, Godmother Frances French by proxy of Mary French.

R. Ainsworth.

* 1802,[132] April 29th, was baptised John Murray, Son of (David) Murray, and Eleanor – born the 26th of the same month. Sponsors Henry Williams and Honor Rabbitt, by me

Ralph Ainsworth.

Aug. 14, 1800. Baptized John Casey, born the 7th instant, Son of Michael and Sally Casey, Godfather John Mungomory, Godmother Mary Casey.

H. Lawson.

Aug. 18th 1800. Baptized Lucy Dalton, born the 25 of July. Daughter of William Dalton and Julia Dalton. Godfather Denie Don, Godmother Catherine Bray.

H. Lawson.

---

[132]   Entered out of chronological order; referred-to infra., p. 94.

Aug. 19, 1800. Baptized John Marony, born the 13 of July, son of James and Mary Marony.

R. H. Lawson.

Anni 1800, Aug. 6, natus Gul. Reyly. Baptisatus die 24. Filius Joannis et Annae Reyly. Matrina Ann. Drew.

R. H. Lawson.

1800, Aug. 27 [altered from 24]. Baptized Mathew O'Duire, born the 23 instant. Son of Timothy and Mary O'Duire. Godmother Eliz. Brown.

R. H. Lawson.

1800, Aug. 27. Baptized John Fryer, born the 18th instant. Son of John and Eliz. Fryer. Godfather R.Ch.[133] Fryer.

R. H. Lawson.

1800, Sep. 4th. Baptized Maria Obrien, daughter of John and Margaret Obrien, born the 20th of August. Godfather Miles McDonnough, Godmother Susanna McDonough.

R. Ainsworth.

1800, Sep. 27th. Baptized John Burgin, son of James and Helena Burgin born Sep. 24th. Godmother Barbara Pierce.

R. Ainsworth.

1800, October 5th. Baptized Henry Gale, son of Henry and Elizabeth Gale, born the 13th of September.

R. Ainsworth.

1800, October 16th. Baptized Joseph Thomas Short, Son of John and Mary Short, born October the 5th. Godfather Raymond Arundel, Godmother Elizabeth Arundel by proxy of Mary Short.

R. Ainsworth.

Henceforth in Calderbank's and Ainsworth's hands, as signed:
1800, Novr. 16th, was baptised Helen Worth, lawful Daughter of Hugh and Mary Worth, Irish Strangers, born Novr. 5th. No Sponsors.

J. Calderbank.

1800, Novr. 26th, was baptised Catharine Brown, lawful Daughter of Thos. and Catharine Brown, born the preceding day. Sponsors Thomas Canning and Theresa Wilkes. Proxies James Ewing, and Ellen Rose.

J. Calderbank.

1801, January 14th, was baptised Mary Dimpsey alias Davies, Daughter of William Dimpsey and Elizabeth Davies, born the preceding day, Sponsor Mary McCambridge.

J. Calderbank.

1801, Jan. 27th. Baptized Francis Murphy, son of Francis and Hannah Murphy, born the 23d of the same month. Godfather Laurence Collaghan, Godmother Susanna Jesop.

R. Ainsworth.

1801, Feb. 1st. Baptized James Woods, son of James and Mary Woods,

---

[133]   Charles, brother of the Rev. William Victor Fryer, mentioned in note 123. See Oliver p. 309; Croft & Gillow, *loc. cit;* *C.R.S.,* 56, p. 172; *C.R.S.,* 63, pp. 400-1.

born the 24th of January. Godfather George Shee by proxy of R. Ainsworth, Godmother Anastasia Shee.

R. Ainsworth.

Vide infra [*i.e. 8 Feb., out of chronological order, below*].

1801, March 1st, was baptized John, Son of Peter and Lucy Anne Coady, born 17th of the preceding Month of February. Sponsors Jas. Dowding and his Daughter Winefride Dowding.

Jas. Calderbank.

Calderbank's hand:
1801, February 8th, was baptised Mary Anne, Daughter of John and Christian Kelly, born December 21st, 1800.

Ralph Ainsworth.

Henceforth in Calderbank's and Ainsworth's hands, as signed:
1801, March 23rd, was baptised Catharine, lawful Daughter of John and Ellen Martin, born early in the morning of the same day. Sponsors John Martin and Mary McCambridge.

Jas. Calderbank.

1801, March 24th, was baptised Timothy, lawful Son of Mr. Charles and Mrs N. Mortimer, born 11th of the same Month. Sponsors Mr. Ross Donnelly and Mrs Jennet Higgins. Proxies Dr Thos. Natten, and Catharine Natten.

Jas. Calderbank.

1801, April 9th, was baptised William, lawful Son of George and Eliz. Foster, born the 6th of the same Month. Sponsors none.

Jas. Calderbank.

1801, April 13th, was baptised Richard, lawful Son of William, and Mary Chapel, born 16th March preceding. Sponsor Anne Geoghan.

Jas. Calderbank.

April 22nd 1801, was baptised Robert, lawful Son of Mr. Christopher, and Mrs Anne Watertown, born 13th of the same Month. Sponsors Mr — Turville and Mrs. Anne Watertown. Proxies Revd. Mr. Martinglay[134] and Lady FitzGerald.

Jas. Calderbank.

May 10th 1801, was baptized Maria Anna Barrelli, daughter of Dominic and Maria Barrelli, born the 5th of the same month. Godfather Dominic Ortelli.

R. Ainsworth.

May the 22d 1801, was privately without the ceremonies baptized Henry Kenelm Best, Son of Henry and Sarah Best, born the 5th of the same month.

R. Ainsworth [*see also 22 May 1802*].

1801, May 24th, was baptised Mary Patience, Daughter of Arthur and Elisabeth Humphreys, born 19th of the same Month. Sponsors William Corry and Mary Mokeley.

Jas. Calderbank.

---

[134] Perhaps John Mattingley, ex-Jesuit, for whom see Foley, VII, p. 494; Kirk, p. 160.

June 1st 1801, was baptized George Higgin, son of Peter and Susannah Higgin, born the 25th of December 1800. Godfather Miles Micdonnough, Godmother Catherine Burke.

R. Ainsworth.

June 2d 1801, was baptized Thomas Macdonald, son of Thomas and Catherine Macdonald, born the 24th of May 1801. Godfather Thomas Fenerty, Godmother Mary Nugent.

Ralph Ainsworth.

June 4th 1801, was baptized Helen Martin, daughter of John and Bridget Martin, born the 3d of May 1801. Godfather Michael O'Brien, God-mother Julia Glasson.

R. Ainsworth.

June 7th, was baptized George Smith, son of Michael and Elizabeth Smith, born May 28th 1801. Godfather Edmund English, Godmother Mary Dean.

R. Ainsworth.

June 7th 1801, was baptized Peter Salmoni son of Peter and Lucy Salmoni, born 18th of May 1801. Godfather James Murphy, Godmother Dorothy Molland.

R. Ainsowrth.

June 8th 1801, was baptized Rose Moyler, daughter of William and Sarah Moyler, born the 24th of March 1800. Godfather John Martin.

Ralph Ainsworth.

1801, July 24th, was baptised Joanna, lawful Daughter of Daniel and Mary Dempsey, born the first of the same Month. Sponsors Thos. Neele and Alice Beggin. Proxy for the latter Alice Tarleton.

Jas. Calderbank.

1801, August 11th, was baptised Edward, Son of Edwd. Murphy and Elisabeth Hambden, born 3rd of the same Month. Sponsor Henrietta Dwire.

Jas. Calderbank.

1801, August 13th. The ceremonies of Baptism were supplied on Laurence Rosalie Haver, lawful Daughter of Julien and Anne Haver; she was baptised the 7th of the preceding Month, the day of her Birth. Sponsors Jacque & Madelaine Gouget.

Jas. Calderbank.

1801, Aug. 18th, was baptised Mary Anne, lawful Daughter of Andrew and Margaret Doran, born 15th of the same Month. Sponsors Timothy Bain and Mary Archer.

Jas. Calderbank.

Calderbank's hand (3 entries):
1801, August 20th, was baptised Margaret, daughter of Thos. and Elizabeth St. John, born the 9th Inst. Sponsors John Crane and Mary Short. By the Rt. Revd. W.G. Sharrock.

1801, September 22nd, was baptised Joseph Henry, lawful Son of Mathew and Anne Madding, born the 4th of the same Month. Sponsor Sarah Love.

Jas. Calderbank.

1801, September 26th, was baptised Mary, lawful Daughter of Dennis and Mary King born 22nd of the same Month. Sponsor Anne Donevant.

Jas. Calderbank.

In the hand of the signatory:

1801, October 21...a été baptisée par nous Curé de la Neuville Dubosc, Diocese d'Evreux en France, soussigné, une fille née d'hier en et du légitime mariage de René Augustin de la Monneraye et de Georgette Marie-Francoise de Kerouarts, qui a été nommée Delphine Adelaide. Le parrain Jean Jacques Ferdinand de la Monneraye, le marraine Delphine Sophie Henriette Delangle.

Le Marquant,[135] Curé de la Neuville Dubosc.

Next nine entries in Calderbank's hand:

1801, Novr. 1st, was baptised Timothy, lawful Son of Thos. and Anne Harley, born 7th of September. Sponsors none. By me,

Jas. Calderbank.

1801, Novr. 10, was baptised Henry, lawful Son of Nicholas and [*blank*] Taffe, born the preceding day. Sponsors [*blank*] Curly and [*blank*] Brown, by me

Jas. Calderbank.

1801, Decr. 13th, was baptised David, lawful Son of John and Mary Ferrers, born the 2nd of the same Month. Sponsors Gerard Barry, and Judith Leaven, by me

Jas. Calderbank.

1801, Decr. 27th, was baptised Stephen, Son of Michael and Mary Barden, born the 24th of the same Month. Sponsors Willm. Gready, and Catherine Hepenstall, by me

R. Ainsworth.

1802, Jan. 1st, was baptised Elisabeth, Daughter of Jas. and Mary Fennerty, born 7th of December 1801. Sponsor Joanna Keafe, by me

R. Ainsworth.

1802, Jan. 6th, was baptised Elisabeth, lawful Daughter of Hugh and Mary Hereon, born 8th of the preceding Month. Sponsors James Maguire and Catharine Neale, by me

Jas. Calderbank.

1802, Jan. 10th, was baptised Anne Mary, lawful daughter of John and Mary Short, born 1st of the same Month. Sponsors Thos. Bates and Elisabeth Pitt. Proxy Ellen Rose, by me

Jas. Calderbank.

1802, January 23rd, was baptised Thos., lawful Son of Joseph and Barbara White, born the 2nd of the same Month. Sponsor Anne Hughes, by me

Jas. Calderbank.

1802, January 24th, was baptised Miles, lawful Son of Miles and Susanna McDonough, born the 15th of the same Month. Sponsors

[135]   Christian names Henri-Jacques; d. Winchester, 1831 (Plasse, *op.cit.*, p. 412; *C.R.S.*, 42, p. 27).

Michael Burne and Henrietta Dwire, by me

Jas. Calderbank.

Next two entries in Ainsworth's hand:
1802, January 29th, was baptized Thomas Phelan, Son of Richard and
Elizabeth Phelan, born the 9th of the same month. Sponsors William
Bugden and Catherine Cellaro [? Cellars].

By me R. Ainsworth.

1802, Feb. 14th, was baptized William Henry Fryer, lawful son of John
and Elisabeth Fryer, born the 30th of November 1801. Godfather Revd.
W. Fryer[136] by proxy.

By me R. Ainsworth.

Next four entries in Calderbank's hand:
1802. Was baptised Feb. 19th, John Baptist, lawful son of Joseph and
Jane Perugie, born the 10th Godmother – Rosanna, by me

Jas. Calderbank.

1802, March 14th, was baptised Mary, Daughter of Dennis Gribbon,
and Mary Richy, born 2nd of the same Month. Sponsor Jac. McMurphy,
by me

Jas. Calderbank.

March 16. Vide infra [*see next entry but one*].

1802, March 19th, was baptised John, lawful son of John and Mary
Daigan; born the 13th of the same Month. Sponsors Timothy Graigan
and Mary Nugent, by me

Jas. Calderbank.

1802, March 16th, was baptised Elisabeth Barry, lawful Daughter of
Garret and Helen Barry, born the 1st of the same Month. Sponsor
Joanna Keif, by

Ralph Ainsworth.

*After this entry, the last on its page, there appears to have been a slip of
paper recording two baptisms. The original is now missing, but according to the transcript at Taunton, it was as follows:*

"1st Child, Ann Monica Combes. Father Lawrence Combes, Mother
Sarah Combes, Godfather Joseph Love, Godmother Lucy Combes.

"2nd Child, John George Perry. Father John Perry, Mother Jane
Perry.[137] Godfather George Harvey, Godmother Eliz. Gill. May 4, 87".

Next nine entries in Calderbank's hand:
1802, April 21st, was baptised Maria, lawful daughter of Peter Paul and

---

[136]   Possibly William Victor Fryer (see note 123) or perhaps his uncle, Dr
William Fryer, President of Lisbon College; cf. Oliver, p. 310; Kirk, pp. 88-9;
Croft & Gillow, *loc. cit.*, Gillow, II, p. 335; *C.R.S.*, 63, p. 401.

[137]   The marriage of John Perry and Jane Hervey on 16 Jan. 1786 is recorded in
R.B.A., p. 309. This and the preceding baptism were originally entered (*supra*,
p. 38) under the correct year: 1787.

Maria McMuttery, born the same Morning. Sponsor John McMuttery, by me

> Jas. Calderbank.

* See 6 leaves back[138]

1802, May 2d, was baptised Joseph, lawful Son of Joseph and Mary Feasana, born the 27th of the preceding Month. Sponsors John and Sarah Dowman. Proxies John and Mary Frances Rose Beasani, by me

> Jas. Calderbank.

1802, May 2d, was baptised Sarah, lawful daughter of Cornelius Sweeny and Margaret his Wife, born the 26th of the preceding Month. Sponsor John Flannyan [? Flannigan], by me

> Jas. Calderbank.

1802, May 27, was baptised Christina Anna, lawful Daughter of James and Martha Whippey, born 10th of the same Month, by

> R. Ainsworth.

1802, June 26th, was baptised Mary Anne, lawful Daughter of Richard and Mary Tabbot, born the 24th of the same Month. Sponsors James Roan and Ellen Roan, proxy Winefride Fenton, by me

> Jas. Calderbank.

1802, May 22nd, Were supplied the ceremonies of Baptism on Henry Kenelm Best, Son of Henry and Sarah Best. Sponsors Sir Thos. and Lady Fleetwood,[139] by

> R. Ainsworth [see also 22 May 1801].

1802, June 28th, was baptised Mary Elisabeth, lawful Daughter of Henry and Sarah Best, born 14th of the same Month, by

> R. Ainsworth. [see also 17 Oct]

1802, July 11th, was baptised Anne, lawful Daughter of Jas. and Mary Parker, born 17th June. Sponsors Mr Solomon and Mrs Catharine Rushell [?]. Proxies Jas. Maguire & Elisabeth Kelsey, by me

> Jas. Calderbank.

1802, August 2nd, was baptised Patrick, lawful Son of Andrew and Margaret Doran, born the 31st of the preceding Month. Sponsors Patrick Coyle and Henrietta Dwire, by me

> Jas. Calderbank.

Next thirteen entries in Ainsworth's and Calderbank's hands, as signed:
1802, August 9th, was baptised Lucia Salmoni, daughter of Peter and Lucia Salmoni, born the 16th of July. Sponsors John Bisani and Maria Rosa Francisca Bisani, by me

> Ralph Ainsworth.

1802, August 22d, was baptized Catherine Barrelli, daughter of Dominic and Maria Barrelli, born the 3d of the same month. Sponsors Dominic Riva and Mary Anne Fasana, by me

> Ralph Ainsworth.

[138] Note in Ainsworth's hand, referring to his entry for 29 April 1802 among those for August 1800 (*supra*, p. 88).

[139] 7th Bart. and his wife Mary, *née* Bostock; see Kirk, p. 86 and, for his death at Bath, 3 Dec. 1802, *infra*, p. 124; *C.R.S.*, 12, p. 85. See also Gillow, *sub* Beste.

1802, August 23d, was baptised Helen Maguire, daughter of Patrick and Catherine Maguire, born the 19th of the same month. Sponsors James and Hannah Maguire, by me

Ralph Ainsworth.

1802, September 7th, was baptised Mary Anne, lawful Daughter of Henry and Mary-Anne Beaumont, born the 1st of the same Month. Sponsors Hugh Jones and Anne Bower, by me

Jas. Calderbank.

1802, Oct. 17th, were supplied the ceremonies of baptism on Mary Elisabeth Best, daughter of Henry and Sarah Best. Sponsors Thomas and Mary Clifford.

R. Ainsworth [see also 28 June].

See next page [note by Ainsworth re entry for 22 Oct., misplaced].

1802, Novr. 9th, was baptised Henry lawful Son of John and Mary Crofton, born 18th of October. Sponsors none, by me

Jas. Calderbank.

1802, Oct. 22d, was baptized Henry Warren, son of Henry and Harriette Warren, born 24th of April. Sponsors none.

R. Ainsworth.

1802, Nov. 13th, was baptized Walter Irvine, son of Christopher William and Jeanne Marie Anne Irvine, born the same day. Sponsors Christopher Irvine and Victoire Julienne.

R. Ainsworth.

1802, Nov. 18th, was baptized Charles Gill, son of Michael and Alice Gill, born the 21st of October. Sponsors none.

R. Ainsworth.

1802, Nov. 22d, was baptized Henry Cooper, son of William and Sarah Cooper, born the 23d of August. Sponsors none.

R. Ainsworth.

1802, Novr. 25th, was baptised Charles Terns Murphy, Son of Francis and Anne Murphy, born the 10th of the same Month. Sponsors Terns Murphy and Margaret Lynch, by me

Jas. Calderbank.

1802, December 5th, was baptised George, lawful Son of George and Anne Handy, born the 4th of June of the same Year. Sponsors none, by me

Jas. Calderbank.

1802, December 12th, was baptized Mary Dubois, lawful daughter of Robert and Anne Dubois, born the 22d of October. Sponsors none.

R. Ainsworth.

1803, Jany. 1st, was baptised Frances McClivery, lawful Daughter of Richard and Anne Dollart, born Decr. of the preceding Year. Sponsors Henry and Margaret Williams, by me

Jas. Calderbank.

Next seven entries in Calderbank's hand:
1803, Jany. 10th, was baptised Margaret, Daughter of John and Barbara

Lewis, born 12th of December of the preceding Month [*sic*]. Sponsors none, by

R. Ainsworth.

1803, Jany. 26th, was baptised Michael, lawful Son of Patrick and Sarah Curly, born 19th of the same Month. Sponsor Rosamond Cosgrove, by me

Jas. Calderbank.

1803, Jany. 30th, was baptised Catharine, lawful Daughter of Daniel and Joanna Ryon, born 21st of the same month. Sponsors none, by me

Jas. Calderbank.

1803, Jany. 31st, was baptised (conditionaliter) Thos., lawful Son of Thos. and Judith Hardy, born 7th of August 1800 [*overwritten upon 1799*]. Sponsors None, by me

Jas. Calderbank.

1803, Feby. 4th, was baptised John, lawful Son of John and Elisabeth Williams, born the same day. Sponsor Elizabeth Browne, by me

Jas. Calderbank.

1803, Feb. 6th, was baptised John Joseph, lawful Son of John and Mary Short, born the 3rd of the same Month. Sponsors John McMuttery Junr. and Martha Hughes, by me

Jas. Calderbank.

(Vide next page) [*note by Ainsworth re misplaced entry for 8 Feb., printed lower on this page*].

1803, Feby. 18th, was baptised James, lawful Son of Thos. and Henrietta Mary Lovely, born the same day. Sponsors Willm. Hopkins and Sarah Lovely, by me

Jas. Calderbank.

Next fifteen entries in Calderbank's and Ainsworth's hands, as signed:
1803, March 12th, was baptized (sub conditione) Joseph Withers.

R. Ainsworth.

1803, March 10th, was baptized (sub conditione) Rebecca Mary Dunning.

R. Ainsworth.

1803, March 19th, was baptised Anne, lawful daughter of John and Ellen Martin, born the preceding day. Sponsors Michael Quinland and Elisabeth Mole, by me

Jas. Calderbank.

Feb. 8th 1803, was baptized Sophia Maria de l'Age daughter of Messire William Francis Count de l'Age and of his lawful wife Sarah Countess de l'Age (formerly Sarah Palmer) born the 16th of December 1802. Sponsors Messire Réné, Marquis de l'Age de la Bretollière, by proxy of Richard Phealan, and Sophia, Viscountess de l'Age, by proxy of Catherine le Roux.

Ralph Ainsworth.

1803, March 21st, was baptized Charles Robert Talbot, Son of John and Harriette Talbot, born the preceding day. Sponsors Charles Talbot

Earl of Shrewsbury[140] by proxy of Ralph Ainsworth, and Fraces [*sic*] Talbot.

Ralph Ainsworth.

1803, March 24th, was baptized Joseph Randall, son of John Randall and Anne, born the 22d of February. No Sponsors.

R. Ainsworth.

1803, April 2nd, was baptised Willm., lawful Son of Will and Elisabeth Parker, aged 4 years and 8 months, and on the same day and at the same Time was also baptised John his Brother aged 7 months. Both (sub conditione) by me

Jas. Calderbank.

1803, April 17th, was baptised James, lawful Son of John and Anne Reily, born 5th of the same Month. Sponsors John Martin and Elisabeth Scanlon, by me

Jas. Calderbank.

1803, April 30th. Baptized William Henry Nugent Jones, son of William Henry and Mary Anne Jones, born the 26th of March. Sponsors John Nugent and Sarah Phebe Nugent.

Ralph Ainsworth.

1803, May 10th, was baptized Anne Batterbury, daughter of Thomas and Charlotte Batterbury, born the 10th of March. Sponsors Richard and Elizabeth Phealan.

R. Ainsworth.

1803, May 22nd, was baptised Hugh, lawful Son of James and Bridget Cambel, born 19th of the same Month. Sponsors Willm. Dunn and Anne Smith, by me

Jas. Calderbank.

1803, May 28th, was baptized Andrew Monk, Son of Andrew and Mary Monk, born the 7th of January. Sponsors Morris Hayden and Lucy Brown.

R. Ainsworth.

1803, June 7th, was baptised Willm., Son of Edward Murphy and Elisabeth Hambden, born 22nd of April of the same Year. Sponsor Rose Tool, by me

Jas. Calderbank.

1803, June 19th, was baptised Mary Anne, lawful Daughter of John and Anne O Neale, born the 16th of the same Month. Sponsor Mrs Callen, by me

Jas. Calderbank.

1803, Septr. 4th, was baptised Edmund Willm., lawful Son of Mr Edmund and Mrs Mary English, born 21st of the preceding Month. Sponsors Mr Edmund and Mrs [*blank*] English Senr., by me

Jas. Calderbank.

Next four entries in Calderbank's hand:

1803, Septr. 13th, was baptised George James, lawful Son of Mr. John

[140]   15th Earl (1753-1827).

and Mrs. Mary Knapp, born 1st of the same Month. Godfather Mr. John Hicks, by

R. Ainsworth.

1803, Septr. 26th, was baptised Anne, lawful Daughter of Edward and Frances Wogan, born the 20th of the same Month. Sponsors Dominick Rosanno and Mary Caverley, by me

Jas. Calderbank.

1803, Octr. 5th, was baptised James, lawful Son of James and Mary Degan, born 30th of the preceding Month. Sponsors Bartholomew Hayes and Mary Lalor, by me

Jas. Calderbank.

1803, Oct. 6th, was baptised James, lawful Son of Philip and Anna Macauley, born 25th of October 1802. Sponsor Ellen Martin, by me

Jas. Calderbank.

Henceforth in Calderbank's and Ainsworth's hands, as signed:

1803, Nov. 18th, was baptised James Murphy, lawful son of Francis and Hannah Murphy, born the 6th of the same month. Godfather John Daley by proxy of Thomas Murphy.

R. Ainsworth.

1803, December 4th, was baptised James, lawful Son of John and Mary Ferrers, born the 18th of the preceding Month. Sponsor Mary Helie, by me

Jas. Calderbank.

1803, December 10th, was baptised Lucia Magdalena Best, lawful daughter of Henry and Sarah Best, born the 23d of November. Sponsors Mr Robert Berkeley and Mrs Eliza French by proxy of Mrs. Apollonia Berkeley, by me

R. Ainsworth.

1804, Jany. 1st, was baptised Simon, lawful Son of George, and his wife Elisabeth Quin, born Novr. 28th of the preceding Year. Sponsors none, by me

Jas. Calderbank.

1804, Jany. 8th, was baptised Charles Dominic, lawful Son of Dominic and Mary Borelli, born Decr. 24th of the preceding Month [*sic*]. Sponsors Joseph Fortelli and Sarah Lovely, by me

Jas. Calderbank.

1804, Jany. 22nd, was baptised Joseph, lawful Son of Peter and Anne Lucy Coady, born the 27th of the preceding Month. Sponsors John Short and Elisabeth Modin, by me

Jas. Calderbank.

1804, Jan. 29th, Baptized Margaret, daughter of William and Elizabeth Cooksey born the 26th of December 1803. No Sponsors.

R. Ainsworth.

1804, Feby. 19th, was baptised Margaret, lawful Daughter of Patrick and Sarah Curly, born the 13th of the same month. Sponsors Nicholas Taafe, and Rose Cosgrove, by me

Jas. Calderbank.

1804, March 4th, was baptized Harriette Catherine Carr, daughter of

[*blank*] and Mary Carr, born the 25th of February. No Sponsors.
                                                            R. Ainsworth.
1804, March 4th, was baptized Sarah Ellison, daughter of James and
Catherine Ellison, born the 14th of February. No Sponsors.
                                                            R. Ainsworth.
1804, March 13th, was baptized George Mostyn, lawful son of Charles
and Mary Mostyn, born the 7th of the same month. Godfather Charles
Browne Mostyn,[141] Godmother Mary Butler.
                                                            R. Ainsworth.
+ 1804, March 13th, was baptized George Jeffers, son of James and
Anne Jeffers, born the 12th of March. Godfather Christopher Loughlan.
                                                            R. Ainsworth.
1804, April 13th, was baptised David, lawful Son of Willm. and Anne
O Hara of Combedown,[142] born a fortnight before. Sponsors None, by
me
                                                            Jas. Calderbank.
1804, April 6th, was baptised John, lawful Son of Michael and Mary
Connor, born 7th September 1802. Sponsors Martha and her Son John
Smith, by me
                                                            Jas. Calderbank.
1804, May 13th. Baptized John Salmoni, lawful son of Peter and Lucy
Salmoni, born the 16th of April. Sponsors Peter Smith and Catherine
Murphy.
                                                            R. Ainsworth.
1804, June 26th, was baptised Anne, lawful Daughter of Nicholas Taffe
and his Wife Anne, born 24th of the same Month. Sponsors John Barrett
and Rose Cosgrove, by me
                                                            Jas. Calderbank.
1804, Oct. 10th, was baptized without the ceremonies John Thomas,
lawful son of Thomas and Sarah Jordan, born the 7th of the same
month,
              by me R. Ainsworth [*see also 26 Oct.*]
1804, Oct. 13th, was baptized Adila, lawful daughter of John and Mary
Knapp, born the 11th of the same month. Sponsors Wm. Day and
Catherine Lewis, by me
                                                            R. Ainsworth.
1804, Oct. 16th, was baptised Edward John Galway, lawful Son of
Captain James Galway and Margary his Wife, born 14th of Septr. Sponsors Christopher MacEvoy Esqr. of the Island of S.Crue, by proxy of
Timothy O'Brien Esqr., and Mrs Catharine O'Brien, by me
                                                            Jas. Calderbank.

[141] Of Kiddington, Oxon. Father of Bishop Francis George Mostyn, Vicar-
Apostolic of the new Northern District, 1840-47; cf. Kirk, p. 170; W. Mazière
Brady, *Annals of the Catholic Hierarchy* (Rome, 1877) pp. 343-4; Stapleton,
Oxfordshire Post-Reformation Catholic Missions, p. 127.
[142] Combe Down, on the outskirts of Bath.

1804, Octr. 16th, was baptised Margaret, lawful Daughter of Jas.
Plunkett Esqr. and his Wife Eliza, born the 2nd of the same Month.
Sponsors Andrew Cummings Esqr. and Mrs Jane Defries, by me
Jas. Calderbank.

1804, Oct. 23d, was baptized (without the ceremonies) Mary Gill, lawful daughter of Michael and Alice Gill, born the 22d of October
R. Ainsworth [see 18 Feb., 1805].

1804, Oct. 26th, were supplied the ceremonies of baptism upon John
Thomas Jordan, son of Thomas and Sarah Jordan. Sponsors James
Goodman and Alice Tarlton.
By me R. Ainsworth [See also 10 Oct].

1804, Oct. 30th, was baptised John, lawful Son of John and Margaret
Tool, born on the 28th. Sponsors Christopher Fox, by proxy of Jas.
Doyle, and Ellenor Hall, by me
Jas. Calderbank.

1804, Novr. 18th, were baptised Charles and Mary, Twins and lawful
Children of Patrick and Catharine Maguire, born the preceding night.
Sponsors James Maguire and Susan Ryan, by me
Jas. Calderbank.

1804, Decr. 1st, was baptised Frederick, lawful Son of Charles and
Elisabeth Wootton, born 4th of June of the same Year. Sponsors Stephen
Wootton and Mary Ann Dale, by me
Jas. Calderbank.

1804, Decr. 26th, was baptised Bartholomew, lawful Son of John and
Anne Helly,[143] born the 15th of the same Month. Sponsors Michael
O'Brien and Margaret Magill, by me
Jas. Calderbank.

1804, Decr. 27, was baptised Frederick, lawful Son of Willm. Errington
Esqr. and Elenor his Wife, born 7th of the same month of December.
Sponsors Malachy O'Conner Esqr. and Mary O'Brien, by proxy of Miss
Monica O'Conner, by me
Jas. Calderbank.

1805, Jany. 3rd, was baptised Elisabeth, lawful Daughter of Nicholas
and Margaret Paillet, born 26th of December 1804. Sponsors Jas. Doyle
and Elenora Hall, by me
Jas. Calderbank.

1805, Jany. 13th, was baptised Elisabeth, lawful Daughter of Thos.
Jenkins and his Wife Martha, born Decr. 24th of the former Year. Spon-
sors Willm. Hopkins and Elisabeth Osmund, by me
Jas. Calderbank.

1805, Jany. 16th, was baptised Winefride, lawful Daughter of Timothy
and Mary Anne Meloni, born 27th of the preceding Month. Sponsor
Jas. Meloni, by me
Jas. Calderbank.

1805, Jan. 18 [date inserted by Ainsworth], was baptised Charlotte,

---

[143] J. Helle, French teacher, of 4 Gloucester St., occurs in *Robbins's Bath
Directory* (Bath, 1800) p. 57.

lawful Daughter of Thos. and Charlotte Barterbury, born 2nd of Decr. of the preceding Year. Sponsors Richard Phelan and Alice Tarleton, by me

                                                           Jas. Calderbank.

1805, Jan. 18th, was baptised Thomas, lawful Son of Daniel and Esther Riordan, born the same day. Sponsor Timothy Oleary.

                                                           R. Ainsworth.

1805, Jany. 22nd, was baptised Mathew, lawful Son of Mathew and Anne Madden, born 18th of the same Month. Sponsor Elisabeth Burt, by me

                                                           Jas. Calderbank.

1805, Jany. 22nd, was baptised George, lawful Son of Edward and Frances Wogan, born the preceding Evening. No Sponsors, by me (Ceremonies omitted)

                                                           Jas. Calderbank.

1805, Feb. 14th, was baptized Mary Anne Fasana, lawful daughter of Joseph and Mary Anne Fasana, born the same day (the ceremonies omitted)

                                                    by me R. Ainsworth.

1805, Feb. 18th, were supplied the ceremonies of baptism over Mary Gill, daughter of Michael and Alice Gill. Sponsor Elizabeth Mouney.

                          R. Ainsworth [*see 23 Oct., 1804*].

1805, Feby. 24th, was baptised Mary, lawful Daughter of Andrew and Mary Murphy, born 10th of the preceding December. Sponsors Christopher Fox and Mary Yates, by me

                                                           Jas. Calderbank.

1805, March 3rd, was baptised Charles James, lawful Son of Patrick, and Elisabeth (his Wife) Fox, born 19th of the preceding Month. Sponsors Francis Kirwan and Margt. Megill, by me

                                                           Jas. Calderbank.

1805, March 4th, was baptised John, lawful Son of John and Catharine Gogin, born 26th of the preceding Month. Sponsors James and Anne Phegan [?], by me

                                                           Jas. Calderbank.

1805, March 21st, was baptised Daniel Benedict Smith, lawful son of Michael and Elizabeth Smith, born the 10th of the same month. Sponsor Helen Rose.

                                                           R. Ainsworth.

1805, March 29th. Baptized at Sodbury, Charlotte Catherine, lawful daughter of William and Catherine Anne Holbrook, born the 10th of January 1804. Sponsor Anne Sceates.

                                                           R. Ainsworth.

1805, April 7th, was baptized Frederick John English, lawful son of Edmund and Mary Elizabeth English, born 23d of February. Sponsors John English and Dorothy Molland.

                                                           R. Ainsworth.

1805, April 8th, was baptised Willm., lawful Son of Terence and Mary Chaumer, born 15th of Jany. Sponsors none, by me

                                                           Jas. Calderbank.

1805, April 14th, was baptised Jane, lawful Daughter of Dominick and Maria Borelli, born 8th of the same Month. Sponsors Francis Borosculli and Margt. Maguire, by me

Jas. Calderbank.

1805, April 14th, was baptised Elizabeth Kintgent, lawful daughter of John and Anne Kintgent, born the 26th of March. Sponsors Joseph Kallenberck and Mary Sennet.

R. Ainsworth.

1805, May 23d, was baptized without the ceremonies Margaret Paula King, lawful daughter of [blank] and Margaret Paula King, born the 19th of the same month.

R. Ainsworth.

1805, May 27th, was baptized in danger without the ceremonies John Foster, lawful son of George and Elizabeth Foster, born the 23d of this month.

R. Ainsworth [See 4 Oct., 1806].

1805, May 28th, was baptized without the ceremonies Lucia Burke, lawful daughter of Edward and Jumima Burke, born the 3d of last March.

R. Ainsworth.

1805, May 30th, was baptized Joseph Love, lawful son of Joseph and Sarah Love, born the 26th of the same months [sic]. Sponsors Julien Havez and Helen Martin.

R. Ainsworth.

1805, June 10th, was baptized Charles Christopher McManus, lawful son of Bernard and Catherine McManus, born the 5th of the same month. Sponsors Christopher Nihele and Julienne McManus. By his Grace Mr. Dillon,[144] Archbishop of Tuam,

signed R. Ainsworth.

1805, June 16th, was baptized Mary Head, lawful daughter of George and Frances Head, born the same day. Sponsors Francis Fletcher and Teresa Maria Metcalfe.

R. Ainsworth.

Next three entries in Rigby's hand:

1805, June 30th, was baptized Joanna, lawful daughter of George and Elisabeth Quin, born 16th of the same month. Sponsor John Smith.

John Rigby.

1805, July 7th, was baptized John, lawful son of William and Nancy O'Haror. Sponsors James Maguire and Mary West.

John Rigby.

1805, July 11th, was baptized John, the Son of Joseph and Judith Smith, born 9th of the same Month. Sponsors Danniel Hanket and Mary-ann Blennerhasset. p. proxin [?] Mary Bomount.

J. Rigby.

---

[144] Archbishop Edward Dillon (d.1809); cf. Sir F. M. Powicke & E. B. Fryde, *Handbook of British Chronology* (Royal Historical Society, 2nd edition, 1961) p. 406; W. M. Brady, *The Episcopal Succession in England, Scotland and Ireland* (Rome, 1876) II, pp. 148, 168.

Next two entries and note in Ainsworth's hand:
1805, Aug. 4th, was baptized at Weymouth (without the ceremonies) James Churchill, son of Martin and Catherine Churchill, born July 13th.
                                            Ralph Ainsworth.
1805, Aug. 17th, was baptized Anne Hogan, daughter of John Hogan and Jane Brealey, born the 6th of Augt. Sponsor Michael Duncan.
                                            Ralph Ainsworth.
See next page but one [*the next page is occupied by the following mortuary list in the handwriting of Dom John Bede Brewer O.S.B.*].
Anno Domini 1780 Apud Philips Norton mortuus est Edwardus Thornton, natus annos [*blank*].
Anno Domini 1780 Die Septembris 19, Bathoniae mortuus est Joannes Walbury Germanus, annos natus 44.
Anno Dni. 1780 Die Septembris 2, mortua est Laetitia Church[145] sex menses nata.
Anno Dni. 1780 Die 22 Octobris, mortuus est Gulielmus Connor natus annos 40.
Anno Dni. 1780 Die Decembris 2, mortua est Catharina Cody annos nata 25.
Anno Dni. 1780 Die Decembris 10, mortua est Charlotta Smith annos nata 74.
Anno Dni. 1780 Die Decembris 30, mortua est Maria Childs annos nata 43.

Next three entries in Ainsworth's hand:
1805, Aug. 25th, was baptized Jane Duncan, daughter of Michael and Sarah Duncan, born the 27th of February 1804. Sponsor Edward Meagher.
                                            Ralph Ainsworth.
1805, Aug. 29th, was baptized John Williams, lawful Son of John and Anne Williams, born the 28th of the same month. Sponsors John Barrett and Elizabeth Abbot.
                                            Ralph Ainsworth.
1805, Aug. 30th, was baptized Charles John Walmesley, lawful son of Charles Esq. and Elizabeth Walmesley, born the same day. Sponsor Susannah Holditch.
                                            Ralph Ainsworth.
Rigby's hand:
1805, Sep. 29th, was baptized James, lawful Son of John and Sarah O'Neal. Sponsors James Murphy and Nancy Hibert.
                                            John Rigby.
Four entries (one deleted) in Ainsworth's hand:
1805, Oct. 1st. Supplied the ceremonies over Christopher Bellew Swift lawful Son of Deane Theophilus and Julia Maria Swift. Sponsors Christopher Dillon Bellew Esq. and Jane Defries.
                                            R. Ainsworth.

[145] Buried in Bath Abbey, 3 Sept. "By Mr Bedingfield's monument" (*R.B.A.*, p. 467).

1805, Oct. 13th, was baptized at Chipping Sodbury Mary Sceats, daughter of William and Mary Sceats, born in the year 1802. Godmother Anne Sceats.

R. Ainsworth.

+ 1805, Oct. 23d, was baptized Henry [*entry deleted*].

1805, Nov. 8th, was baptized Mary Abbot, lawful daughter of Richard and Elizabeth Abbot, born yesterday the 7th. Sponsors William Charlton and Mary Trafford by proxy of Margaret Williams.

R. Ainsworth.

Rigby's hand:
1805, Novr. 15, was baptized Caroline, lawful Daughter of Francis and Ann Murphy. Sponsors, James Doyle, Mary Munth.

John Rigby.

Ainsworth's hand:
1805, Nov. 22d, was baptized without the ceremonies George Flanagan, lawful son of Michael and Margaret Flanagan, born the 21st.

Ralph Ainsworth [*see 23 Dec*].

Three entries in Rigby's hand:
1805, Decbr. 8, was baptized Edmund, the lawful son of Philip and Mary Hogan. Sponsors Math. Campbell and Mary Anne Garland.

John Rigby.

1805, Oct. 20, was baptized Mary, lawful daughter of William and Mary Hillard.

John Rigby.

1805, Decr. 11th, was baptized Sarah, lawful Daughter of John and Mary St. John. Sponsors James Curtin and Anne Sullivan.

John Rigby.

Ainsworth's hand:
1805, Dec. 23d, were supplied the ceremonies of baptism over George Flanagan, lawful son of Michael and Margaret Flanagan, born 21st of Nov. Sponsor William Rian.

John Rigby.

Rigby's hand:
1806, Feb. 14, was baptized Joseph, lawful Son of Peter and Lucy Salmoni. Sponsors [Peter *deleted*] Joseph and Honoria Herbert.

John Rigby.

Words italicised in Ainsworth's hand; others in Calderbank's:
1806, Feb. 27th. was baptized Clement John Michael, son of John Garcias and Jane Percy, born 23rd. God Mother Sarah Lozano [?].

R. Ainsworth.

Next seven entries in Rigby's hand:
1806, March 18, was baptized Catherin Reyly, lawful daughter of Mr. and Mrs. Reyly (N.B. without the Ceremonies), by me

John Rigby.

1806, March 16, was baptized without the Ceremonies Joanna, lawful daughter of James and Ellen Richards. Sponsors James Quin and Joanna Whitehead, by me

John Rigby.

1806, Ap. 20, was baptized Daniel, lawful Son of John and Mary Lynch. Sponsor Mary Read.

John Rigby.

1806, May 6, was baptized Richard, lawful Son of Richard and Susanna Archer. Sponsor Ellen Rose.

John Rigby.

1806, May 25, was baptized (sub Cond.) Robert, lawful Son of Hubert Dubois, aged 6 years.

John Rigby.

1806, May 25, was baptized Henry (Sub Cond.), lawful Son of Hubert Dubois, aged 6 months.

John Rigby.

1806, May 25, was baptized John Oliver, lawful Son of Robolphus and Elizabeth Kent, born 19th of the said month. Sponsors John Howard Kyan by proxy of Thos. Sutton Kyan, and Delia Fairklough by Proxy of Phillis Mary Anne Kyan.

R. Ainsworth.

Next three entries in Ainsworth's hand:

1806, June 1st, was baptized Matthew Toole, lawful son of Richard and Margaret Toole, born the 19th of March. Sponsors Alexander Macdonald and Julia Earls.

R. Ainsworth.

1806, June 7th, was born and baptized without the ceremonies William Jordan, lawful son of Thos. and Sarah Jordan.

R. Ainsworth [*see 24 June*].

1806, June 22d, was baptized James Henry Cody, lawful son of Peter and Lucy Cody, born the 2d of the same month. Sponsors Michael Carroll and Jane Brooke.

R. Ainsworth.

Two entries in Bridsall's hand:

1806, June 21st, was baptized John, lawful son of Will. and Eliz. Penny, born June 15th. Sponsor Lucy Waren.

John Birdsall.

1806, June 22d, was baptized William, lawful son of William and Mary Sceats, 6 years old, at Chipping Sodbury. Sponsor his Grandmother Ann Sceats.

John Birdsall.

Ainsworth's hand:

1806, June 24th, were supplied the ceremonies of Baptism over William Jordan, lawful son of Thomas and Sarah Jordan, born the 7th of the same month. Sponsors William Hopkins and Laetitia Smallman.

R. Ainsworth [*see 7 June*].

Next four entries in Birdsall's hand:

1806, July the 6th, were supplied the Ceremonies of Baptism over Margaret Castello, lawful daughter of Matthew and Ann Castello. Sponsors Richd. Phelan and Eliz. Phelan.

John Birdsall

1806, Augt. 22d, was baptized Mary, lawful daughter of George and

Jane Dewerdeck, born Augt. the 1st. Sponsor Mary Hensie.

John Birdsall.

Sepr. 10th 1806, was baptized Catharine, lawful daughter of Nicolas Paillet and Margaret Paillet, born Augt. 31st 1806. Sponsors John Brenan and Rosanna Howard.

John Birdsall.

1806, Sepr. 28th, was baptised James, lawful Son of Richard and Ann Pursel, born about a fortnight before. Sponsor Arabella Kelly.

John Birdsall.

Ainsworth's hand:
1806, Sep. 29th, was baptised Richard Walmesley, lawful son of Charles Walmesley Esqr. and Elizabeth his wife, born the 28th of the same month. Godfather William Gerard Walmesley by proxy of R. Ainsworth.

R. Ainsworth.

Next thirteen entries in Ainsworth's and Birdsall's hands, as signed:
1806, Octob. the 4th, were supplied the ceremonies of baptism, without Sponsors, over John Foster, born May 27th 1805. Vide May 27, 1805.

John Birdsall.

1806, Oct. 3d, was baptised James Jerome Short, lawful son of John and Mary Short, born the 30th of September. Sponsors James Doyle and Helen Rose.

Ralph Ainsworth.

1806, Octr. 12th, was baptised Maria Kentchins, lawful daughter of John and Ann Kentchins, born Sepr. 18th 1806. Sponsors Hubert Dubois and Sarah Wright.

John Birdsall.

1806, Novr. 19th, was baptised Lazarus, lawful Son of John Bennet Walsh, and Elizabeth his Wife, born Novr. 9th 1806. Without Sponsors, he being a travelling Irishman, by

John Birdsall.

1806, Novr. 26th. Baptised, and Decr. 28th supplied the Ceremonies over William Charles Fasana, born Novr. 22d 1806, lawful son of Joseph and Mary Ann Fasana. Godfather Giovanni Biscani, Godmother Maria Francesca Bisani [*sic*].

John Birdsall.

1806, Nov. 30th, was baptised Henry Renison English, lawful son of Edmund and Mary Elizabeth English, born the 30th of October 1806. Sponsors Robert and Sarah English.

by Ralph Ainsworth.

1807, Jany. 15th, was baptised by Ralph Ainsworth without the Ceremonies, and Jany. 19th received the Ceremonies, Henry, lawful Son of David and Elizabeth Henty, born Jany. 13th. Sponsors James Birkit M.D. and Frances Bradshaw, from

John Birdsall.

1807, Feb. 5th, was baptised William, lawful son of Thomas and Charlotte Batterbury, born December the 20th 1806. Sponsors Jean De La Lée and Isabella Clarke.

Ralph Ainsworth.

1807, March 14th, was baptised Frances Bick, lawful daughter of John and Mary Bick, born the 12th of February. Sponsors Thomas Ross and Sarah Thacker by proxy of Edward Kelly and Margaret Hines,

by Ralph Ainsworth.

1807, March 17th, was baptised Mary Ashman, widow of David Ashman and Daughter of John and Ann French, at Frome, aged about 70. Sponsor, her Sister Mrs More.

John Birdsall.

1807, March 29th, was baptised Mary, lawful daughter of Maurice and Eliz. Quin, born March 9th. Sponsor Cornelius Sweeny, by

John Birdsall.

1807, April 5th, was baptised (sub cond.) William, lawful Son of Laurence and Eleonora Birch, born Augt. 18th 1804. Sponsor Mathew Cammel.

John Birdsall.

1807, March 20th, was baptised (sub cond.) Will. Penny aged about 30 years, and March 29th Mary Browne aged about 20 years (sub cond.); both converts.

John Birdsall.

Ainsworth's hand:
1807, April 18th, was baptised without the ceremonies Matthew, lawful son of Matthew and Anne Costello, born the same day.

By John Birdsall [*see 27 April*].

Next nine entries in Ainsworth's and Birdsall's hands, as signed:
1807, April 19th, was baptized Elizabeth Fox, lawful daughter of Patrick and Elizabeth Fox, born the 6th of the same month. Sponsor William Cane.

Ralph Ainsworth.

1807, April the 20th, was baptised John Denny, lawful son of William and Mary Denny, born the 13th of the same month. Godfather Daniel Shean, Godmother Abbe Connor.

Ralph Ainsworth.

1807, April 27th, were supplied the ceremonies over Matthew Costello, baptised the 18th of the same month. Sponsor Patrick Dooling.

Ralph Ainsworth [*see 18 April*].

1807, April 29th, was baptized Mary Hogan, lawful daughter of Charles and Mary Hogan, born the 23d of the same Month. Sponsors James Quin and Jane Kavannah.

Ralph Ainsworth.

1807, May 31st, was baptised John, lawful Son of John and Mary Ferrers, born May 7th 1807. Sponsors James Mulleny and Annora Hagerty.

John Birdsall.

1807, June the 4th, was baptised John, lawful son of Edmund and Jemima Burke, born the 26th of last February. Sponsors John and Mary Short.

Ralph Ainsworth.

1807, June 17th, was baptised Richard, lawful Son of James and Judith

Carrol of Dublin in Ireland, born the same day; without Sponsors.

John Birdsall.

1807, June 19th, were supplied the Ceremonies over Elizabeth, lawful Daughter of John and Ellen Martin, born and baptised June 17th 1807. Sponsors John Martin and Catherine Sullivan.

John Birdsall.

1807, June 14th, was baptised (sub con.) on her being received into the church, Elizabeth O'Neil, aged 30 years.

John Birdsall.

Next six entries in Birdsall's hand:
1807, June 23rd, was baptised Frederic, lawful Son of Charles and Elizabeth Friar, born the 12th of this month. Sponsor Anne Denie.

Ralph Ainsworth.

1807, June 27th, was baptised (sub cond.) on her being received into the Church, Jane Carpenter, aged 37 years.

John Birdsall.

1807, June 28th, was baptised James, lawful Son of James and Ellen Hand, born June 12th last. Sponsor Matthew Camel.

John Birdsall.

1807, June 28th, was baptised Elizabeth Gill, lawful Daughter of Michael and Alice Gill, born June 26th last. Sponsors John and Mary Short.

John Birdsall.

1807, July 6th, was baptised Joseph, lawful Son of Richard and Eliz. Abbot, born the day before. Sponsors Thos. Murphy, and Margt. Williams.

John Birdsall.

1807, Augt. 9th, was baptised Charles O'Neal, lawful Son of John and Sarah O'Neal, born the 17th of July preceeding [*sic*]. Sponsor [*blank*].

John Birdsall.

Ainsworth's hand:
1807, Aug. 22d, was baptised Mary Anne Smith, lawful daughter of Joseph and Joanna Smith, born the 10th of this month. Sponsors James Clancey and Phillis Kyan.

Ralph Ainsworth.

Next six entries in Birdsall's hand:
1807, Augt. 23rd, was baptised Charles, lawful Son of Cornelius and Mary Dowding, born Augt. 2. Sponsors John Short and Lucy Cody.

John Birdsall.

1807, Augt. 23rd, was baptised Henry Michael, lawful Son of Michael and Frances Carrol, born Augt. 19th. Sponsor Victoire Julien.

Ralph Ainsworth.

1807, Sepr. 19th, was baptised Elizabeth Mulloy upon her being received into the Church, aged 29 years (sub cond.).

John Birdsall.

1807, Sepr. 20th, was baptised Ann, lawful Daughter of Matthew Madden, born Sepr. 15. Sponsor Elizabeth Bert.

John Birdsall.

1807, Octr. 4th, was baptised Elizabeth Gibbs upon her being received into the Church, aged 24 years (sub cond.).

John Birdsall.

1807, Octr. 17th, was baptised Elizabeth, lawful Daughter of Michael and Judith Bready, born in January last, without Sponsors, being on their road to Ireland.

John Birdsall.

Next eight entries in Ainsworth's and Birdsall's hands, as signed:

1807, Oct. 16th, was baptised John Errington, lawful son of William and Eleanor Errington, born the 4th of the same month. Godmother Monica O'Connor.

Ralph Ainsworth.

1807, Oct. 19th, was baptised Joseph Hanna, lawful son of Joseph and Isabella Hanna, born the 21st of December 1805. Godmother Margaret Hanna.

Ralph Ainsworth.

1807, Oct. 26th, was baptised Frederic Balsh, Son of [*blank*] Balsh[146] and Ann Campbell, born Octr. 13th 1799. Godmother Mrs Burn.

John Birdsall.

1807, Novr. 1st, was baptised Ann Lewis, lawful Daughter of Randall and Mary Lewis, born the day before. Godmother Catharine Hall.

John Birdsall.

1807, Nov. 2d, was baptized John Salmoni, son of Peter and Lucy Salmoni, born the 28th of September. Sponsors Antonius Strata and Catherine Murphy.

Ralph Ainsworth.

1807, November the 14th, was baptised Henry Joseph Knapp, lawful son of John and Mary Knapp, born the 12th of the same month. Sponsor William Day.

Ralph Ainsworth.

1807, Novr. 25th, was baptised Ann, lawful daughter of Henry Frain and Jane Frain, born Octr. 3rd preceeding [*sic*]. Godfather and Godmother Daniel and Catharine Gleeson.

John Birdsall.

1807, Decr. 20th, was baptised John, lawful Son of William and Elizabeth Rodway, born at Horton near Sodbury, Gloucestershire, Novr. 18th. Godmother Ann Winbow.

John Birdsall.

Calderbank's hand:

1807, Decr. 31, was baptised immediately after Birth, Elisabeth, lawful Daughter of Joseph and Mary Feasana. Sponsors Giovanni and Maria Francesca Biscani, by me

Jas. Calderbank.

Next nineteen entries in Birdsall's hand:

1808, Jany. 12th, was baptised Hannah, lawful Daughter of John and

---

[146]   Balch, or Baltch, was the surname of a Wiltshire Catholic family; cf. *C.R.S. Monograph 1*, pp. 199, 219, 249.

Ruth Wheelan, born Decr. 23 ann. pr. Sponsors Patrick McKeon and Catharine Hunt.

John Birdsall.

1808, Jany. 19th, was baptised Henry, lawful Son of Richard and Ann Pursel, born Jany. 17th. Godmother Mary Fielding.

John Birdsall.

1808, Jany. 22d, was baptised John, lawful Son of Richard and Elizabeth Greenman, born March 1st 1807. Godmother Jane Bateson.

John Birdsall.

1808, Feb. 1st, was baptised William, lawful Son of Richd. and Margaret Toole of Tiverton,[147] born Jany. 18th. Godfather David Fielding. Godmother M. Ann Cowean.

John Birdsall.

1808, Feby. 20th, was baptised Andrew Nicholas Browne, lawful Son of Nicholas and Ellen Brown, born the same day. Sponsors Sir Thos. Burke Bart. and Mrs Mary Martyn by proxy of Miss O'Driscoll.

Ralph Ainsworth.

1808, Feb. 28th, was baptised Frances, lawful Daughter of Abram and Ann Flower, born the 27th Augt. Godfather James Quin.

John Birdsall.

1808, March 10th, was baptised James, lawful Son of Jeremiah and Ellen Doolen, born Mar. 6. Godfather Daniel Buckley, Godmother Ellen Doyle.

John Birdsall.

March 13th 1808, was baptised Jane, lawful Daughter of James and Catharine Taylor, born Feby. 29th. Godmother, her Sister Mary Taylor.

John Birdsall.

April 10th 1808, was baptised Patrick, lawful Son of Michael and Marcella Cole, born 17th March 1808. Sponsor Miss Teresia Hyde.

Ralph Ainsworth.

April 26th 1808, was baptised Catharine, lawful Daughter of Phillip and Catharine Sheridan, born April 7th. Sponsor John Wheelan.

John Birdsall.

April 27th 1808, was baptised John, lawful Son of James and Ellen Richardson, born 23rd April. Sponsor Mary Lewis per proxy of Johanna Quirk.

John Birdsall.

April 27th 1808, was baptised Mary Anne, Daughter of George Williams and Lia West, born the same day. Sponsor Mary West.

John Birdsall.

1808, April 29th. Baptised without the Ceremonies Elizabeth Nowlen, lawful Daughter of James and Ann Nowlen, born the day before.

John Birdsall [see 30 Sept., 1809].

May 1st 1808, was baptised J. Baptist, lawful Son of Antonius and Catharine Strata, born March 1st. Godfather Petrus Salmoni, and Elizabeth Phelan.

John Birdsall.

---

[147] Although written thus, the place meant may be Twerton, Bath.

May 2d 1808, was baptised without the ceremonies, William, lawful Son of Thos. and Sarah Jordan, born Apr. 29th.

Ralph Ainsworth [*see 15 May*].

May 6th 1808, was baptised William, lawful Son of Charles and Ann Smallcomb, born April 22d. Godmother Elizabeth Keane.

John Birdsall.

May 15th 1808, were supplied the Ceremonies over William Jordan, baptised 2d Inst. Godfather William Hopkins.

J. Birdsall [*see May 2nd*].

May 18th 1808, was baptised by Bishop Sharrock without the Ceremonies, and the following day received the Ceremonies, William, lawful Son of Robert and Mary Croning, born May 7th. Godmother Mary West.

J. Birdsall.

1808, June 5th, was baptised Hannah, lawful Daughter of David and Elizabeth Henty, born May 23rd. Godfather Richard Phelan, Godmother Mary Brown.

John Birdsall.

Ainsworth's hand (2 entries):

1808, June 19th, was baptised Edward Stewart, Son of Richard and Catharine Stewart, born the 6th of April. Godmother Teresa Hyde.

Ralph Ainsworth.

1808, July 1st, was baptised Thomas Smith, son of Michael and Elizabeth Smith, born 12th of June. Sponsors Michael Long and Catherine Roussel.

Ralph Ainsworth.

Next thirteen entries in Birdsall's hand:

1808, July 3rd, was baptised Catharine, lawful Daughter of William and Mary Hillard, born June 17th. Sponsors Matthew Halpen and Margaret Lynch.

John Birdsall.

1808, July 3rd, was baptised Mary Elizabeth, lawful Daughter of Peter and Lucy Cody, born June 26th. Sponsors Cornelius Dowding and Ann Dowding.

John Birdsall.

1808, July 27th, was baptised Nicolas, lawful Son of Nicolas and Margaret Paillet, born July 11th. Godfather Patrick Mulloy, Godmother Catherine Ward.

Ralph Ainsworth.

1808, Augt. 5, was baptised Ann, lawful Daughter of Timothy and Judith Tafe, born the day before. Godmother Winefrid More.

John Birdsall.

1808, Augt. 26th, was baptised Frederic, Son of David and Christiana Brayes, born 16th of the same month. Godmother Mary James.

John Birdsall.

1808, Augt. 28, was baptised (sub cond.) George, lawful Son of Thomas and Elizabeth St. John, aged about 11 years.

John Birdsall.

1808, Sepr. 19th, was baptised Mary Ann, lawful Daughter of Robert and Mary Whately, born the day before. Godmother Margt. Clareson.

John Birdsall.

1808, Sepr. 27th, was baptised Mary, lawful Daughter of Peter and Ellen Lauton, born Feb. 6 last (sub cond.). Godmother Ann Sullivan.

John Birdsall.

1808, Oct. 28th, was baptised James, lawful Son of George and Frances Head, born the same day. Godmother Mary Kingstone.

John Birdsall.

1808, Oct 30th, was baptised Peter, lawful Son of Richard and Bridget Dowling, born the 24th of the same Month. Godmother Margaret Sweeny.

John Birdsall.

1808, Novr 6th, were baptised Catharine and Bridget, lawful Daughters of Patrick and Catharine Hunt, born Oct. 27. Sponsors to the first Philip Sheridan and Honora [blank], to the second Matthew Fagan and Bridget Bisset.

John Birdsall.

1808, Novr. 13th, was baptised Thomas, lawful Son of John and Mary Short, born Novr. 11th. Godfather William Penny, Godmother Sarah Pitt by proxy of Mary Short.

John Birdsall.

1808, Novr. 13th, was baptised (sub cond. on her being received into the Church) Mary Ann Dowding, aged 21 years.[148]

John Birdsall.

Next eight entries in Ainsworth's and Birdsall's hands, as signed:
1808, Novr. 27th, was baptised (sub conditione) Mary Anne Louisa Bailey, lawful daughter of William and Elizabeth Bailey, born Nov. 1st. Sponsors Christopher Irvine and Victoire Julien.

Ralph Ainsworth.

1808, Dec. 1st, was baptised Elizabeth Battleberry, lawful daughter of Thomas and Charlotte Battleberry, born the 19th of October. Sponsors Richard Phelan and Anne Row.

Ralph Ainsworth.

1808, Dec. 1st, was baptised Mary English [*sic, with dotted line beneath*] English, lawful daughter of Edmund and Mary Elizabeth English, born the 3d of July. Sponsors Thomas English (by proxy of Robert English) and Mary Anne Marveil.

Ralph Ainsworth.

1808, Decr. 28, was baptised Christina, lawful Daughter of Thomas and Henrietta Loveless, born the 22 of the same month. Godmother Henrietta Church by proxy of Ann Church.

John Birdsall.

1809, Jany. 1st, was baptised Cornelius, lawful Son of Cornelius and Mary Dowding, born Decr. 14. Godfather Joseph Dowding and [*sic.*] Lucy Cody.

John Birdsall.

1809, Jany. 1st, was baptised Lewis Don Julian, lawful Son of Santonge and Mary Simeon, born July 17th last. Godfather Lewis Antoine Simeon

[148]   Also in list of converts, *infra.*, p. 119.

du Hamel, Godmother Mary Henneker by proxy of Louisa Simeon.
> John Birdsall.

1809, Jan. 8th, was baptised James, lawful Son of Joseph and Ann Dowding, born the 3rd of this month. Sponsors Cornelius Dowding and Lucy Cody.
> John Birdsall.

1809, Jan. 29th, was baptised Elizabeth, lawful Daughter of Maurice and Elizabeth Quin, born the 21st of the same month. Godmother Margaret Sweeny.
> John Birdsall.

Next six entries in Birdsall's hand:
1809, March 4th, was baptised Henry, lawful Son of John and Elizabeth Fryer, born Feb. 25. Godfather John Denie, Godmother Winefred Denie.
> Ralph Ainsworth.

1809, March 12th, was baptised Sarah, lawful daughter of John and Ann Kentchens, born Feb. 23. Godfather Cornelius Dowding, Godmother Arabella Kelly.
> John Birdsall.

1809, March 18th, was baptised William, lawful Son of Robert and Martha Moon, born the day before. Godmother Mary Carrol.
> John Birdsall.

1809, March 19th, was baptised Augustine, Son of James Dowding and Mary Hall, born March 5th. Godfather John Kentchens, Godmother Mary Dowding.
> John Birdsall.

1809, Mar. 26th, was baptised (sub cond.) upon her being received into the church, Mary Hall, aged 27.
> John Birdsall.

1809, April 16th, was baptised Maria, lawful Daughter of Peter and Lucy Salmoni. Sponsors Peter Flenigen Esq. and Eliz. Willan.
> Ralph Ainsworth.

Coombes's hand:
1809, May 7th, was baptised Thomas, lawful son of Richard and Elizabeth Phelan, born May 5th. Sponsors Wm. Bugden and Mary Chopping.
> W. H. Coombes.[149]

Next twelve entries in Ainsworth's and Birdsall's hands, as signed:
1809, May 22d, was baptised Elijah, lawful Son of Abram and Ann Flower, born April 6th. Sponsor James Quin.
> J. Birdsall.

1809, May 16th, was baptized Frederick, lawful son of John and Mary Knapp, born May 15th. Godmother Catherine Knapp.
> Ralph Ainsworth.

1809, May 24th, was baptized Michael, lawful son of Peter and Helen Lawton, born the 5th of the same Month. Sponsors William Askins and Catherine Taylor.
> Ralph Ainsworth.

[149] William Henry Coombes D.D.; see *C.R.S.*, 65, note 341 to Introduction.

1809, July 11th, was baptised Martha Moon, aged 43 (sub cond.) upon her being received into the Church.

                                                                    John Birdsall.

1809, July 26th, was baptised Ann, lawful Daughter of John and Mary St John, born July 19th. Godfather Matthew Camel, Godmother Elizabeth Smith.

                                                                    John Birdsall.

1809, July 27th, was baptised (sub cond.) on her being received into the Church, Ann Nowlen, aged 31.

                                                                    John Birdsall.

1809, August 15th, was baptised (sub cond., he having had private baptism by some protestant Minister) George, lawful Son of Edwd. and Elizabeth Murphy, born June 4th 1808. Godmother Eleanor Nowlin.

                                                                    John Birdsall.

1809, Augt. 15th, was baptised Charles, lawful Son of Edward and Elizabeth Murphy, born July 18th 1809. Godmother Eleanor Nowlin.

                                                                    John Birdsall.

1809, Augt. 16th, were supplied the ceremonies over Ann, lawful Daughter of James and Sarah Douglass, born Decr. 2, and baptised in the Isle of Mann Decr. 12. Godfather Timothy Gaffeney, Godmother Jane McCastling.
                                                                    John Birdsall.

1809, August 19th, was baptised Henry, lawful Son of William and Ellenore Errington, born Augt. 3rd. Godfather Mr Malachy O'Connor, Godmother Mrs Comerford.

                                                                    John Birdsall.

1809, August 30th, was baptised Mary, lawful Daughter of Thomas and Mary Welsh, born Jany. 4th, 1807. Godmother Ann Hayes.

                                                                    John Birdsall.

1809, Sepr. 10th, was baptised Joseph, lawful Son of Joseph and Mary Long, born July 20th this year. Sponsor Mary Meyers.

                                                                    John Birdsall.

Birdsall's hand (3 entries):
1809, Sepr. 13th, was baptised Ellen, lawful daughter of Philip and Bridget Ryan, born the 6th of this month. Godmother Mary Hoy.

                                                                    Ralph Ainsworth.

1809, Sepr. 13th, were supplied the Ceremonies of baptism (sub cond.) over William, Son of Matthew Somerfield and Harriet Osmund, born Oct. 31, 1808. Godfather Patrick Murphy, Godmother Catharine Conway.
                                                                    John Birdsall.

1809, Sepr. 30th, were supplied the ceremonies over Elizabeth, lawful daughter of James and Ann Nowlen, born April 28th, 1808 and baptised the following day. Godmother Elizabeth Mulloy.

                                            John Birdsall [*see 29 April 1808*].

Next eight entries in Calderbank's hand:
1809, was conditionally baptised Anne, lawful Daughter of Wm. and Elizth. Parker, born 1st April. Spons. Anne Nagle.

                                                                    J. Calderbank.

1809, Octr. 20th, was baptised conditionally Francis, lawful Son of Francis and Honora Halworth, born 9th Decr. 1808. Sponsor Timothy Taaffe.

J. Calderbank.

1809, Nov. 12, was bapt. Charles, Son of Thos. and Jane Prince, born 22nd Octr. Spons. Richd. Pheilan and Elizth. Henly.

J. Calderbank.

1809, Novr. 19, was bapt. Charles, Son of Peter and Elizth Mullighan, born 1st Decr. 1806. Spon. John Short and Mrs Margt. Tunstall.

J. Calderbank.

1809, Novr. 20, was bapt. Maria, Daughter of Laurence and Elenor Kelly, born 18th. Octr. Spons. Elizth. O'Leary.

J. Calderbank.

1809, Novr. 25, was bapt. Andrew, Son of Alexander and Ellen Conolly, born 24th. Spon. John Mutry and Elizth. Sweeny.

J. Calderbank.

1809, Novr. 28th, was bapt. Sarah, Daughter of John and Sarah Hill, born 23rd.

J. Calderbank.

1810, Feby. 6th, were supplied over the above mentioned Sarah Hill the Ceremonies of the church. Sponsors on the occasion were Henrietta Church and Cornelius Dowding, by me

Jas. Calderbank.

Here follow twelve blank pages, then, in Wilks's hand:
Status Congregationis
Anno 1788.

1,2. Thomas Moore and Wife
  3. Jane Harrish
  4. Miss Robinson
4,5. [*sic*] Sumner and Wife
  6. – Bryan
  7. Miss FitzGerald's man
8,9,10. Mr Donnelly and Wife and Daughter
11. – McDermot, Devizes
12. Irish tailor at Murphy's
13. Lady Shrewsbury[150]
14. George · · · · footman
15. Maid and housemaid

16. Mrs Cahegan
17. Edward Wogan
18. Miss Webb
19,20. Mr and Mrs Tadlock
21. Frances Forsar
22. Marie Louise Herriez

Here follow three blank pages, then lists of converts, beginning in Brewer's hand:
Anno Dni. 1780, Die Octobris 9. In Gremium Ecclesiae admissa est Anna Austin, annos nata 17.

---

[150]   Elizabeth, *née* Dormer, widow of the 14th Earl, whose nephew was the 15th Earl (*supra,* pp. 96-7). For Lady Shrewsbury see *C.R.S. Monograph 1*, pp. 117, 248. She died in 1809 and there is a memorial-inscription to her in Bath Abbey.

1780, Die Octobris decimo septimo, admissus in Gremium Ecclesiae Gulielmus Connor.
Die Decembris 20, admissa est Maria Childe.
Anno Dni. 1781, Die Martii 13, admissa est Anna Tudor, Vidua.

Pembridge's hand (the first six entries repeat those on page 15):
Received into the Church.
1782, Feby. 23, Diana James. Present William and Mary Howell
    March 14, Miss Mary Proctor   Present   Mrs Martin and Blake
            And Mary Elliot   Mary Goodacre
    May 16, Peter Green of Dunkerton, present Thos. Brown
    Dec. 8, Charles Francis of Wellow, present Mrs Martin
    Dec.   John Mills, Bath
1783, Nov. 1, Emma Barbara Dutton
1792, Augst. 8, Mary Wilcock; present Simon Hensy, Mary Short and
    John Mills.

                                             M. Pembridge.
Henceforth in various hands, as signed:
1793, Aug. [*blank*] received into the Church William Batchelor. Present Jacob West etc.

                                             H. Lawson.
1794. Received into the Church Sep. 8, Anna N. Gage. Present Jacob West.

                                             H. Lawson.

1795. Received into the Church June 20th, J. Pike. Present Jacob West.
                                             R.H. Lawson.
1796. Received into the church January 25, Richard Howell. Present Mr Feray, French Priest.

                                             R.H. Lawson.
1797. Received into the Church August 8th, Elizabeth Howell, Arabella Kelly, Jane James. Witness T. Mulligan.

                                             R.H. Lawson.
1799. Received in the Church in the presence of the congregation, Francis Melmoth and Elizabeth Heith the 9th of March.

                                             R. Henry Lawson.
1800, June 26th. Received into the Church Mary Seifreid.

                                             R. Ainsworth.
1800, June the 5th. Rebecca Dunning and Sarah Feeling.

                                             R.H. Lawson.
Received into the Church upon sundry occasions: Maria Catherine Smith, Mary Mackey, Catherine Phelon, Winefrid Moore, Elizabeth Browne, Sarah Bourk, Sarah Meagher, Elizabeth Weston, Anne Rowe, James Rowe, N.N.Taffe, Charlotte Merrick.

                                             R. Ainsworth.
1800, September 28th. Received into the Church Mrs N – Dorel, by the Rd. R. Rev. D.D. G.W. Sharrock, Ep.Telmess. Present Mrs Porter and Hales, and Constantia and Maria Walsh [*in Ainsworth's hand.*]

1800, Oct. 16th, Received into the Church Charlotte Brooks; present Mary Hencey and Helen Rose.

R. Ainsworth.

February 9th 1801, received into the church Mary Golding, aged 23 years, in the presence of Helen Rose, by me

Jas. Calderbank.

March 26th 1801, was received into the church Elisabeth Ketcherside, aged 56 years, by me

Jas. Calderbank.

April 11th 1801, was received into the church Elizabeth Kent, aged 19 years, in the presence of Anne Hughes and a Stranger, by me

Jas. Calderbank.

April 29th 1801, was received into the church Jas. Davies, aged 20, in the presence of Honble. Robert Plunket, his Master.

Jas. Calderbank.

August 12th 1801, was received into the church Winefride Morgan, aged 30 years, by me

Jas. Calderbank.

Next ten entries in Calderbank's hand:

1802, was received into the church Mary Fazana by

Ralph Ainsworth.

1802, April 6th, was received into the church Catharine Connor, aged 78 years, in the presence of Michael O'Brien, by me

Jas. Calderbank.

1802, July 8th, was received into the Church Thos. Jenkinson, aged 75, by me

Jas. Calderbank.

1802, October 28th, was received into the Church Miss Rebecca Ketcherside, aged 26, in the presence of Madame de Mansigny, by me

Jas. Calderbank.

1803, January 16th, was received into the Church by Joseph Withers by

R. Ainsworth.

1803, April 1st, was received into the Church James Goodman, aged 23, by me

Jas. Calderbank.

1803, April 23rd, was received into the Church John Mathews, aged 25, by me

Jas. Calderbank.

1803, October 26th, was received into the Church Anthony Holloran, aged 28, by me

Jas. Calderbank.

1803, Novr. 1st, was received into the church Philip Wright, aged 36 years, by me

Jas. Calderbank.

1803, Novr. 16th, was received into the Catholic church Mary Sparke, aged 26, by me

Jas. Calderbank.

Ainsworth's hand:
1803, Oct. 28th, was received into the Catholic Church Jane Byrne, aged 36.
                                                        R. Ainsworth.

Calderbank's and Ainsworth's hands, as signed:
1803, Nov. 21st, was received into the Catholic church Mrs L. Elisabeth Hobbs, aged 25 years, by me
                                                        Jas. Calderbank.
1804, January 1st, was received into the Catholic Church Mrs Sarah Best, aged 27, in the presence of Mr Henry Best, her Husband, Mr David Rochfort and several other persons, by me
                                                        Jas. Calderbank.
1804, Feb. 10th, was received into the Church Anne Cassell, aged 27, in the presence of Helen Rose, by me
                                                        R. Ainsworth.
1804, April 7th, was received into the Catholic church Elisabeth Gilpin, aged 28, in the presence of a Stranger, by me
                                                        Jas. Calderbank.
1804, May 5th, was received into the Church Anne Cassell, by me
                                      R. Ainsworth [*entry deleted*].
1804, [May *deleted*] 31st, was received into the Catholic Church Jane Read, aged 31, by me
                                                        R. Ainsworth.

Birdsall's hand; see death-entry, 13 June (sic.) 1806, infra., p. 127.
1806, July the 10th, was received into the Church John Leech, of Irish extraction, lying sick of a consumption at his lodgings at Twerton, aged about 60 years.
                                                        John Birdsall.
Some time before this was received into the Church Charlotte Higgins who long remained in a dying state after Revd. John Rigby had received her. [*in Birdsall's hand; see death-entry, 24 November 1807, infra., p. 128*].

Henceforth in Ainsworth's, Birdsall's and Calderbank's hands, as signed:
1806, Octob. 7th, was received into the Catholic Church Richard Hancock, aged 66 years.
                                                        John Birdsall.
1806, Novr.16th, was received into the Catholic Church Charles Higgins, aged 17 years.
                                                        John Birdsall.
1806, Novr. 23rd, was received into the Catholic Church Mary Browne, aged 20 years.
                                                        John Birdsall.
1806, Decr. 10th, was received into the Catholic Church William Penny, aged 25 years.
                                                        John Birdsall.
1807, March 19th, were received into the Catholic Church Mark Abbot, aged 18, and Frances Boyce, aged 19 years.
                                                        Ralph Ainsworth.

1807, June 14th, was received into the Catholic Church Elizabeth O'Neil, aged about 30 years.

John Birdsall.

1807, June 27th, was received into the church Jane Carpenter of Shoccerwick[151] near Bath, aged 37 years.

John Birdsall.

1807, June 28th, was received into the Church Stephen Davies, aged 17 years, in the presence of Mark Abbot and others of the Congregation.

John Birdsall.

1807, July 12th, was received into the Catholic Church Leonora Birch, aged 32 years, in the presence of her Husband.

John Birdsall.

1807, Sepr. 13th, were receive [sic] into the Church Elizabeth Mulloy and Elizabeth Gibbs, the former aged 29 years, the latter 24, in the presence of Patrick Mulloy and Mrs Hebdin and others.

John Birdsall.

1807, Decr. 16th, was received into the Catholic Church Jemima Burke in the presence of her Husband Edwd. Burke and Mrs Callan.

John Birdsall.

1808, May 6th, was received into the Catholic Church Elizabeth Dutton, aged 64, in the presence of her Husband and others.

John Birdsall.

1808, Novr. 13, was received into the Catholic Church Mary Ann Dowding,[152] aged 21 years, in the presence of Mr H. Williams.

John Birdsall.

1809, Feb. 8, was received into the Catholic Church, Sarah Praid, aged 28 years. She died the following day.

By John Birdsall.

1809, March 26th, was received into the Catholic Church Mary Hall, aged 27 years, in the presence of Mrs Hebdin and others of the Congregation.

John Birdsall.

1809, July 10th, was received into the Catholic Church Martha Moon, aged 43 years, in the presence of Ann Box and Mary Carrol.

John Birdsall.

1809, July 27th, were received into the Catholic Church Mr Thomas Ketcherside, aged 66, and Mrs Ann Nowlen, aged 31, in the presence of each other and Miss Rebecca Ketcherside.

John Birdsall.

1810, June 9th, was recd. into the Catholic Church Robt. Moon, aged 56 years, by me

Jas. Calderbank.

1810, June 16th, was recd. into the Catholic church Richd. Clarke, aged 16 years, by me

Jas. Calderbank.

---

[151] Shockerwick.

[152] See also *supra*, p. 112 (baptismal entry).

1810, Septr. 14th, was received into the Catholic Church Helen Barry, aged 51, by me

Jas. Calderbank.

Pembridge's hand (following 12 blank pages):
Obituary Register 1792.
April 26. Deceased: James Ruddic, Inglisbach.
   28. The Revd. Mr Hugo Heatley, Resident for the Out-Mission, Age 33. R. In P. Buried in the Abbey Church, left hand Isle, May 2, 1792, close to the Wall, under Dr Bostock's Monument.[153]
June 4, Joanna Moore, Age 14.
July 4, Honora Harrogan, Aged 78.
July 12, John Doyer, Age 40.
July 16, Michael Meare, Infant Age 6 Months 2 Weeks.
Sept.19, Willm Doyle, Infant Age 3 Weeks.
Oct. 1, James Bryen, Infant, 2 Months, Bath.
Oct. 20, Timothy Murphy, Weston.
Dec. 1, Mathew Micmurtry, Bath, 17, Bath.
Dec. 10, Mr Edmund Teaffe,[154] Ir. Stranger, 63, Bath.
Dec. 21, William Brown, Infant, 9 Months, Bath.
Dec. 23, Elizabeth Hall, 50, Bath.

1793
Jany. 14, Mary Anne Metcalf,[155] Infant, 3 Months 10 Days.
Jany. 23, Helena Thornton, 56, Bath.
Feby. 1, Mary Rosano, Child, 3 years, Bath.
Feby.23, Elizabeth Dowding, 9 years, Bath.

1793. *[Date and 5 entries in Ainsworth's hand]*
April 5th Mary Leech, aged 42, Bath.
      13,   John Jennings, aged 36, Bath.
      15,   Mr: Le Marquis Du Gage, aged *[blank]*
      17,   Mrs Elizabeth Eyre, aged 49, Bath.
May   9th, Miss Catherine Leonora Walsh[156], aged 28, Bath.

Lawson's hand (4 entries):
July 22,   Marcella Desmonds, aged 22, Bath.
July 25,   William Lowndes, aged *[blank]*, Bath.
August 7,   Luke Connoway, aged 22, Bath.
Aug. 10,   Anne Thomas, aged 24, Bath.

---

[153] "Ricardus Bostock M.D., olim de Wixall in comitatu Salopiae, obiit 16 Mar. 1747" (Davey, p. 63). But *R.B.A.*, p. 475 dates the burial May 3rd "Under Samuel Wilson, Esqre, his stone." Birt, p. 117 gives 1757 as the year of Heatley's birth.

[154] Buried at St James's, Bath, 13 Dec., as Taaffe — the usual spelling of this name (*The Genealogist*, New Series, IX, p. 111). Doubtless "Ir." means Irish.

[155] Buried in Bath Abbey, 18 Jan. (*R.B.A.*, p. 476).

[156] Buried in Bath Abbey, 14 May (*ibid.*).

Ainsworth's hand (7 entries):
Aug. 19th, James Dane, aged 60, Bath.
Aug. 29th, William Darling, aged 27, Bath.
Sep. 12th [? *10th*] , Thomas Day, aged 63, Ingsbach.
Sep. 16th, Frances Nagle,[157] Aged –, Bath.
Sep. 11th, James Quince, aged 23, Pickwick.
Oct. 21st, John Fogarthy, aged –, Bath.
Oct. 21st, Thomas Metcalfe Esq., aged 36.[158]

Lawson's hand (3 entries):
Oct. 28th, Margaret Foresight.
April 16 (*1794?*) John N. Died, Bath.
1794, March, Died Riquetts, Bath.

                1794. [*Date and 2 entries in Ainsworth's hand.*]
March 4th. Died Susanna Day, aged 72, Ingsbach.
March 9th. Died [*blank*] Cranfield, aged [*blank*] , Bath.
Lawson's hand:
March 11. Died [*blank*] Simon Quin, Bath.
Ainsworth's hand (12 entries):
April 30th. Died Elizabeth Clothier, aged 17, Bath.
May. 6th. Died Anne Howard,[159] aged 59, Bath.
May 10th. Died Honora Maulin, aged [*blank*] , Bath.
June 27th [?] , Died Mary Denie, aged 6, Bath.
July 31st. Died Ray. Thos. Hugo Arundel,[160] aged 2 Months, Bath.
Aug. 21st. Died Robert Madan Esq.,[161] aged 64, St., Bath.
Nov. 18th. 1794. Died Miss Mary Anne French,[162] aged 30, Bath.
Dec. 12th 1794. Died John Tobin Esq., aged 61, Bath.
Dec. 25th 1794. Died James Dowling, aged –, Stranger.
Jan. 1st   1795. Died Michael Monks, aged –, Soldier.
Jan. 2d   1795. Died Bartholomew Cranfield, aged –, Bath.
Jan. 29th 1795. Died Margaret Lyons, aged –, Bath.
Lawson's hand (8 entries):
Jan. 1795. Died Margaret Howard, Bath.
Jan. or Feb. Died at Horton, Mrs Manning.

[157]   Buried in Bath Abbey, 23 Sept., as "Neagle" (*ibid.*).

[158]   For his memorial-inscription in the Abbey, see Davey, p. 71.

[159]   Wife of Philip Howard of Corby Castle, Cumberland; cf. genealogy in C.B.J., Lord Mowbray, Segrave & Stourton, *History of the Noble House of Stourton* (1899) II, p. 851; also *R.B.A.*, p. 477 (burial, 10 May 1794).

[160]   In *R.B.A., loc. cit.,* is a burial-entry: "Aug. 4. J. B. Arundell". See also note 120.

[161]   Buried in Bath Abbey, 26 Aug., as Madden (*R.B.A., loc. cit.*). "St." in this entry is probably an abbreviation for "Stranger". His *Laity's Directory* obituary is reprinted in *C.R.S.,* 12, p. 51.

[162]   Buried in Bath Abbey, 22 Nov. (*R.B.A., loc. cit.*).

March 24, 1795. Died Rev. Mr Geary, O.S.B.,[163] Bath, aged 82.
March 27, 1795. Died James Goffe, Bath.
April 14, 1795. Died Francis Loons, Bath.
April 15, 1795. Died Mary Darling, Bath.
April   1795. Died Mary Martin, Bath.
April 16, 1795. Died Thomas Moore, Bath.

1795 [*Date and 2 entries in Ainsworth's hand.*]
May 20th. Died the Rev. Mr. Thos. Moore,[164] aged 73, Bath.
July 3d 1795. Died Anne Pit, aged 26, Bath.
Lawson's hand:
May Died Philip Grace, aged 16, Bath, Soldier.
Ainsworth's hand (3 entries):
Aug. 6th. Died the Rev. Thos. Ballyman,[165] aged 60, Bath
      10 Died Anthony Gale, aged —, Bradford.[166]
May 25th 1796. Died Mary Murphy, aged [*blank*], Bath.
Lawson's hand:
June 24. Died Mrs Malpews [?], aged [*blank*], Bath.
Henceforth in Ainsworth's hand:
1796, July 7th. Died Jacquette De Kerouartz, daughter of James,
      Count De Kerouartz, president of the Parliament of Britany,
      and of Mary Reine De Kergouet, wife of Charles Count
      D'Hector, Lieutenant-general of the Navy of the King of
      France, Commander of the naval force of Britany, and was
      buried the 10th of the same month.
1796, July 31. Died Maria Ellen Brown, aged 14 Months, Bath.
1797, May   7th. Died Brigit Dalton,[167] aged 72, Bath.
      May 25. Died Catherine Nagle,[168] aged 35, Bath.
      June 1st Died Sarah Bell,[169] aged 53, Stranger.
      Aug. 16th. Died Elizabeth Barber, Bath.
November 25th 1797. Died the Right Revd. and venerable prelate
      Doctor Charles Walmesly, Bp. of Rama and Vicar Apostolic of
      the Western District, in the 75th year of his age and the 40th
      of his Episcopacy, Bath.
March 3d 1798. Died Mrs — Jay, aged —, Bath.

[163]   Dom John Anselm Geary, for whom see Birt, p. 119 and *C.R.S.,*65, pp. 56-7; also *C.R.S.,* 12, p. 50. He was buried in the Abbey on 27 March (*R.B.A., loc. cit.*).
[164]   Ex-Jesuit. See *C.R.S.,* 65, p. 73; Foley, VII, p. 520; *C.R.S.,* 12, p. 50.
[165]   Benedictine. See Birt, p. 120; *C.R.S.,* 12, p. 50; *R.B.A.,* p. 477 (Bath Abbey burial 8 Aug. 1795); Kirk, p. 9.
[166]   Bradford-on-Avon. See also note 55.
[167]   *née* More. See *C.R.S.,* 65, p. 73 & references there given; *C.R.S.,* 12, pp. 62, 64 (*Laity's Directory* obit.); *R.B.A.* p. 478 (Abbey burial, 16 May); Davey, p. 71 (memorial-inscription in Bath Abbey).
[168]   Buried in Bath Abbey, 1 June (*R.B.A., loc. cit.*).
[169]   Buried in Bath Abbey, 8 June (*ibid.*).

10th 1798, Died William Muffy, aged 56, Bath, Stran.

13th 1798. Died Miss Eliza Grace, aged —, Bath, Stranger.

June 5th 1798. Died Mrs Elizabeth French,[170] aged 69, Bath.

Lawson's hand (2 entries):

July the 17th 1798. Died Miss Charlotte Grace, aged 16, Hotwells.[171]

July the 29th 1798. Died Miss Anne Grace, aged 17, Holwells [sic].

Next eleven entries in Ainsworth's hand:

Aug. 7th 1798. Died Catherine Ware, aged —, Bath.

Aug. 8th 1798. Died James [*illegible* ?Casry], aged —, Bath.

Aug. 8th 1798. Died Catherine Nailling, aged —, Bath.

Oct. 9th 1798. Died Celia Taffe, aged —, Bath.

Jan. 12th 1799. Died Margaret Steward, aged 69, Sion Hill, Stranger

Jan. 15th 1799. Died James Brown, aged 38, Bath, Stranger.

Jan. 17th 1799. Died Elizabeth Barnes, aged 66, Bath.

Jan. 18th 1799. Died William Robinson,[172] aged 61, Bath.

Jan. 21st 1799. Died the Reverend James Jennison,[173] aged 61, Bath.

Jan. 23d 1799. Died William Larcon, aged —, Bath.

Jan. 25th 1799. Died Helen Hignett,[174] aged 31, Bath.

Lawson's hand (2 entries):

March 22 [*altered from* 23] 1799. Mic. Nolin, aged 63, Bath.

April 19, 1799. Eliz. Oran [?], aged 32, Bath.

Ainsworth's hand (2 entries):

June 30th 1799. Died Mary Butler,[175] aged 69, Bath.

July 6th 1799. Died Frances Martyn,[176] aged 80, Bath.

Next seven entries in Lawson's hand:

Aug. 1799. Died Sarah Mahony, aged 14, Bath.

August 1799. Died Robert Baker, aged 17, Bath.

September 6th 1799. Died Mary Woodam, aged 61, Horton Common.

1799. Decem. Died W. Conolly, aged 38.

1799. At the Hotwells, Miss Francis [sic] Grace, 19.

January 2, 1800, At Bath, Cath. Martin.

1800, January the 14th. Died the Honorable Miss Margaret Preston,[177]

---

[170]   Buried in Bath Abbey, 12 June (*R.B.A.*, p. 479).

[171]   Presumably Bristol Hotwells.

[172]   *C.R.S.*, 12, p. 64, dates his death 18 Dec. 1798. Perhaps father of Dom Thomas Gregory Robinson who became a Benedictine after serving as a naval surgeon (see his baptismal entry, 12 Oct. 1780, *supra*, p. 10).

[173]   Ex-Jesuit. See *C.R.S.*, 65, p. 73; *R.B.A.*, p. 479 (burial, 25 Jan., as "Jeaneson").

[174]   In *C.R.S.*, 12, p. 72, as "Hegnett".

[175]   Mrs Mary Butler (*ibid.*).

[176]   Buried in Bath Abbey, 13 July (*R.B.A., loc. cit.*)

[177]   Aged 54 (*C.R.S.*, 12, p. 74). Other Catholic deaths in Bath, not among these few register-entries, are: Fitzgerald Groghean (*sic*) Nagle, buried 3 Dec. 1799 (*R.B.A.*, p. 480; see also *supra*, p. 81) and Mrs Mary Townshend, d. 29 May 1800 (*C.R.S.* 12, p. 78).

Daughter of James Preston, Viscount Gormanston, and the
Honorable Thomasin Barnewall, both of the Kingdom of Ireland.
Bath.

Ainsworth's hand (2 entries):
1800, Oct. 22d. Died Mary Hughes, aged 19, Bath.
1800, Nov.10th.Died Sarah Hughes, aged 18,Bath.

Calderbank's hand (name italicised in Ainsworth's):
1801, February 10th. Died Dr. *Meagher*, agd. [blank].

Next fourteen entries in Calderbank's hand:
1801, February 19th. Died Mrs. Dunn.
1801, February 24th. Died Patrick Sullivan, aged 27, Bath, R.I.P.
1801, May 6th. Died Willm. Perry, aged 38, Bath, R.I.P.
1801, August 8th. Died Mrs Decima Smith, aged 74, Bath, R.I.P.
1801, Aug. 10th. Died Peirce Walsh Esqr., aged [blank], Bath, R.I.P.
1801, Aug. 21st. Died Mary Anne Doran, aged 7 days, Weston.
1801, Septr. 23rd. Died Francis Curly, aged 62, Bath, R.I.P.
1801, October 16th. Died John Campbell, ag'd 61, Bath, R.I.P.
1801, Decembr. 4th. Died Mrs Porter,[178] aged 57, Sion Hill, Bath, R.I.P.
1802, January 17th. Died Mary Lawlos, aged [blank], Bath, R.I.P.
1802, Feb. 15th. Died Miss Barbara Dorrel, aged 4 years, Bath.
1802, March 4th. Died Mary Mullighan, aged 57, R.I.P.
1802, March 10th. Died Jacob Saifraid, aged 89, Bath, R.I.P.
1802, April 21st. Died Mrs Jane J.Burke, aged 80, R.I.P.

Ainsworth's hand:
1802, May 19th. Died Thos. Brown, aged 50, Bath, R.I.P.

Calderbank's hand (2 entries):
1802, June 5th. Died David Welsh, aged 46, Bath, R.I.P.
1802, June 21st. Died Thos. Phelan, aged 5 months. Bath.

Ainsworth's hand (3 entries):
1802, Sep. 21. Died Mary Johnson, aged –, Bath.
1802, Sep. 25th. Died Mrs -- Glasson, aged –, Bath.
1802, Oct. 5th. Died John Trowbridge, aged –, Bath.

Next nine entries in Calderbank's hand:
1802, Decr. 3rd. Died Sir Thos. Fleetwood[179] Bart., aged 61, Bath.
1802, Decr. 6th. Died John Weldon Esqr., aged 49, Bath, R.I.P.
1802, Decr. 10th. Died Jas. Dunn, aged 45, Bath, R.I.P.
1802, Decr. 12th. Died [blank] Kellenbrek, aged [blank], Bath, R.I.P.
1802, Decr. 13th. Died Thos. Clarke, aged 91, Widcomb, R.I.P.

[178] *née* Mary Nevill; cf. Egerton Castle (ed.) *The Jerningham Letters,* II, p. 400.
[179] Also in *C.R.S.,* 12, p. 85.

1803, Jany. 14th. Died Michael OBrien, aged [blank], Bath, R.I.P.
1803, Feby.1st. Died John Murray, aged [blank], Bath, R.I.P.
1803, Feb. 3rd. Died Denis Morand, aged [blank], Bath, R.I.P.
1803, Feby.8th. Died Thos. Hardy, aged 3 years, Bath.

Ainsworth's hand (2 entries):
1803, March 3d. Died Margaret [blank], aged 76, Bath.
1803, March 17th. Died Catherine Pope, aged 68, Bath.

Next eight entries in Calderbank's hand:
1803, March 23rd. Died Revd. William Wilkinson Fletcher,[180] aged 81,
                Bath, R.I.P.
1803, June 10th. Died Henry Cooper, aged 10 months, Bath.
1803, July 2nd. Died Mrs Anne Madden,[181] aged 70, Bath, R.I.P.
1803, Augst. 21st. Died Jane Buckley, aged 63, Bath, R.I.P.
1803, Aug. 27th. Died Anne Jobson, aged 51, Bath, R.I.P.
1803, Sep. 19th. Died Anne Cliffe, aged 73, Bath, R.I.P.
1803, Octr. 4th. Died Mrs Susan Day, aged 78, Bath, R.I.P.
1803, Octr. 9th. Died Mrs Elenora Walsh, aged 67, Bath, R.I.P.

Ainsworth's hand (2 entries):
1803, Oct. 12th. Died Mrs Mary Hussey, aged 85, Bath, R.I.P.
1803, Oct. 26th. Died Mary Jones, aged 58, Bath, R.I.P.

Calderbank's hand:
1803, Novr. 20th. Died Anthony Holloran, Serjeant in the Army, aged 28
                years, R.I.P.

Ainsworth's hand (2 entries):
1803, Dec. 13th. Died Mary Heaney, aged 62, Bath, R.I.P.
1803, Dec. 17th. Died Bernard Byrne, aged 48, Bath, R.I.P.

Calderbank's hand (3 entries):
1803, Decr. 27th. Died Edd.Kirby, aged 53, Stranger, R.I.P.
1804, Jany. 8th. Died Magt. McGauley, aged 60, Bath, R.I.P.
1804, Feby. 23rd. Died Pascal Ballieul, French, agd. 29, R.I.P.

Ainsworth's hand (3 entries):
1804, Mar. 26th. Died Nicholas Molland, aged 66, Bath, R.I.P.
1804, March 13th. Died Elizabeth Campbell, aged 60, R.I.P.
1804, March 16th. Died George Jeffers, aged 3 days.

---

[180]   Formerly President of St Omer's; cf. Gillow, II, p. 298 (*sub* Fletcher); Kirk,
p. 250 (*sub* Wilkinson, with date of death as 24 March); *C.R.S.,* 63, p. 430. The
mortuary-entries for the Spring of 1803 reflect no increase in deaths coinciding
with the "influenza" epidemic then raging in Bath; cf. E. J. Climenson, *Passages
from the Diaries of Mrs Philip Lybbe Powys* (1899) p. 352.

[181]   In *C.R.S.,* 12, p. 86, as "Madan".

Calderbank's hand (3 entries):
1804, March 30th. Died the Right Honble. Lord Dormer,[182] aged 78, Bath, R.I.P.
1804, April 9th. Died M. Rose Ashton, aged 93, R.I.P.
1804, April 9th. Died Maurice Hayden, aged 50, R.I.P.

Ainsworth's hand (2 entries):
1804, April 26th. Died Antony Garvey Esq., aged 67, Stranger.
1804, May 29th. Died Mrs Anne Ennever, aged 33, Bath, R.I.P.

Next eight entries in Calderbank's hand:
1804, June 2nd. Died Garrett Barry, aged 14 years and 5 months, Bath, R.I.P.
1804, June 22nd. Died John McGrath, aged 60, R.I.P.
1804, July 1st. Died William Cooper, aged 54, Bath, R.I.P.
1804, July 1st. Died William Batchelor, aged 84, Bath.
1804, July 14th. Died Joseph Winbow, aged 52, Horton, R.I.P.
1804, July 28th. Died Michael Conner, aged 52, Bath, R.I.P.
1804, August 30th. Died Anne Love, aged 66, Bath, R.I.P.
1804, Septr. 9th. Died Catherine Hogden, aged 30, Stranger, R.I.P.

Ainsworth's hand (2 entries):
1804, Oct. 8th. Died John Flanagan, aged 44, Bath, R.I.P.
1804, Oct. 9th. Died Nicolas Taffe, aged 44, Bath, R.I.P.

Calderbank's hand:
1804, Decr. 30th. Died Catharine Browne, aged 41, Bath, R.I.P.

Ainsworth's hand
1805, Jan. 17th. Died Margaret English, aged 53, Bath, R.I.P.

Calderbank's hand:
1805, Jany. 29th. Died Elizabeth Taylor, aged 76, Bath, R.I.P.

Ainsworth's hand (2 entries):
1805, Feb. 4th. Died Juliet Leathem, aged 70, Bath, R.I.P.
1805, Feb. 5th. Died Mary Macartey, aged 52, Bath, R.I.P.

Calderbank's hand (2 entries):
1805, March 14th. Died Daniel Conner, aged 80 [75 *deleted*], Bath, R.I.P.
1805, March 15th. Died Mary Burke, aged [*blank*], R.I.P.

Ainsworth's hand:
1805, March 7th. Died James Rowe, aged 61, Bath, R.I.P.

Calderbank's hand (3 entries):
1805, March 23rd. Died George Wogan, infant of 11 weeks.

[182] Memorial-inscription in Bath Abbey (printed by Davey, p. 83).

1805, April 19th. Died Frances Wogan, aged [*blank*], Bath, R.I.P.
1805, April 29th. Died John Callers (drowend), R.I.P.

Ainsworth's hand (4 entries):
1805, May 16th. Died Charlotte Duval, aged [*blank*], Bath, R.I.P.
1805, May 20th. Died Samual Abraham, a Black, aged 63, Bath, R.I.P.
1805, May 21st. Died Mary Mitchell, aged 26, Bath, R.I.P.
1805, June 3rd. Died Henry Nugent McGary, Soldier, aged 28, Stranger,
          R.I.P.

Rigby's hand (3 entries):
1805, June 26. Died Denis Sheean, aged 54, Bath, R.I.P.
1805, June 20. Died Walter Cooksey, aged 10, Bath, R.I.P.
1805, July 6. Died Michael O'Doherty, aged 61, Bath, R.I.P.

Next six entries in Ainsworth's hand:
1805, Oct. 18th. Died Thos. Sword Esq., aged 52, Ir. St.,[183] Bath, R.I.P.
1805, Dec. 6. Died Mrs Cosgrove, aged 78, Bath, R.I.P.
1805, Dec. 19th. Died Mary Seifreid, aged 72, Bath, R.I.P.
1806, Jan.   8th. Died Mary Norris, aged 67, Bath, R.I.P.
1806, Jan.   8th. Died Mary Doyle, aged 70, Bath, R.I.P.
1806, Feb. 16th. Died Bartholomew Costello Esqr., aged 69, Stranger,
          Bath, R.I.P.

Birdsall's hand (4 entries):
1806, June the (say 11th). Died a child (infant) of Hubert Dubois.
1806, June the 26th. Died Mary Coster, Widow, who is believed to have
          fled from France with her husband and Daughter in the beginning
          of the revolution about the year 1792. R.I.P.
1806, June[184] 13. Died John Leech, aged about 60, a convert, R.I.P.
1806, July 26. Died Mary Maguire, aged 20 months.

Ainsworth's hand:
1806, Aug. 28th. Died Jane Byrne, aged 39, a convert, R.I.P.

Next five entries in Birdsall's hand:
1806, Sepr. 11th.   Died Richd. Crowch, aged 76, R.I.P.
1806, Sepr. 19th.   Died Martha Saw, aged about 32, R.I.P.
1806, Octob. 9. Died Richard Hancock, aged 66, a Convert, R.I.P.
1806, Oct.   17th.   Died Revd. Antony Chemite,[185] a French Emigrant
          of the Province of Picardy, and was buried at Walcot,
          aged 52, R.I.P.
1806, Novr. 19th.   Died William Tulley, aged about 60, R.I.P.

[183]   Irish Stranger.
[184]   Clearly June in the register but evidently a slip for July; see entry in converts-list, *supra*, p. 118.
[185]   In *C.R.S.*, 12, p. 99 as "Chemitte".

Ainsworth's hand:
1806, Nov. 20th. Died the Revd. Michael Benedict Pembridge,[186] aged
                82, R.I.P.

Next seven entries in Birdsall's hand:
1806, Decr. 17. Died Sarah Odber, aged 17, R.I.P.
1806, Decr. 23. Died James Pursel, an infant.
1807, Jany. 14. Died Elizabeth Foster, aged about 36, R.I.P.
     item   Thos Day at Inspach,[187] aged 58, R.I.P.
     item   Giles Hall, Bath, aged 12, R.I.P.
1807, Jany. 26. Died Mrs Mary Smythe, aged 72, R.I.P.
1807, Jany. 29. Died Ellen Quin, Bath, aged 52, R.I.P.

Ainsworth's hand (3 entries):
1807, Feb. 5th. Died Eleanor Barrett, aged 72, R.I.P.
1807, Feb. 11th. Died Catherine Burn, Bath, aged 84, R.I.P.
1807, March 8th. Died William Micmuttry, Bath, aged about 65, R.I.P.

Henceforth in Birdsall's hand:
1807, Mar. 9th. Died John Sullivan, born at Cork in Irel., at Bath, agd.
                25, R.I.P.
     eodem die John Keegan [blank] Bath, agd. 70, R.I.P.
1807, March 29th. Died John Bick, Bath, agd. [blank], R.I.P.
1807, Apr. 8th. Died James Enwright, Bath, agd. 60, R.I.P.
     eodem die   Monsr. Cousselle of France, at Bath, agd. about 45,
                R.I.P.
1807, May 20th. Mary Dickson, Bath, agd. [blank], R.I.P.
1807, May 17th. Catharine Maguire, Bath agd, 41, R.I.P.
1807, June 22d. Died James Burke, Bath, agd. 50, R.I.P.
1807, July 1st. Died Jane Carpenter at Shockerwick, agd. 37, R.I.P.
1807, July 14th. Died James Curtin, Bath, agd. 35, R.I.P.
1807, July 16th. Died Ambrose, Baron de la Tour, Bath, agd. 70, R.I.P.
1807, July 23rd. Died Frances Donavon, Bath, agd. 46, R.I.P.
1807, Sepr. 2d. Died Mr Richard Crowch, Bath, agd. 17, R.I.P.
1807, Sepr. 30. Died Mrs Wilmore in the poor house, agd. 72, R.I.P.
1807, Oct. 6th. Died Charlotte Connor, Bath, agd. 78, R.I.P.
1807, Novr. 17th. Died Mary Kennedy   do. agd. 46, R.I.P.
1807, Novr. 24th. Died Charlotte Higgins do. agd. 50, R.I.P.
1807, Decr. 17th. Died Jemima Burke, Bath, agd. 30, R.I.P.
1807, Decr. [blank] Died Mary Tobin, Bath, agd. 72, R.I.P.
1808, Jany. 4th. Died Ed. Carrol, Bath, aged 58, R.I.P.
1808, Jany. 14th. Died Sarah Clarke, Bath, aged 50, R.I.P.
1808, Feb. 29th. Died Mad. Adelaide du Longchamp, agd. 60, R.I.P.
1808, April 24th. Died Matthias Reilly, Bath, agd. 47, R.I.P.

[186] See also *C.R.S.*, 65, pp. 67, 70-72.
[187] Englishbatch; see note 18.

1808, July 24th. Died Thos. Jenkinson, Bath, agd. 81, R.I.P.
1808, July 30th. Mrs Anastasia Charker,[188] Bath, agd. 57, R.I.P.
1808, Augt. 10th. Died Miss Cath. Mostyn,[189] Bath, agd. 30, R.I.P.
1808, Oct. 25th. Died Mrs Elizabeth Hudson[190] do. agd. 45, R.I.P.
1808, Novr. 4. Died Mr Ambrose O'Ferrall, Bath, Agd. 66, R.I.P.
   and Mr Giovanni Bisani, Bath, Aged [blank], R.I.P.
1808, Novr. 19th. Died Mr Willm. Norris, Bath, Aged [blank]
   and Monsr. Imbert Columés, aged 82, R.I.P.
1809, Jan. 31. Died Mr Ogfried Hassall, agd. 86, Bath, R.I.P.
   Feb. 9. Died Mrs Sarah Praid, Bath, agd. 28, R.I.P.
   Mar. 22. Died William Moon, an infant, Bath

Next three entries in Ainsworth's hand:
May 15. Died Mary Travers, aged 68, Bath, R.I.P.
April 24th. Died Mary Short, Aged [blank], Bath, R.I.P.
May 27th. Died Sarah Rourke, aged [blank], Bath, R.I.P.

Next three entries in Birdsall's hand:
June 28. Died Laurence Birch, aged 38, Bath, R.I.P.
July 28. Died Joseph Kattenback, aged 45, Bath, R.I.P.
   30. Died James Darnley, aged 41, Bath, R.I.P.

Next five entries in Calderbank's hand:
Octr. 4th. Died Dominick Resana, aged 59, Bath, R.I.P.
   7th. Died Mary Anne Heron, aged 13-9m.,[191] Bath, R.I.P.
   17th. Died Rt. Revd. Dr. G.W. Sharrock, aged 67, Bath, R.I.P.
   His Lordship had been consecrated Bishop 28 years and had
   governed the Western District almost 12.
   19. Died Joseph Love, aged 74, Bath, R.I.P.
   22. Died Jane Dowling, aged 77, Bath, R.I.P.

Ainsworth's hand (2 entries):
1812, Oct. 8th. Died Thomas Hathaway, aged 45, Bath, R.I.P.
1812, Oct. 13th. Died Hannah Maillard, aged 35, Bath, R.I.P.

With the exception of the two for 1812, printed above, the mortuary-entries from the end of 1809 are continued in the second register (infra., p. 186 ff.). The items which follow are no longer in the first register, but are here printed from the Taunton transcript:-

[188] In *C.R.S.*, 12, p. 103.
[189] Buried in Bath Abbey; cf. Davey, p. 68; also *C.R.S.*, 12, *loc. cit.*
[190] In *C.R.S.*, 12, p. 105.
[191] i.e. 13 years, 9 months; see baptismal entry, 23 Jan. 1796, *supra*, p. 76.

"Loose sheets in the register". [*Now missing; see supra, p. viii*].
"(1) Names of children to be Confirmed, no date[192]

"Peter McMurtry	aged 12 years		
Matthew McMurtry	aged 14		
John McMurtry	aged 10		
James Pope	aged 15		
John Hughes	aged 13		
Cornelius Dowden	aged 11		
Charles Jakes	aged 10		
Ambros Jakes	aged 8		
George Perry	aged 8		
William Perry	aged 6		
Alexander Murphy	aged 6		
Charles Robins	aged 6		
Robert Baker	aged 10		
Ann Baker	aged 12		
Maria Farrell	aged 13	Francis Foresayth	aged 7
Ann Pope	aged 16	Ann White	aged 7
Mary Moore	aged 15	Charles Dowden	aged 13
Joanna Moore	aged 13	Ann Bave [?]	aged 14
Elizabeth Moore	aged 10	Charlotte Applebe	aged 12
Thomas Moore	aged 6		
William Culbert	aged 12		
Deborah Culbert	aged 7		
Robert Foresayth	aged 12		
Thomas Foresayth	aged 10"		

"(2) Certificate of Registry of Death

Slatvia Thomas of Walcot	14 of July 1845
	Mr T. Hiscox. Registrar"

"(3) A list of a few books of Mr Simpson's,[193] taken by Bishop Sharrock". [*no actual list included.*]

"(4) Four other papers relating to baptisms" [*no actual papers*].

END OF FIRST REGISTER

[192] Evidently this list was drawn up in 1792; three of the children described as "aged 10" were born between November 1781 and March 1782 (John McMurtry, Charles Jakes and Robert Baker, for whom see pp. 12, 16). Ambrose Jakes, here "aged 8", was born on 4 March 1784 (*supra,* p. 20) and Francis Foresayth, "aged 7", on 28 Feb. 1785 (*supra,* p. 25). Very few of those listed here do in fact occur in the confirmation-lists printed *supra,* pp. 66-9.

[193] Doubtless John Cuthbert Simpson, O.S.B. (see Index).

Entries in Calderbank's hand until stated otherwise.

[*p.1*] Baptismall Register Commencing with the Opening of the new Chapel at Bath, December 3rd 1809.

[*p.2*] 1809, Decr. 15, were supplied the Ceremonies of Baptism over Paul George, Son of John Francis Dugout, Marquis de Casaux, and of Madame Henrietta de Freneaux, his lawful Wife. Sponsors Leon Augusten de Casaux and Georgina de Richmont, by

R. Ainsworth.

The names Casaux and Freneaux, above, are as substituted, in another hand, for Calderbank's original versions: "Caysaux" and, perhaps, "Ferneaux". The next 15 pages are tabulated, as below.

Birth	Baptism	Name of Child	Parents	Sponsors	Priest
	1809				
Decr. 17th	Decr. 24	Helen Murphy	Michael and Mary Murphy	Thos. Fenton and Mary Fenton	Jas. Calderbank
Decr. 15	Decr. 24	John Felix St Ange Simeon	Felix St Ives St Ange; Mary Margt. Felicia Simeon	John Denie Mary Margt. Simeon	Jas. Calderbank
1810 Jany. 14	1810 Jany. 21	Mary Hackett	Wm. and Catherine Hackett	Julien Havey Margt. Hynes	Jas. Calderbank
1810 Jany. 16	1810 Jany. 28	James Doran	Patrick and Eliza Doran	Philip Hogan and Bridget Gillan	Jas. Calderbank
1809 December 29	1810 Jany. 29	James Taaffe	Jas. and Mary Taaffe	Andrew O'Conner and Elenora Birch	Ralph Ainsworth
1810 Jany. 22	1810 Jany. 31	Anne Nolan	James and Anne Nolan	Without ceremonies. Supplied 8th Oct. 1810. Mich. Fortrey and Margt. Paillet	Jas. Calderbank
1809 Decr. 26th	1810 Feby. 4th	Catharine Maria McCarthy	John and Catharine McCarthy	Without ceremonies	Ralph Ainsworth
1810 Jany. 18th	1810 Feby. 4th	Margt. Hilliard	Wm. and Mary Hilliard	Charles and Sarah Kelly	Ralp [*sic.*] Ainsworth
Feby. 13	Feby. 27	Daniel McCarthew	Daniel and Catharine McCarthew	Bridget Cane	Jas. Calderbank

Next entry in Ainsworth's hand apart from words italicised, in Calderbank's hand.

131

Birth	Baptism	Name of Child	Parents	Sponsors	Priest
1810 Jany. 3d	1810 Feby. 28th	Frances Peard	Richard and Fraces [sic.] Peard	Without ceremonies. *Supplied March 18th. Anne Nagle*	Ralph Ainsworth

Henceforth in Calderbank's hand up to and including the baptism on 26 Feb 1812, apart from words italicised on 4 June 1810, in Baines's hand — presumably added some years later.

Birth	Baptism	Name of Child	Parents	Sponsors	Priest
1810 March 5th	1810 March 11th	James Sydney Jordan	Thos. and Mary Jordan	James Jordan and May Jordan. Proxies Philip Hogan, Letitia Smallman	Jas. Calderbank
1810 March 16	1810 March 16th	Mary Short	John and Mary Short	Without ceremonies. Supplied April 2nd. Wm. Alpin and Anne Pike	Jas. Calderbank
March 8th 1810	1810 March 18th	Margt. Purcell	Richd. and Anne Purcell	Anne Whelan	Jas. Calderbank
1809 Decr. 8th	1810 April 6th	Elizabeth Browne	Wm. and Mary Browne	Ellen Donohoe	Jas. Calderbank
1810 March 6th	1810 April 26	Edwd. Paillet[1]	Nichas. and Margt. Paillet	Jas. Gouget and Ellen Dowling	Jas. Calderbank
1810 April 1st	1810 May 1st	Frances Murphy	Andrew and Mary Murphy	Edwd. Kelly and Margaret McMahon	Jas. Calderbank
1807 April 14th	1810 May 1st	Nicholas Murphy. Conditionally baptised	Andrew and Mary	Jas. Hagerton	Jas. Calderbank
1810 April 26	1810 May 7th	Wm. Ryan	Michael and Margaret Ryan	Bridget Cane	Jas. Calderbank
1810 May 26th	1810 May 31	Maurice O'Connell	John O'Connell Esqr. and Elisabeth his Wife	Mauric [sic.] O'Connell Esqr. and Mrs Jane Coppinger. Proxies Timothy O'Brien Esqr. and Mrs Elizth. Coppinger	Jas. Calderbank

[1]   Became a Benedictine; cf. Birt, p. 161; Oliver, pp. 369-70.

Birth	Baptism	Name of Child	Parents	Sponsors	Priest
1810 June 3rd	1810 June 4th	Theresa Francisca Goldfinch	Charles and Rachel Goldfinch	Without ceremonies. *Supplied the 8th of July.* *Sponsors James Burke and Frances Lacy*	Jas. Calderbank
1810 May 26th	1810 June 10th	Robert Norris	Robt. and Anne Norris	Cornelius Sweiny	Jas. Calderbank
1809 [?1807] Novr. 3d	1810 June 15th	Eliza Winefride Overton Parish of[2]	George and Mary Overton	Miss Winefride Denie	Jas. Calderbank
1810 Feby. 10	1810 June 16th	Mary Overton, Sister to the above	George and Mary Overton	Mrs Anne Denie	Jas. Calderbank
1810 June 21st	1810 June 21st	Charles Fitzherbert	Thos. Fitzherbert Esqr. and Mary Anne Fitzherbert	Thos. Clifford Esqr. and Mrs. Lucy Weld. Proxies Wm. Day Esqr. and Miss Frances Talbot	Jas. Calderbank
1810 July 12th	1810 July 13th	Mary Williams	Wm. and Elizth. Williams	Mary Harvey	Jas. Calderbank
1810 [*blank*]	1810 Aug. 5th	Clare Styles	Wm. and Elizth. Styles	Joseph Maverly, Dolly Lens. Proxies [*blank*] Ward and Margt. William [*sic.*]	
1810 Aug. 3rd	1810 Aug. 31st	Mary Lucy Jane Phipps	Thos. Henry Hele and Mary Phipps	Mr. Jo. Dalton and Miss Lucy Dalton by proxy of Mr Jo. Stoner and Ellen Stoner	R. Ainsworth
1810 Aug. 26	1810 Aug. 29	John Finnerty	Thos. and Mary Finnerty	Philip Hogan and Honora Hagerty	Jas. Calderbank
1810 Aug. 20th	1810 Septr. 16th	Henry Philips	Wm. Philips and Elisabeth	Owen Brenen and Mary Slone	R. Ainsworth
1810 Aug. 19	1810 Septr. 16th	George Coady	Peter and Lucy Coady	John Dowding and Victoire Julien	Jas. Calderbank

[2] Apparently "Pindeiran", followed by an illegible word, somewhat smudged; perhaps Calderbank's version of Pendarren, S. Wales.

Birth	Baptism	Name of Child	Parents	Sponsors	Priest
1810 Septr. 18	1810 Octr. 24	George Ballerby	Thos. and Charlotte Ballerby	Richd. Whelan and Anne Melor	Jas. Calderbank
1810 Octr. 22	1810 Octr. 28	Mary Magdalen Gerald	Peter and Frances Gerald	Francis la Corte and Mary Magdalen Desor	Jas. Calderbank
1810 Novr. 2nd	1810 Novr. 5th	Frances [? Francis] Martin	John and Elenor Martin	Without ceremonies. Supplied 18th Decr. 1810. Cornelius Murphy and Margt. Clarkson.	Jas. Calderbank
1810 Octr. 28	1810 Novr. 18	Michael Dowding	Cornelius and Mary Dowding	Michael Laler and Arabelle Kelly	Jas. Calderbank
1810 Octr. 31	1810 Decr. 2	Wm. Alworth	Francis and Honora	Bridget Dowling	R. Ainsworth
1810 Novr. 7th	conditionally Decr. 2	Mary Flynn	Jas. and Frances Flynn	Bridget Dowling	Jas. Calderbank
Novr. 25th 1811 [sic.]	Dec. 18 1810	Cathne. Tobin	Edwd. and Cathne. Tobin	Jas. Lyons, Martha Stein	Jas. Calderbank
Jany. 1st 1811	Jany. 13th 1811	Joanna Connell	John and Elizth. Connell	Anna Connell	R. Ainsworth
1811 Feby. 7th	1811 Feby. 7th	Edwd. Knapp	John and Mary Knapp	Catharine Knapp. Proxy Wm. Day	R. Ainsworth
1811 Feby. 16	1811 Feby. 17	George Henshall	Ralph and Elisabeth Henshall	Jas. Burke and Eliza Maria Husenbeth for whom was proxy Margt. Donahoe	Jas. Calderbank
1811 Feby. 24	1811 March 2nd	Bartholomey Broderick	Thos. and Margt. Broderick	Jeremiah Hayes, Ester Joiner	Jas. Calderbank
1811 March 6th	1811 March 9th	Richd. Anthony O'Reily	Mathew and Margt. O'Reily	Most Revd. Dr. Richd. O'Reily,[3] by proxy of Revd. Jas. Calderbank, and Anna Maria O'Reily	Jas. Calderbank

[3] Archbishop of Armagh; cf. Sir F.M. Powicke & E.B. Fryde, *Handbook of British Chronology* (1961 edition) p. 384; W.M. Brady, *The Episcopal Succession in England, Scotland and Ireland* (Rome, 1876) I, pp. 231, 357

Birth	Baptism	Name of Child	Parents	Sponsors	Priest
1811	1811				
March 9th	March 11th	Mary Anne Mateoli	Nichcolas [sic.] and Anne Mateoli	Joseph Fesanna and Anne Rozanna	Jas. Calderbank
1811	1811				
March 3rd	March 11th	Winefrid Sarah Pepper	Henry and Sarah Pepper	Thos. Pepper and Winefrid Dto.	Jas. Calderbank
1811	1811				
Feby. 21st	March 14th	John Edwd. Crosby	John and Anne Crosby	John Lysath and Mary Tracey	Jas. Calderbank
1811	1811				
Feby. 20th	March 17th	Edmd. Francis English	Edmd. and Mary Elizth. English	John and Frances English	Jas. Calderbank
1811	1811				
March 16th	March 20th	Wm. Hilliard	Wm. and Mary Hilliard	Jas. Carver and Lucy Anne Coady	Jas. Calderbank
1811	1811				
March 21st	March 31st	John Benedict Kentgons	John and Anne Kentgons	Proxies Ricd, Whelan, Mary Alanson. John Dowding and Martha Smith[4]	R. Ainsworth
1811	1811				
April 2nd	April 17	Helen Hunt	Patrick and Cathne. Hunt	John Alpen and Mary Lyon	Jas. Calderbank
1811	1811				
March 29	April 21st	Wm. Canvan	John and Mary Canvan	Michael Henery and Mary Racket	R. Ainsworth
1811	1811				
April 19	April 21	Edwd. Short	John and Mary Short	Samuel and Anne Rowe, proxies Joseph Short Matilda Hatch	J. Calderbank
1811	1811				
May 7th	May 8th	Jane Porter	Wm. and Jane Porter	John Doyle and Mary Anne Doyle	R. Ainsworth
1811	1811				
March 3rd	May 14th	Dennis Traesey	Dennis and Jane Traesey	Thos. Blake and Margt. Blake. Proxies George Whelan Sara Tivitre	R. Ainsworth
1811	1811				
April 14th	May 14th	Michl. Magrath	Michl. and Sara Magrath	Wm. and Elizth. Magrath	R. Ainsworth
1811	1811				
May 16th	May 16th	George Head	George and Frances Head	Cornelius Murphy and Theresa Adams	R. Ainsworth
1811	1811				
April 7th	June 10th	Thos. Dulworth	Thos. and Frances Dulworth	Mary Hearne	Jas. Calderbank

[4] It is not clear who are the proxies; presumably the first two, whose names immediately follow the word "Proxies".

Birth	Baptism	Name of Child	Parents	Sponsors	Priest
1811 May 7th	1811 June 13th	Thos. Lawton	Peter and Eleanor Lawton	Julien Havey	R. Ainsworth
1811 June 2nd	1811 June 25th	Jane Quigley	Thos. and Jane Quigley	Richard Riley and Cathne. Quigley by proxy of Mary Coffy	Jas. Calderbank
1811 June 24th	1811 July 7th	John Quinn	George and Elizth. Quinn	Daniel Buckley Mary Heley	Jas. Calderbank
1808 Decr.	1811 August 11	Sarah Battle (conditionally)	John and Sarah Battle	Michael Ryan Bridget Cane	Jas. Calderbank
1811 April[?] 30	1811 August 11	Elizth. Battle	John and Sarah Battle	Michael Ryan and Bridget Cane	Jas. Calderbank
1811 Augt. 2	1811 Augt. 13	Mary Anne Murphy	Edwd. and Elizth. Murphy	Michl. Carr [? Case] and Elizth. Montalbat	Jas. Calderbank
1811 Septr. 2nd	1811 Septr. 2nd	Cecilia Frances English	Mr John and Frances English	Edmd. English and Elizth. Huddlestone by proxy of Miss C. Trapps	R. Ainsworth
1811 Augt. 27	1811 Septr. 8th	Eleana Mabry	John and Jane Mabry	Edwd. Kelly, Elen. Mylim	Jas. Calderbank
1811 Septr. 8	1811 Septr. 9	Lucy Maria Loveless	Thos. and Henrietta Loveless	Wm. Hopkins and Matilda Hatch	Jas. Calderbank
1811 Augst. 21	1811 Sept. 17th	Jas. Nowlan	Jas. and Anne Nowlan	Hugh Reynolds Mary Lester	Jas. Calderbank
1811 Septr. 15	1811 October 9th	Mary Anne Smith	Michael and Elizth. Smith	Anne Denie	R. Ainsworth
1811 Novr. 1	1811 Novr. 4	Frances Bellon	Thos. and Frances Bellon	Edwd. McMullin and Bridget Marr	Jas. Calderbank
1811 Novr. 11	1811 Novr. 30	Jas. Redman	Jas. and Anne Redman	Jas. Dowding and Sarah Metcalfe	Jas. Calderbank

1811, Decr.—. Was baptised David Joseph Godwin, born 24th day of June 1809, the son of [*blank*] Godwin. Sponsor Margt. Tunstall, by me
Jas. Calderbank.

December

1811, Decr. 12. Were baptised Jane and Susanna Higgins, the former born June 28th 1807, the latter April 9th 1810, Children of Peter and Susanna Higgins. Sponsors Laurence Geaghan and Christina Strowbridge, by me
Jas. Calderbank.

1811, Decr. 17th. Was baptised Anne, Daughter of Peter and Lucy Salmoni, born Novr. 17th. Sponsors Julian Havez and Cathne. Murphy, by me
Jas. Calderbank.

Feby, 4. 1812. Baptised (sub conditione) George Columbel, aged 6 years, son of George and Bridget Columbel, by
J. Birdsall.

Same day was baptised (sub conditione) David Creven, Son of David and Mary Creven, aged 5 years, by
J. Birdsall.

Baptised Martha Dexter, Son [sic.] of Edwd. and Anne Dexter, born Feby. 2d. God Mother Anne Wilcock, by
J. Birdsall.

1812 ... Baptised John White, son of Patrick and Catharine White, born the 16th of Febry. Sponsors Matthew Lynam and Mary Lynch, by
R. Ainsworth.

1812, Febr. 27th. Baptised Mary Anne Jordan, Daughter of Thos. and Sarah Jordan, born yesterday. Sponsors William Hopkins and Anne Dto., by
R. Ainsworth.

1812, Feby. 26. Baptised Jas. Raarden, Son of Patrick and Catherine Raarden, born the 9th. Sponsors Richard Reynolds, by proxy of Michael Carr, and Margt. Lynch, by
R. Ainsworth.

The next five entries are in a different hand, presumably Feraud's:
The 25th day of March 1812 was baptized Amelia Purselcox, the Daughter of Richard and Anne Purselcox, born the 4th day of March 1812. Godfather Phillip Sillamon, by
Charles Feraud,[5]

On the same day was baptized Mary Finarty, the daughter of Thos. and Anne Finarty, born on the 30th day of January 1812. Godmother Elizabeth Quin, by
Chas. Feraud.

The 15th day of April 1812 was baptized Edwin Joseph Godwin, the Son of Elizabeth Godwin, born on the 21st day of June 1800. Godmother Margaret Tunstall, by
Chas. Feraud.

On the same day was baptized Elizabeth Mary Godwin aged 40 (a converted Quakeress). Godmother Margaret Tunstall, by
Chas. Feraud.

[5] Dom Charles Ambrose Feraud O.S.B. (Birt, p. 146). See also Baines's journal, 4 March 1818 (*C.R.S.*, 65, pp. 222-3).

The 4th day of May 1812 was baptized privately (mortis periculo) Bartholemew O'Neille, the Son of Richard and Bridget O'Neille, born on the same day. Godmother Elizabeth Phelan, by

Chas. Feraud.

Henceforth in Calderbank's hand:
1811. Was baptised Mary Christina Ernestine, Daughter of Samuel and Ernestine Rose, born at Castle Coombe July 2nd of the same year. Sponsors Henry Arundell and Christina Arundell, by

Monsr. de Bo[*illegible*].[6]

1812. Was baptised Elenora, Daughter of Thos. Raymund Arundell Esqr. and Eliza his Wife, born 17th of March of the same year. Sponsors Sir Edwd. Smythe Bart. and Lady Clifford, by

W'am Barnes.[7]

1812, June. Was baptised Jas. Bernard Dowding, Son of Cornelius and Mary Dowding, born June 13th. Sponsors Thos. Mierscought and Mary Brown, by

R. Ainsworth.

1812, July 4th. Was baptised Hugh, Son of Andrew and Mary Murphy, born 27 of May. Sponsors Daniel Hackett and Honora Hagerty, by me

Jas. Calderbank.

1812, July 11th. Was baptised Catharine, Daughter of Francis and Mary Alworth of Twerton, born 13th June. Sponsor Mary Coffey, by me

Jas. Calderbank.

1812, Augst. 5th. Was baptised Frances, Daughter of Thos. and Frances Dulworth, born 19th of [December *deleted*] July. Sponsor Margt. O'Leary by me

Jas. Calderbank.

1812, August 16th. Was baptised John, Son of Jas. and Frances Flyn, born the 9th Inst. Sponsors Jas. Rice and [*blank*] his Wife, by me

Jas. Calderbank.

1812, Augst. 20th. Was baptised Benjamin, Son of Thos. and — Tobin, born 27th April. Sponsor Catharine McGuire, by me

Jas. Calderbank.

Septr. 7th 1812. Was baptised Jas., Son of Jas. and Ellen Purcell, born 1st Septr. Sponsors Julien Havey and Ann Galway, by

R. Ainsworth.

Septr. 20th 1812. Was baptised Mary, Daughter of Paul and Hannah Vaughan, born the 12th August. Sponsors Bartholomew Vaughan and Catharine Mary Vaughan, by me

Jas. Calderbank.

Septr. 26, 1812. Was baptised Charles, Son of Luke and Martha Sinnett, born 15th Augt. Sponsor Catharine Taylor, by me

Jas. Calderbank.

Octr. 11th 1812. Was baptised Anne, Daughter of Peter and Lucy

---

[6] In Calderbank's superficially neat, but often barely legible hand, this looks like "Boske".

[7] Secular priest. See Oliver, p. 239.

Coady, born 13th of Septr. Sponsors Mathew Alpin and Mary Demontier, by me

Jas. Calderbank.

Octr. 11th 1812. Was baptised Wm., Son of David and Elisabeth Henty, born 5th of the same month. Sponsors Noah Osmund and Theresa Osmund, by me

Jas. Calderbank.

1812, Octr. 20th. Was baptised Jas., Son of Jas. and [blank] Lawton, born 18th. Sponsors Michael Conroy and Elenor Newell, by

R. Ainsworth.

1812, Novr. 24. Was baptised Jas., Son of Michael and Margaret Ryan, born 15th. Sponsors Daniel Hacket and Elisabeth West, by me

R. Ainsworth.

1812, Decr. 10th. Was baptised Margt., Daughter of Timothy and Elisabeth Larkin, born 2nd. Sponsor Mary Barry, by me

J. Calderbank.

In a different hand (not Ainsworth's):

1812, Sept. 30. Was baptised Charles Robert English, son of Edmund and his wife Mary Elizabeth English, born on the 15 inst. Sponsors Robert English, proxy for Thomas English, and Margaret Paula King, by

R. Ainsworth.

Henceforth in Calderbank's hand:

Decr. 14th. Was baptised Mary, Daughter of James and Mary Cooper. Sponsor Julien Havey (sine Ceremoniis), by me

Jas. Calderbank.

Decr. 18th 1812. Was baptised Thos. McGuire, Son of Michael and Mary McGuire, born 11th. Sponsor Elizth. Phealan, by

R. Ainsworth.

1813

Jany. 11th. Was baptised Simon, Son of Maurice and Elizth. Quin, born 3rd Inst. Sponsors Richd. James and Theresa Osmund, by me

J. Calderbank.

Jany. 11th. Was baptised Agnes Mary, Daughter of Mr. John and Mrs. English, his wife, born the preceding Evening. Sponsors Edwd. Huddlestone Esqr. and Miss Sarah English. Proxy for Mr. H., Wm. Day Esqr., by me

Jas. Calderbank.

Jany. 14th. Was baptised Frances, Daughter of Wm. and Mary Hillier, born Novr. 27, 1812. Sponsors Thos. St John and Margt. Ford, by me
Jas. Calderbank.

Jany. 23rd 1813. Was baptised Francis Fabian Sabastian, Son of John and Mary Short. Sponsors Maurice Green and Anne Bull, born 20th. Proxy Mary Demontier for Anne Bull, by me

Jas. Calderbank.

1813, Jany. 26th. Was baptised James, Son of James and Martha Johnson, born 18th. Sponsor Mary Cooper (sine ceremoniis) by me
Jas. Calderbank.

1813, Jany. 31. Was baptised Victoire Anne, Daughter of Pierre Gerard

and Euphrosine Hussenot. Sponsor Charles Antoine Graue [?] and
Victoire Julienne Femairee [?] by

R. Ainsworth.
Feby. 24, 1813. Was baptised John, Son of John and Mary Anne Fare,
born 15th. Sponsors Wm. Marten and Catharine Sullivan, by me

J. Calderbank.
1813, March 2nd. Was baptised Anne, Daughter of Thos. and Mary
Anne FitzGerald, born Jany. 1st. Sponsors Michael Lalor and Elisabeth
Lalor, by me

J. Calderbank.
1813, March 14th. Was baptised Arthur, Son of Daniel and Bridget
Donelly, born 18th of Feby. Sponsors Patrick and Bridget Kearney, by
R. Ainsworth.
1813, March 29th. Was baptised John Edwd., Son of John and Ellen
Denie, born same day. Sponsors Edwd. Glover[8] and Barbara Denie, by
R. Ainsworth.
1813. Was baptised April 4th, Thos., Son of Jas. and Elisabeth,[9] his
Wife, born 10th of March, same year, Sponsors John Collighan and
Margt. Paillet (sine Ceremoniis), by me

Jas. Calderbank.
1813, April 15th. Was baptised James, Son of Patrick and Honora
Walker, born 14th. Sponsors Patrick Fabray [?] and Mary Kingston, by
me

Jas. Calderbank.
1813, April 19th. Was baptised John, Son of Thos. and Margaret
Rodden, born the preceding day. Sponsors Michael Ryan and Miss
Emilia Hartsinke, by me

Jas. Calderbank.
1813. Was baptised George, Son of Patrick and Mary Kavannah, born
21st [?].[10] Sponsors Patrick and Catharine Hagerty, by me

Jas. Calderbank.
1813, May 17th. Was baptised Harriet, Daughter of John and Jane
Deavy, born 3rd Inst. Sponsors Garret Barry and Harriet Barry, by

R. Ainsworth.
1813, Mary 23rd. Was baptised Mary Anne, Daughter of John and
Catharine Fulley, born 28th of April. Sponsors Bartholomew Vaughan
and Ellen Dowling, by me

J. Calderbank.
1813, May 30th. Was baptised James Stewart Nelley, Son of John and
Charlotte Nelley, born 27th of April. Sponsor James Stewart, by proxy
of Julien Havey, by

R. Ainsworth.
1813, June 6th. Was baptised Jane Thompson, Daughter of Henry and

---

[8] ? the Benedictine. See Birt, p. 139; also Baines's journal, *passim* (in *C.R.S.*, 65).

[9] Surname omitted.

[10] Month omitted.

Joanna Thompson born 21st of May. Sponsors Andrew Lauley and Honor Hagerty, by

R. Ainsworth.

1813, June 13th. Was baptised Elenor Sophia, Daughter of George Burke Kelly Esqr. and Mary his Wife, born 21st May. Sponsors Edmund P. and Matilda Kelly his Sister, by me

Jas. Calderbank.

1813, June 13th. Was baptised Owen, Son of Patrick and Jane Ryley, born Jany. 15th. Sponsors Wm. and Lucy Coady, by me

Jas. Calderbank.

1813, July 19th. Was baptised Mary, daughter of Mary and Willm. Parker born 7th Inst. Sponsors Thos. Quinn and Elenora Lawton, by

R. Ainsworth.

1813, July 25. Was baptised Anne, daughter of James and Mary Slack, born 19th. Sponsor Martha McGuire, by me

Jas. Calderbank.

1813, August 1st. Was baptised Wm,, Son of John and Anne Kentchens, born 26 July. Sponsors Mathew Alpin and Theodosia Hayward, by

R. Ainsworth.

1813, August 12th. Was baptised Mary Anne, daughter of Andrew and Mary McNally, born at Calne in Wiltshire, July 26. Sponsor Bridget Mahony, by me

Jas. Calderbank.

1813, August 15th. Was baptised Cornelius, Son of Bartholomew and Margt. Leary, born 24 July. Sponsors — Sullivan and Helen Martin, by me

Jas. Calderbank.

1813, Septr. 10th. Was baptised Edmond, Son of David and Mary Barratt, born 6th. God Mother Mary Wroughton,[11] by

R. Ainsworth.

1813, Septr. 15th. Was baptised Jas., Son of Wm. and Mary Fisher, born 7th. Sponsors Michael Ryan and Ellen Oxford, by me

Jas. Calderbank.

---

[11] Not "the famous Evergreen of Bath", mentioned in *C.R.S.*, 65, p. 74; her Christian name was Susannah, according to a pedigree in the Wiltshire Archaeological Society's collections at Devizes, kindly communicated by the Hon. Librarian, Mr R.E. Sandell. This records her death in 1825 at Wilcot, Wilts., where she was lady of the manor, though she also lived at no. 2, Catherine Place, Bath, and was prominent in Bath society for half a century. Contemporary references to her, apart from that already cited, occur in *Dr. Campbell's Diary of a Visit to England in 1775* (ed. J.L. Clifford, 1947) p. 89; in R. Warner, *Bath Characters* (1807; annotated copy in Bath Reference Library), pp. 15-17; in *Passages from the Diaries of Mrs Philip Lybbe Powys* (ed. E.J. Climenson, 1899) pp. 327, 352; in J. Britton, *Beauties of Wiltshire*, III (1825) p. 346; in Bath *Directories*, 1805-24 (usually as "Mrs Wroughton") and in *The Bath Chronicle* (obituary in issue of 5 May 1825). See also G. Monkland, *Supplement to the Literature and Literati of Bath* (1855) pp. 49-50. None of these printed sources reveals Susannah's Christian name, though the *Directory* for 1812 (p. 113) gives its initial, but misprints her surname as "Wrington".

1813, Septr. 15th. Was baptised Charles, Son of Wm. and Mary Fisher, born 7th. Sponsors Michael Ryan and Ellen Oxford, by me
Jas. Calderbank.
1813, Septr. 19. Was baptised Frances Mary, Daughter of Thos. and Henrietta Mary Loveless, born 14th. Sponsors John Palmer and Henrietta Church, by me
Jas. Calderbank.
1813, Sept. 29. Was baptised Mary, daughter of Philip and Bridget Riley, born 18th. Godmother Sarah Caezby [?].
R. Ainsworth.
1813, Octr. 20th. Was baptised Jane, daughter of Jas. and Anne Redmond. Godmother Mary Burn, by
R. Ainsworth.
1813, Octr. 21st. Was baptised Elizth., daughter of Willam. and Catharine Hawkins, born the preceding day. Sponsors John Marten and Catharine Corbin, by
R. Ainsworth.
1814, Febr. 5th. Was baptised Isabella Jane,[1][2] Daughter of Mr and Mrs John English, born the same day. Sponsors Richd. Rawe Esqr. and and Charlotte Georgiana, Lady Bedingfield; proxies Revd. R. Ainsworth and Miss Constantia Walsh, by
R. Ainsworth.
1814, April 3rd. Was baptised Felix William, Son of Louis Felix Gloude Simeon and Rowena [?] his Wife, born 22nd Feby. Sponsors St Ange Felix Ives Simeon and Mary Simeon; proxy John Vandenhoff, by me
J. Calderbank.
For the next two entries, see also infra., p. 192.
1814, March 17th. Was baptised Dennis Henry, Son of Edward and Elizth. Murphy, born Decr. 26, 1813. Sponsors Patrick Hoy and Henrietta Loveless, by me
J. Calderbank.
1814, March 9th. Was baptised Wm., Son of George and Sarah Stacey, born Feby. 28. Sponsors Cornelius Dowding and Henrietta Loveless, by me
J. Calderbank.
1814, April 23. Was baptised Mary Anne, Daughter of Cornelius and Mary Anne Dowding, born 14th. Sponsors Jas. Dowding and Mary Brown, by me
J. Calderbank.
1814, May 22nd. Was baptised Mary, Daughter of Thos. and Margt. Broderick, born 19th. Sponsors Jas. and Jane McGuire, by me
J. Calderbank.

[1][2] Later Countess English, a title conferred on her by Pope Pius IX; she was a great benefactress to the Church. See Davey, pp. 63-4; Roche, *History of Prior Park*, pp. 256-8; *A History of the English Benedictine Nuns of Dunkirk Now at St Scholastica's Abbey, Teignmouth, Devon* (edited by the Community, 1958) pp. 152-3, 198-9. For her godmother, see *C.R.S.*, 7 and E. Castle (ed.) *The Jerningham Letters* (2 vols., 1896).

Next entry in Rishton's hand:
1814, June 1st. Was baptised Richard, Son of Thos. and Charlotte Batterbury, born April 21st. Sponsors Richard Phelan and Mary Short, by me

Thos. Rishton.[13]

Calderbank's hand:
1814, June 26th. Was baptised Elizabeth, Daughter of Henry Claude Raimond de Beaufort Esqr. and his wife Rosalie Elizabeth Wilhelmina, born the 5th. Sponsors Sir Richd. Bedingfield Bart. et Madame Henriette de Caysau, by me

J. Calderbank.

Henceforth in Rishton's hand:
1814, July 18th. Was baptized James, Son of James Flin and his Wife Frances, born the 11th. Sponsors George and Elizabeth Quin, by me

Thos. Rishton.

1814, Aug. 14th. Was baptized Henry, Son of John and Anne Kentjean (born the 7th); the Sponsors Henry Bodsen and Theodosia Haywood, by me

Thos. Rishton.

1814, Aug. 24th. Was baptized Francis Edward, Son of [*blank*] Mounteworth

by me Thos. Rishton.

Sep.15, Dead.

1814, Aug. 28th. Were baptized Sarah, born Apl. 18th 1810, and Enoch. born Jany. 1st 1813, Daughter and Son of Isaac and Lucy Freeman; Sponsors to the former were Peter Lawton and Margaret Edwards, to the latter, the said Peter Lawton and Sarah Edwards

by me Thos. Rishton.

1814, Sepr. 7th. was baptized Thos., Son of Edward and Mary Cary (born Sepr. 3). Sponsors Murtagh Malone and Helen Oxford

by me Thos. Rishton.

1814, Sepr. 9th. Was baptized Joseph, the Son of Joseph and Elizabeth Henty, born Sepr. 6th. Sponsors Richard Phelan and Mary Anne Brown, by me

Thos. Rishton.

1814, Sepr. 11th. Was baptized John, the Son of Richard and Mary Pasey, born Augst. 28th. Sponsors James Nagle and Anne Sheean, by me

Thos. Rishton.

1814, Sepr. 16th. Was baptized Catharine, daughter of Thomas and Elizabeth Geogan, born Aug. 15th. Sponsors Michael and Margaret Ryan, by

James Calderbank.

1814, Sepr. 28th. Was baptized George Frederick, Son of Frederic and

[13]   Dom Thomas Clement Rishton O.S.B., for whom see *C.R.S.*, 65, p. 81.

Elizabeth Slade (born Sepr. 18th). Sponsors Richard Phelan and Mary Trowbridge, by me

Thos. Rishton.

1814, Sepr. 30th. Was baptized Caled [*sic*], the son of Thos. and Elizabeth Edwards (born Sepr. 29th). Sponsors Richard Phelan and Anne Baker, by me

Thos. Rishton.

1814, Oct. 17th. Was baptized William, the son of Maurice and Elizabeth Quin, born Octr. 9th. The Sponsors Cornelius and Mary Anne Dowding, by me

Thos. Rishton.

1814, Octr. 20th. Was baptized [*blank*], Son of [*blank*] and Ellenor Lorton,[14] by me
(Died an infant)   Thos. Rishton.

1814, Octr. 24th. Was baptized Ellen Clare, the Daughter of John and Ellen Denie (born the same day). Sponsors Jeremiah Cairns and Winefrid Denie, by me

Thos. Rishton.

1814, Novr. 5th. Was baptized Edward Joseph, the son of John and Mary Short (born Novr. 4th); the Sponsors Edward Bates and Elizabeth Bates, by me

Thos. Rishton.

1814, Novr. 21st. Was baptized Thos., Son of Thomas and Margaret Mara, without ceremonies, by

James Calderbank.

1814, Decr. 5th. Were baptized Lawrence and Charles, the Sons of Patrick and Mary Walsh (born Decr. 1st); the Sponsors Richard Reynolds and Ellenor Moylan, by me

Thos. Rishton.

1814, Decr. 11th. Was baptized Walter, the Son of William and Elizabeth Baily, born Novr. 4th; the Sponsors Matthew Halpin and Julienne Victoire, by me

Thos. Rishton.

1814, Decr. 20th. Was baptized Bridget, the daughter of Michael and Margaret Ryan (born Decr. 14th); the Sponsor Mary Fagan, by me

Thos. Rishton

1814, Decr. 20th. Was baptized Anne, the Daughter of William and Mary Boyd, born Decr. 14th; the Sponsors Michael Ryan and Mary Fisher, by me

Thos. Rishton.

1814, Decr. 30th. Was baptized Sarah, the Daughter of Andrew and Mary Murphy, born Decr. 20th; the Sponsors Francis and Mary Bence, by

James Calderbank.

[14] Or Lawton; she died three days later. The mortuary register records her death (*infra*, p. 188) but not the child's.

1815, Jany. 15th. Was baptized Anne, the Daughter of William and Teresa Heskins born Jany. 6th; the Sponsors Thos. Maverly and Mary Osmund, by

James Calderbank.

1815, Jany. 24th. Was baptized William, the son of John and Mary Anne Fair (born Jany. 6th); the Sponsors Richard Phelan and Ellenor Martin, by me

Thos. Rishton.

1815, Jany. 27th. Was baptized Mary, the Daughter of Francis and Margaret Ward, born Jany. 25th; the Sponsors Sir Thos. Hugh Clifford Bart. and Miss Mary Barbara Clifford, by

James Calderbank.

1815, Feby. 5th. Was baptized (conditionally) Maria, the Daughter of Thomas and Mary Bailie, born Decr. 21st 1814, by me

Thos. Rishton.

1815, March 5th. Was baptized Elizabeth Helen, the Daughter of John and Isite O'Brien, born Feby. 23rd; the Sponsors James Flin and Elizabeth Shean, by me

Thos. Rishton.

1815, March 15th. Was baptized Alban Huddleston, the Son of John and Frances English, born the same day; the Sponsors the Revd. Samuel Spooner[15] and Miss Mary Huddleston; Proxies Mr Wm. Day and Miss Winefrid Barrett, by

James Calderbank.

1815, March 22nd. Were baptized Caroline Helen and Emily Theresa Theodon, twin Sisters, Daughters of Jean Francois Theodon and Marie Rose Theodon, born March 14th, by

James Calderbank.

Next two entries in Calderbank's hand:
1815, April 16th. Was baptised George, Son of Richd. and Letitia Abbot, born 12th. Sponsors Richd. Phelan and Mary Trafford, by

Jas. Calderbank.

1815, April 17th. Was baptised George, Son of Thos. and Mary FitzGerald, born 4th. Sponsors Jas. Hagerty and Elizth. Osmund, by

Jas. Calderbank.

Rishton's hand:
1815, July 17th. Was baptized Bridget, the Daughter of Thos. and Mary McDermot (born June 20th) by me

Thos. Rishton.

Henceforth in Calderbank's hand:
1815, August 1. Baptised Mary, Daughter of Bartholomew and Margt. O'Leary, born 27 July. Sponsor Mary Parker, by me

Jas. Calderbank [*see also 27 Aug.*].

---

[15] Secular priest, "steadfast in the faith" but "better suited for an actor than a missionary" (Oliver, p. 414). See also J.B. Dockery, *Collingridge* (Newport, Mon., 1954) *passim; C.R.S.*, 65, p. 231.

August 2nd 1815. Was baptised Henry, Son of Barbara Cooper, born 28 July, by me

Jas. Calderbank.

Augst. 15th 1815. Was baptised Anthony, Son of Francis and Eliza Montaberte, born 13th. Sponsor Mary West, by me

J. Calderbank.

Augst. 16, 1815. Was baptised Mary Theresa, Daughter of Charles Eyston Esqr. and his Wife Maria Theresa, born 15th Inst. Sponsors Basil Eyston Esqr. by proxy of the Revd. Jas. Calderbank, and Mrs Theresa Metcalfe,[16] by me

Jas. Calderbank.

Augst. 27. Supplied the ceremonies of Baptism on Mary O'Leary, baptised 1st. Sponsors Peter Lawton and Catharine Sullivan, by me

J. Calderbank.

1815, Septr. 8th. Was baptised Henry, Son of Mathew and Mary Campbell, born 7th. Sponsors Michael Ling and Anne Gilepsie, by me

J. Calderbank.

1815, Septr. 20th. Was baptised Mary Anne Henrietta, daughter of John and Henrietta Palmer, born 18th. Sponsors Peter Smith and Henrietta Maria Loveless, by me

J. Calderbank.

1815, Octr. 1. Was baptised Henry, Son of John and Anne Kengkins, born Septr. 25. Sponsors Cornelius Dowding and Mary West, by me

Jas. Calderbank.

1815, Octr. 25. Fut baptisée Sabine Anne Therese de Tinseau, fille légitime de Charles Marie Therese Leon de Tinseau et de sa femme Anne O Leary de Tinseau, née le 27 du Mois de Septembre de la même Année. Le parrain Charles Antoine Balthazar de Tinseau; Marraine Antoinette Victoire Rosamonde de Tinseau, qui tous deux étant absents, furent remplacés pp. l'un par le Revd. Mr. Calderbank et l'Autre par Mde. Anne O Leary, par moi

J. Calderbank.

1815, Novr. 26. Was baptised Theresa Hartley, Daughter of [blank] Patison and Esther his Wife, born 21st. Sponsors Julien Havery and Henrietta Church, by me

Jas. Calderbank.

1815, Decr. 3. Was baptised John, Son of Michael and Elizabeth Fonttelie [?], born 29th Novr. Sponsors John Kengkins and Mary Anne Kengkins, by me

Jas. Calderbank.

Next five entries in Rolling's hand (the first three clearly relate to one family):
1815, Decr. 5th. Was baptized Rebecca, Daughter of William and Harriet Henly, born Aug. 19th 1810. Sponsor Cornelius Railly, by me

Thos. Rolling.

---

[16]   See notes 90 & 95 to first register; also marriage-entry, 12 Oct. 1814 (*infra,* p. 192) and Baines's journal, 30 Dec. 1817; burial of "little Miss Eyston" (*C.R.S.,* 65, p. 222).

1815, Decr. 5th. Was baptized Mary, Daughter of Wm. and Harriet, born Oct. 19th 1812. Sponsor Cornelius Railly, by me

Thos. Rolling.

1815, Decr. 5th. Was baptized Elizabeth, Daughter of Wm. and Harriet, born [blank] 1814. Sponsor Cornelius Railly, by me

Thos. Rolling.

1815, Decr. 22nd. Was baptized Mary Ford, Daughter of James and Rosana Ford, born Decr. 13th 1815. Sponsor Mary Dillon

Thos. Rolling.

1815, Decr 25th. Was baptized Ann, Daughter of John and Mary Kearton (2 years of age). Sponsors [blank], by me

Thos. Rolling.

Calderbank's hand (2 entries):
1816, Jany. 29th. Was baptised John Francis, Son of John Wright Esqr. and Mary Catharine his Wife, born the same morning. Sponsors John Wright Senr. Esqr. by proxy of Edwd. Wright Esqr. and Mrs [blank] Wright, by

Jas. Calderbank.

1816, Feby. 21. Was baptised Lucy, Daughter of George Dyer and Lia West, born 18th. Sponsor Elizabeth West, by me

Jas. Calderbank.

Next ten entries in Rolling's hand:
1816, Jany. 21st. Was baptized Ellen Denton, Daughter of Charles and Ellen Denton (2 years of age). By

Thos. Rolling.

1816, Febry. 4. Was baptized Daniel, the Son of Daniel and Margaret Keasy. Born Jany. 26th 1816. Sponsors Anne Egan, T. Edwards. By me

Thos. Rolling.

1816, Febry. [blank]. Was baptized Joseph, the son of Silis and Mary Parfitt, born the 11th. Sponsor [blank] Taylor

Thos. Rolling.

1816, Febry. 24th. Was baptized Grace, Daughter of John and Margaret Coen, born 23. (Father a Man of Colour). By me

Thos. Rolling.

1816, Febry. 27th. Was baptized William, the Son of William and Francis [sic.] Edwards, born 23 Inst. Sponsor Mary Edwards. By me

Thos. Rolling.

1816, March 4. Was baptized Mary Ann Aylesbury, Daughter of George and Ann his Wife, born 3rd Inst. Sponsors Thomas Aylesbury and Elizabeth Wright.

Thos. Rolling.

1816, March 10th. Was baptized James, the Son of Cornelius Dowding and Mary his Wife, born the 7th. Sponsors Richard Clarke and Elizabeth Corbett, by

Jas. Calderbank.

1816, Mch. 14th. Was baptized Thos. Quigly, the Son of Thos. and Jane his wife, born born [sic.] Febry. 8th. Sponsors Michael Smith and Mary Carrol. By me

Thos. Rolling.

April 10th/16 [16 *underlined; i.e. 1816*]. Was baptized James Daniels, the Son of John and Winifred Daniels. Born April 4th. Sponsors William Allner and Jane Moyer. By

Jas. Calderbank.

April 15th. Was baptized Mary Cecily Short, the Daughter of John and Mary Short, born April 13th. Sponsors Michl. Creagh and Mary Lewis. By me

Thos. Rolling.

The part italicised below is in Rolling's hand, the remainder by Calderbank.
1816, April 15th. Was baptized Vincent John, Son of Mr John English and his Wife Frances, born the same day. Sponsors Mr Robt. English and Mrs Mary Bostock by proxy of Mr Wm. Day and Miss Mary Gibson, by me

Jas. Calderbank.

15 April. Was baptized [*incomplete entry by Rolling*].

Calderbank's hand (2 entries):
1816, Decr. 2nd. Was baptised Mary Emilia Bibiana Alexina, Daughter of Benjamin and Anne Langley, born same day. Sponsors Revd. Alexander Alexis Valgalier[17] and Miss Emilia Hartsinck, by me

Jas. Calderbank.

1816, Decr. 22nd. Was baptised Hector St. Cyr, Son of Nicholas Philippe Constant Caffeari [? *Initial letter indistinct*] et Mary his wife, born the same day (without ceremonies) by me

Jas. Calderbank.

Henceforth in Rolling's hand:
April 14. Was Baptized Theresa, Daughter of Charles and Catharine Evans, Born 22 March. Sponsor Mrs Moon

By me Thos. Rolling.

+ 1816. In the month of June was baptized Anthony Devereux Strata, Son of Antonio and Mary Strata, born March 13th 1816. Sponsors Richard Whelan and Eliza Anello.

By Thos. Rolling.

+ 1816, June 28. Was baptized Mary Ann Thompson, Daughter of Born 4 Inst. [*sic.*]. Sponsors Jas. Hagarty and Mary Sullivan.

By me Thos. Rolling.

July 4. Was baptized Mary Baily, Daughter of John and Mary his wife. Born 10th June. Sponsors Michal Smith and Jane Quigly.

By me Thos. Rolling.

July 31. Was Baptized Maurus Quin, Son of Maurus and Mary his Wife, born July 30th. Sponsors Michl. Craigh and Ellen Crowly.

By me Thos. Rolling.

July 20. Was baptized John F. Connor, Son of John and Ellen his Wife, born 12 Inst. Sponsors Jas. Hagarty and Rebecca Ketcherside.

By me Thos. Rolling.

---

[17]   Abbé Valgassier (*C.R.S.*, 12, p. 227).

July 19. Was baptized Francis Quin, Son of Peter and Esther his Wife, born 17 Inst. Sponsor Mrs Taylor.

By me Thos. Rolling.

Aug. 4. Was baptized Maurus Flin, Son of Jas. and Frances his Wife, born 1st. Sponsors John Obrian [?] and Mary Crowly.

By me Thos. Rolling.

Aug. 27. Mary Ann Goddard, Daughter of Sarah G. and Edward Williams, born Septr. 21 – 15 [*presumably 1815*].

By me Thos. Rolling.

1816, Augst. 20. Was baptized Edward Henty, Son of David and Elizabeth born on 2nd of same Month.

By J. Calderbank.

Septr. 16. Was baptized Helen Park, Daughter of Joseph[18] and Mary his Wife. Sponsors Ed'ad. Gillespie and Sarah Orrel by proxy of Alice Rutherford.

By Jas. Calderbank.

Octr. 15. Was baptized Austin [?] Joseph Alner, Son of William and Esther his Wife, born 14. Sponsors John Timberry and Mary Molineux.

By me Thos. Rolling.

21. Ann Carrol, Daughter of Jas. and Mary. Born 19. Sponsor Ann Hegan.

By me Thos. Rolling.

[*The above is exactly repeated after the next entry.*]

18. Cecily Freeman, of [*sic.*] Isaac and Lucy his wife. Born 16. Sponsors Nicolas Mathioli and Ann Rosanna.

By me Thos. Rolling.

29. William Wickham, Son of John and Mary. Born 28. Sponsors John Flanighan, Mary Capel.

By Jas. Calderbank.

+ Nov 1st. Was baptized Joseph Baker, Son of Thos and Mary his wife, born 26.

By me Thos. Rolling.

2. Was baptized Michl. Burk, Son of Miles and Mary B. his wife, born Oct. [*exact date indistinct; possibly 12th or 13th*]. Sponsors Patrick Mabella and Bd. Kelly

By me Thos. Rolling.

13th. William Henly, Son of William and Harriet. Born, died on Same Day, viz. 13th Nov.

By me Thos. Rolling,

Nov 3. Cath. Sealy Curtis, Daughter of Robert and Mary. Sponsor Ann Sealy. Born 2nd.

By Jas. Calderbank.

13 Novr. Was baptized Jas. Porch [?] Son of Jas. and Mary P. his wife, born 10th.

By me Thos. Rolling.

---

[18]   Joseph Park, carpenter and joiner of Larkhall, Bath, occurs in the *1819 Directory*, p. 83.

17. Thos. Ryan, Son of Michl. and Margaret his wife. Born 1st. Sponsors Dominic Drury and Cath. Drury.

By me Thos. Rolling.

26. Was baptd. John Russell Burke, Son of J. and Mary his wife. Born 24th.

By me Thos. Rolling.

Next eleven entries in Calderbank's hand:

1816, Decr. 27th. Was baptised George, Son of John and Mary Anne Fare, born 16th Inst. Sponsors Wm. Edwards and Elenor Martin, by me

Jas. Calderbank.

1817, Jany. 9. Was baptised John, Son of John and Anne Randell, born 17th April 1816. God Mother Catharine Taylor, by me

Jas. Calderbank.

1817, Jany, 24. Was baptised Edward, Son of Wm. and Mary Capel, born 8th of the Same Month. Sponsor Sarah Hutchings, by me

Jas. Calderbank.

1817, Feby. 5th. Was baptised Joseph Patrick, Son of Patrick and Mary O'Connor, born 16th Augst. 1816. Sponsor Lucy Williams (sine ceremoniis), by me

Jas. Calderbank.

1817, Feby. 20th. Was baptised Honoria, Daughter of Michal and Honoria Nolan, born 4th Inst. Sponsor Anne Wickham, by me

Jas. Calderbank.

1817, Feby. 22. Was baptised conditionally Loftus Michael, Son of Loftus and Mary Ann Fenning. Sponsor Henrietta Henry. The child was born 3rd Augst. 1814; by me

Jas. Calderbank.

1817, March 9th. Was baptised Mary, daughter of Thos. and Frances Dulworth, born 29th Jany. 1816. Sponsor Margt. Leary, by me

Jas. Calderbank.

1817, March 30th. Was baptised Wm., Son of John and Catharine Hancock, born 16th. Sponsor Maria Moon, by me

Jas. Calderbank.

1817, April 4th. Was baptised William Gregory, Son of William and Elizabeth Bailey, born 13th of March. Sponsors Walter Irvine and Harriet Smith, by me

Jas. Calderbank.

1817, April 8th. Was baptised James, Son of Thos. and Anne Earles, born 8th of March. Sponsors Michael Lalor and Dorothy Lalor, by me

Jas. Calderbank.

1817, April 11th. Was baptised Henrietta Maria, Daughter of John and Henrietta Maria Palmer, born the preceding day. Sponsors Mathew Campbell and Louisa Guista, by me

Jas. Calderbank.

Next eight entries in Rolling's hand:

17 [*underlined; i.e. 1817*] Jany. 26. Was baptized Jas. Ellington, Son of Richard and Ann Ellington, born 24 Inst. Sponsor Mary Carrol.

By me Thos. Rolling.

Do. Was baptised Richard, Son of John and Margaret Waters. Sponsor Ann Hegan.

By me Thos. Rolling.

1817, March 3. Was baptized William Smith, Son of Hugh and Jane Smith of Chipping Sodbury.

By me Thos. Rolling.

1817, March 4th. Was baptized Thos., Son of James and Ellen Smith, about a fortnight old.

By me Thos. Rolling.

1817, March 12. Was baptized Thos., Son of Thos. and Mary Broudrick. Born on the 8 of the same Month. Sponsors Thos. Leagheay and Mary Tracy.

By me Thos. Rolling.

1817, March 25. Was baptized Mary Ann Thompson, Daughter of William and Elizabeth Thompson (Protestants). Child's age 2 years.

By me Thos. Rolling.

1817, April 30. Supplied the Ceremonies of baptism on Clare Orcher Catherine English, Daughter of John and Frances English. Sponsors Francis Caning Esq. and Mrs Jane Caning. Sponsors per proxies John Easton Esq. and Miss Talbot.

By me Thos. Rolling.

May 3rd 1817. Was baptized Thos. Conlan, Son of Luke Conlan and Elizabeth Ladell. Born April 29. Sponsors Daniel Manning and Sarah Gill.

By Thos. Rolling.

Calderbank's hand (3 entries):

1817, May 8th. Was baptised William Henry, Son of Samuel and Elizth. Mary Shirley, born 5th of April of the same year. Sponsors Joachim Ribello Palharosos [?], by proxy of Dr Jas. Birket[19], and Elizth. Shirley, by me

Jas. Calderbank.

1817, May 26th. Was baptised Richd. Augustine, Son of Richd. and Letitia Abbott, born the same day. Sponsors Wm. Edwards and Mary Power, by me

Jas. Calderbank.

1817, May 29th. Was baptised Charles Joseph, Son of John Baptist Joseph Denie and of Ellen his wife, born the same day. Sponsors Revd. Vincent Glover[20] and Mr Deane by proxy of Wm. Day Esqr., by me

Jas. Calderbank.

Rolling's hand (4 entries):

1817, June 15. Was baptized Owen Ryan, son of William and Mary Ryan, born June 7. Sponsors Michl. Ryan and Theresa Hesking.

By me Thos. Rolling.

1817, June 22. Was baptized Elen Flin, Daughter of John and Ann Flin born 19 Inst. Sponsors William and Mary Carrol, by

Thos. Rolling.

[19] Or Birkitt, 19 St James's Parade (*ibid.*, p. 46).

[20] Benedictine (see index to *C.R.S.*, 65).

1817, June 25. Was baptized Charles, Son of Joseph and [*blank*] Fasana, born May 30th. Sponsors Anthony Fasana (by proxy of Thos. Rolling) and Mdm. de Beaurepere, by me

Thos. Rolling.

1817, June 26. Was baptized Henry, Son of John Wright Esqre. and Mary Catharine his wife, born the same Day. Sponsors Sir Henry Englefield and Mrs Catharine Charlton (Proxies Miss Eliza Wright and T. Rolling).

By me Thos. Rolling.

Calderbank's hand (3 entries):
1817, June 29. Was baptised Joseph Henry, Son of John and Isate O'Brien, born 22nd. Sponsors James Haggerty and Barbara Cooper by me.

Jas. Calderbank.

1817, June 29. Was baptised John Cornelius, Son of Patrick and Esther Crowley, born 23d. Sponsors Maurice and Elizth. Quinn, by me

Jas. Calderbank.

1817, June 30th. Was baptised John Lattin, Son of Alexander Mansfield Esqr. and his wife Paulina, born 14th. Sponsors Patrick Lattin Esqr. and Miss Fanny Mansfield, by me

Jas. Calderbank.

Next eight entries in Rolling's hand:
1817, June 30. Was baptized William Paul Fitzpatrick, son of William and Catharine. Born the same Day. Sponsors Thos. and Lucy Williams.

By me Thos. Rolling.

1817, July 6. Was baptized Edwin Rial, Son of Patrick and Jane Rial his wife. Born 6 December 1814. Sponsors William Allner and Mary Gill.

By me Thos. Rolling.

1817, July 6. Was baptized Mary Ann Gill, Daughter of Sarah Gill and Laurence Stones. Born 15 March 1817.

By me Thos. Rolling.

1817, July 10. Was baptized William Bland, son of William and Sarah, born June 1st.

By me Thos. Rolling.

1817, July 12. Was baptized Joseph Rebottaro, Son of Paschal Rebottaro and Mary Cambruzzo. Born the same Day.

By me Thos. Rolling.

[*This replaces a similar entry, scratched out, in which "his wife" occurs after the mother's name.*]
1817, August 5. Was baptized Richard Ryan, Son of Patrick and Joana Ryan, born 3d Inst. Sponsors Michael Ryan and Catharine O'Neil.

By me Thos. Rolling.

1817, Augst. 10. John Magary, Son of John and Mary Magary, born July 30. Sponsors John and Ann Wickham.

By me Thos. Rolling.

1817. Was baptized Juliania Cecilia, Daughter of Rosalie and Henry De Beaufort, born July 1st. Sponsors [*blank*].

By me Thos. Rolling.

Next nine entries in Baines's hand:
1817, Augt. 6th. Was baptized Charles Conolly, Son of Charles and
Eliza Conolly. Sponsors Mr Conolly of Mitford [*sic.*] Castle[21] and
Lady Blount, by me

Peter Baines.

1817, Augt. —. Was baptized [*blank*] Cambell [*blank*] of Math. and
Mary Cambell. Sponsors Henry Williams and Ann Rate.

By me Peter Baines.

1817, August 14th. Was baptized Catharine Flinn, daughter of Mr —
Flin and Catharine his wife.

By me Peter Baines.

1817, Sepr. 29th. Was baptized Margaret Dolwell, aged 2½ years,
daughter of Thos. and Frances Dolwell. Sponsors Philip Sulivan and
Marg. O'Leary, by

Thos. Brindle.

1817, Octr. 1st. Was baptized Catharine Brown, daughter of Thos. and
Ann Brown, born Sepr. 27th of this year. Sponsor Ann Wickham, by

Thos. Brindle.

1817, Octr. 9th. Were [*sic.*] baptized Edwd. Rundell, born April 7th
1814, son of John and Ann Rundell. Sponsor Louisa Dovrell[?], by

Thos. Brindle.

Also Eliza Henley, daughter of James and Hariet Henley, born Octr. 5th.
Sponsor Maurice Quin, by

Thos. Brindle.

Also John Burns, son of John and Mary Burns, born May 22d 1809; also
James Burns, son of the same, born Jany 11th 1812, by

Thos. Brindle.

"Conditionally" written alongside the above two baptisms.

1817, Novr. 5th. Was baptized Charles John Eyston, son of Charles
Eyston Esqr. and Teresa Mary Eyston his wife.[22] Godfather Sir John
Throckmorton Bart. Godmother Mary Jane Eyston. By proxy of Mr
John Wright and Miss Georgiana Cary.

by me Peter Baines.

Henceforth in Baines's and Brindle's hands, as signed:
1817, 7[?] of Novr. Was baptized Eliz. Fautsch, daughter of Michael
and Eliz. Fautsch, born Novr. 5, 1817. Sponsors John and Ann Kentchens, by me

Thos. Brindle.

1817, Novr. 18. Was baptized David Thomas, Son of William and Mary
Frances Thomas. Sponsors William Thomas and Eliz. Arnoud, by me

Thos. Brindle.

1817, Decr. 13. Was baptized Mary Sheehy, Daughter of Michael and
Eliz. Sheehy, born Decr. 1, 1817. Sponsor Mrs Loveless, by me

Thos. Brindle.

[21] Midford Castle; see *C.R.S.*, 65, p. 90.
[22] See Baines's journal, same date (*C.R.S.*, 65, p. 212).

1817, Decr. 19. Was baptized Eliz. Tuins, Daughter of Charles and Catharine Tuins, born Septr. 23, 1817. Sponsor Martha Moon, by me
Thos. Brindle.

1817, Decr. 20th. Was baptized Caroline Eliza Wilkes, daughter of James and Eliza Catharine Wilkes. Sponsors Mr George Dun, Mrs Ann Melloa
by me Peter Baines.

1817, Decr. 27. Was baptized Wm. Patrick Rigall, son of Wm. Patrick and — Rigall, born Decr. 23, 1817. Spons. Ann Hypsly and James Heagelty,

by me Thos. Brindle.

1818, Jany. 4. Was baptized Den. McHoue, son of Den. and Mary McHoue, born Decr. 29, 1817. Spons. Mary Moony,

by me Thos. Brindle.

1818, Jany. 5. Was baptized Catharine Baily, daughter of Thos. and Eliz. Baily, born Jany. 2, 1818. Spons. Mary Russel,

by me Thos. Brindle.

1818, Jany. 7. Was baptized Joseph Navanne, Son of Innocents and Jane Navanne, born March 11. Spons Mrs Hipsly.

by me Thos. Brindle.

1818, Jany. 18. Was baptized Thos. Fitzgerald, son of Thos. and Mary Fitzgerald, born Jany. 1, 1818. Spons. Thos. Neill and Ellen Dunivan,
by me Thos. Brindle.

1818, Feby. 1. Was baptized Catharine Donoghue, daughter of Jeffery and Mary Donoghue, born Jany. 28, 1818. Spons. John Magary and Mary Wood,

by me Thos. Brindle.

1818, Feby. 7. Was baptized Bridget Howe, daughter of Denis and Martha Howe, born Aug. 29, 1817. Mrs Hipsly,

by me Thos. Brindle.

1818, Feby. 22d. Was baptized Charles Hagan, Son of Ann and John Hagan, born Jany. 27, 1818. Sponsors Wm. Bootfellow and Sarah Leonard,

by me Thos. Brindle.

1818, March 4. Was baptized Mary Eliz. Verstein, daughter of George and Mary Verstain, born March 3d 1818. Sponsors Elizabeth and Henry Williams,

by me Thos. Brindle.

1818, March 5. Was baptized William Quin, Son of Mary and William Quin, born Feby. 28, 1818. Spons. Mrs Hyppsly, by me

Thos. Brindle.

1818, March 13. Was baptized Teresa Ann Dowding, daughter of Cornelius and Mary Dowding, born March 9, 1818. Spons. Mrs Hippsly and Maurus Quin,

by me Thos. Brindle.

1818, March 19. Were baptized Joseph and James Wickham, Twins, Sons of John and Ann Wickham, born March 18, 1818. Sponsors James [? Janet] Davies for Joseph and El. Mylon for James Wickham.

by me Thos. Brindle.

1818, Apl. 1. Was baptized Sarah Smith, daughter of — Smith and Ellen his wife, born March 30, 1818. Spons. Bedy [?] Weston,
by me Thos. Brindle.

1818, Apl. 5. Was baptized Charles Canor, Son of John and Ellen Canor, born Apl. 4. Spons. John Handy and Mary Riurden,
by me Thos. Brindle.

See below [*in Brindle's hand, referring to Baines's entry for 13 April.*]

1818, April 17. Was baptized Catharine Margaret Whyte, daughter of Captn. Edward Whyte R.N. and Mary his Wife, born April 13, 1818. Spons. Nicholas Charles Whyte Esqr. and Mrs Catharine Hall and Mrs Alice Osborne,
by me Thos. Brindle.

1818, April 17. Was baptized Ann Western, daughter of William and Eliz. Western, born Feby. 14, 1818. Spons. Mary Parfitt,
by me Thos. Brindle.

1818, April 26. Was baptized Ann Martha Dobson, daughter of Joseph and Eliza Dobson, born March 29, 1818. Spons. Teresa Heskins and Owen Rian,
by me Thos. Brindle.

1818, June 4. Baptized Daniel Tunly, son of Michael Tunly and Mary Widcomb, born May 18, 1818. Spons. Maria Manly and Thos. Calverwell
by me Thos. Brindle.

1818, April 13. Baptized William Archer English, son of John and Frances English, born the same day. Sponsors, Captain Thos. Couche, Mrs Sarah Neve by proxy of Miss Esther Mary Ferrers,
by me Peter Baines.

1818 [*no date*]. Baptized Margaret Dowlen, daughter of Andrew and Elizabeth Dowlen. Sponsors, Bernard Earls, Catharine Madden. Proxy Thos. Neil,
by me Peter Baines.

1818 [*no date*]. Was Baptized (sub conditione) John Rooney, son of John and Julia Rooney, born April 7th 1817. Sponsor Mrs Short,
by me Peter Baines.

1818 [*no date, but see* Baines's journal, *19 May*]. Were Baptized Frances Maria and Ann Constantia Welby, daughters of Benjamin and Maria Ann Welby. Sponsor Mrs Corbin,
by me Peter Baines.

1818, June 3d. Was Baptized James Kentgens, son of John and Ann Kentgens, born May 31st 1818. Sponsors, Joseph Green, Ann Hippisly.
by me Peter Baines.

1818 [*no date*]. Was Baptized Mary Ann Reorden, daughter of Timothy Reorden and Elizabeth Spencer. Sponsors Peter Cody and Ann Reorden,
by me Peter Baines.

1818, June 27th. Was baptized Sarah Hill, daughter of Joseph and Margaret Hill, born June 14th last. (No Godfather or Godmother.)
by me Peter Baines.

1818, June 27th. Was baptized John Baptist Thomas, son of – and Margaret Thomas. Sponsor Mary Ann Bodmin,

                                        by me Peter Baines.

1818, July 9. Was baptized Charlotte Brereton Bailie, daughter of Mary and Thomas Bailie, born June 2, 1818. Spons. William Lill Brereton and Mary Ann Bowment [?],

                                        by me Thos. Brindle.

1818, Augt. 3. Was baptized Edward Wright, Son of John and Mary Catharine Wright, born Augt. 3d 1818. Spons. Gerard Edwd. Strickland and Miss Eliz. Wright,

                                        by me Thomas Brindle.

1818, Aug. 9. Was baptized Eliz. Casy, daughter of Daniel and Margaret Casy, born July 30, 1818. Spons. Alb. Kenmouth and Cath. Allan,

                                        by me Thos. Brindle.

Next four entries in Barber's hand:

1818, Aug. 24. Was baptized Sebastian Joachim Allner, Son of William and Esther Allner, born August 22d 1818. Sponsors William Rose and Martha Steene,

                                        by me Luke Barber.[23]

1818, Aug. 26. Was baptized Margaret Mulguiney, daughter of Thomas and Elizabeth Mulguiney. Sponsor Patrick Omaney,

                                        by me L. Barber.

1818, Sepr. 5. Was baptized Patrick MacNalty, Son of John and Sarah MacNalty, born August 24. Sponsors Mrs Smith and Miss Smith,

                                        by me L. Barber.

1818, Sepr. 7. Was baptized Patrick Dexeter, Son of Edward and Ann Dexeter, without Sponsors,

                                        by me L. Barber.

Henceforth in Baines's and Brindle's hands, as signed:

1818, Sepr. 15th. Was baptized Charles John Thomas Conolly, son of Charles Conolly Esqr. and Eliza his wife. Sponsors John Clifton Esqr. by proxy of Charles Clifton Esqr. and Mrs Conolly of Mitford [*sic.*] Castle,[24]

                                        by me P. Baines.

The above infant was born Saty. the 12th inst.

1818, Augt. 24. Was baptized John Thomas Peacock, born Augt. 10, 1818, son of John and Margaret Peacock. Spons. Mary Edwards,

                                        by me Thos. Brindle.

1818, Septr. 18. Was baptized George Johnson, son of William and Ann Johnson, born June 14th 1818. Spons. Lucy Williams,

                                        by me Thos. Brindle.

1818, Septr. 24. Was baptized John Blackin, Son of John and Mary Blackin, born Septr. 21, 1818. Spons. Catharine Sanders,

                                        by me Thos. Brindle.

[23] Dom Luke Bernard Barber O.S.B., Prior of Downside (Birt, p. 149; Oliver, p. 238).

[24] Midford Castle.

1818, Septr. 24. Was baptized Leonard Mulone, Son of James and Elizabeth Mulone, born Septr. 5, 1818. Spons. Murtegh Mulone and Mary Reef,
by me Thos. Brindle.

1818, Septr. 24. Was baptized Mary Fuz, daughter of John and Ann Fuz, born Septr. 20, 1818. Spons. Mrs Hippisly,
by me Thos. Brindle.

1818, Septr. 26. Was baptized Mary Ann Mollineux, daughter of Danl. and Mary Ann Mollineux, born Septr. 14, 1818. Spons. Mary Marra and Thos. Broderick,
by me Thos. Brindle.

1818, Septr. 26. Was baptized Thomas Linus Quin, Son of Maurus and Eliz. Quin, born 23 of Septr. 1818. Spon. Brigit Timins [?] , by proxy of Honora Hegarty, and Cornelius Dowding,
by me Thos. Brindle.

1818, Octr. 15. Was baptized Brigitt Earl, daughter of Ann and Thos. Earl, born Septr. 12, 1818. Spons. Sarah Lalor and Math. Hudson,
by me Thos. Brindle.

1818, Octr. 19. Was baptized Hannah Purtill, daughter of James and Hannah Purtill, born Octr. 2d 1818. Spons. Maurus and Eliz. Quin,
by me Thos. Brindle.

1818, Novr. 2. Was baptized Mary Ryan, daughter of Michael and Margaret Ryan, born Octr. 25, 1818. Spons. Jane Wall and Thos. Earl,
by me Thomas Brindle.

1818, Novr. 11th. Was baptized Charles James Barret, son of Thos. and Ellen Barret. Sponsors James Nagle and Catharine Martin,
by me Peter Baines.

1818, Novr. 14th. Was baptized Mary Teresa Palmer, daughter of John and Henrietta Palmer, born yesterday. Sponsors Peter Smith and Harriet Ann Smith,
by me Peter Baines.

1818, Novr. 15. Was baptized Thomas Heskins, son of Noah and Mary Heskins, born Octr. 20, 1818. Spons. William and Teresa Asburn,
by me Thomas Brindle.

1818, Novr. 15. Was baptized John Magee, Son of Michael and Margaret Magee, born Novr. 2d 1818. Spons. Lucy Lambert,
by me Thomas Brindle.

1818, Novr. 19. Was baptized Henry Kelly, Son of John and Ann Kelly, born Novr. 17, 1818. Spons. Lucy Freeman,
by me Thos. Brindle.

1818, Decr. 13th. Was baptized Mary McCarthy, daughter of John and Sarah McCarthy. Sponsor Lucy Freeman,
by me Peter Baines.

1818, Decr. 24. Was baptized Eliz. Thompson, daughter of Henry and Joana Thompson, born Novr. 1, 1818. Spons. James and Honora Hegarty,
by me Thos. Brindle.

1818, Decr. 26th. Was baptized Thos. Flynn, Son of James and Frances

Flynn, born the 18th of Decr. 1818. Sponsor Ann Hippisly,

by me P. Baines.

1818, Decr. 30. Was baptized Eliz. Coalman, Daughter of John and Mary Coalman, born Decr. 28, 1818. Spons. Cath. Brennan and Pat. Murphy,

by me Thos. Brindle.

1818, Decr. 30. Was baptized Mary Coalman, Daughter of John and Mary Coalman, born Decr. 28, 1818. Spons. Ann Thomas, and Pat. Murphy,

by me Thos. Brindle.

1819, Jany. 6. Was baptized Bridget Maccarthy, daughter of Ellen and Patk. Maccarthy, born Jany. 2d. Spons. Ann Butler and Denis Kett,

by me Thos. Brindle.

1819, Jany. 15. Was baptized Hannah Madden, daughter of Mathew and Ann Madden, born July 16, 1815. Spons. Ann Hippisly,

by me Thos. Brindle.

1819, Feby. Was baptized Caroline Burk, daughter of Miles and Mary Burk, born Jany. 8, 1819. Spons. Margaret Ryan and William Crow,

by me Thos. Brindle.

1819 —. Was baptized John Brickell, Son of Thos. and Ellen Brickell, born Feby. 6. Spon. Lucy Freeman, this day Feby. 7, 1819,

by me Thos. Brindle.

1819, Feby. 26. Was baptized Eliz. O'Leary, daughter of Bartholomew and Margaret O'Leary, born Feby. 20, 1819. Spons. John Jeffers and Mrs Hippisly,

by me Thos. Brindle.

1819, March 7. Was baptized without ceremonies Jane West, daughter of [blank] and Martha West, born 24 of Feby. 1819,

by me Thos. Brindle.

1819, March 12. Was baptized without ceremonies Alfred Tuins, Son of Chas. and Cath. Tuins, born 19 of Feby. 1819. Spons. Mary Kingston,

by me Thos. Brindle.

1819, March 19. Was baptized Mary Henesy, daughter of William and Eliz. Henesy, born 15th of Jany. 1819. Spons. Ann Reardon,

by me Thos. Brindle.

1819, March 19. Was baptized Catharine Kilmud, daughter of Albert and Cath. Ellen. Kilmud, born 22d of Jany. 1819. Spons. — Marshall,

by me Thos. Brindle.

1819, March 20th. Was baptized (sine ceremoniis) Henry Edwards, in the moment of Death,

by me Thos. Brindle.

1819, March 21. Was baptized John Connel, son of Peter and Joana Connel, born 16 of March 1819. Spons. Daniel and Margaret Cacy,

by me Thos. Brindle.

1819, March 21. Was baptized (sine ceremoniis) Robt. Rendell, Son of William and Ann Rendell, born 8 of March, 1819. Spons. [blank] and Lucy Williams,*

by me Thos. Brindle.

* Ceremonies supplied the following day.

1819, April 3d. Was baptized without Ceremonies Mary Ann Jones, Daughter of Charlotte and John Jones, born March 12, 1819,
by me Thos. Brindle.

1819, April [blank] was baptized John MacCloskey, Son of John and Mary McCloskey, born Feby. 21, 1818.
by me Thos. Brindle.

1819, April 23d. Was baptized Eliz. Campbell, Daughter of Mathew and Mary Campbell, born April 20, 1819. Spons. Miss Williams and Mr Palmer,
by me Thos. Brindle.

1819, April 25. Was baptized James Cacy Dulworth, Son of Thomas and Frances Dulworth, born 7 of April 1819. Spons. Sarah and James Cacy,
by me Thos. Brindle.

1819, May 4. Was baptized Walter Rowland Jones, Son of Walter Rowland Jones and Mary Madeleine Jones. Godmother Lucy Freeman,
by me P. Baines.

1819, May 15. Was baptized without ceremonies William Black, Son of Richd. and Margaret Black,
by me Thos. Brindle.

1819, May 21. Was baptized Catharine Smyth, Daughter of Sarah and Hugh Smyth, born May 14, 1819. Spons. Mary Coalman,
by me Thos. Brindle.

1819, May 23. Was baptized Eleanor Murphy, Daughter of Jeremiah and Jane Murphy born May 9, 1819. Spons. Ann and James Pyke,
by me Thos. Brindle.

1819, May 23d. Was baptized John Huncock, son of John and Catharine Huncock. Sponsors Patrick Cullen and Mary Hunt,
by me P. Baines.

1819, June 9. Was baptized Ferdinand Edward English,[25] Son of Mrs F. and Mr J. English, born the same day. Spons. Rt. Revd. Dr Ed. Slater[26] and Miss Winifred English,
Vide 1825[27]
by me Thos. Brindle.

1819, June 17. Was baptized George Magrath, Son of Michael and Sarah Magrath, born June 11, 1819. Spons. Har't. Loughlin and Bernard Ryly,
by me Thos. Brindle.

1819, June 20. Was baptized William Long, Son of John and Sarah Long,

---

[25] The future Archbishop; cf. Oliver, p. 297; Roche, *Prior Park, passim.* His parents' Christian names were Frances (*née* Huddleston) and John; see entry of their marriage, 29 Aug. 1810, *infra,* p. 191, and note 12 above *re* his sister, the Countess.

[26] Bishop Edward Bede Slater O.S.B., Vicar-Apostolic of Mauritius (Birt, p. 139).

[27] This entry is re-written after a deleted 1825 entry, *infra,* p. 185, and is crossed-out in the register (as is an immediately preceding one which duplicates that of 21 May 1819) but is here reproduced in its correct chronological position.

born June 6, 1819. Spons. Denis Kett and Hannah Crook,
                                        by me Thos. Brindle.
1819, June 22. Was baptized Ell. Dunavan, daughter of Michael and
Martha Dunavan, born June 11, 1819. Spons. Ann Cox,
                                        by me Thos. Brindle.
1819, June 24. Was baptized Mary, Daughter of John and Sarah Shires,
born May 30, 1819. Spon. Pat. and Ann Macmillan,
                                        by me Thos. Brindle.
See Register of Mary Parfit at June 1820 [*Baines's hand*].

1819, July 11th. Was baptized George Henry Martin, Son of John and
Ann Martin. Sponsors Julian Havé and Ann Sullivan,
                                        by me Peter Baines.
1819, July 11th. Was baptized Elizabeth Frances Fare, daughter of
John and Mary Ann Fare. Sponsors William and Catharine Martin,
                                        by me Peter Baines.
1819, July 28th. Was baptized Martin Broadrick, son of Thomas and
Margaret Broadrick. Sponsors Martin Killfoyle and Ann Hippisly,
                                        by me Peter Baines.

Joseph Orange — see register at June 1820 [*Baines's hand*].

Augt. 1st 1819. Was baptized (sub conditione) Mary Watts, daughter
of William and Clarice Watts, born June 30th 1818. Sponsor Julian
Havé,
                                        by me Peter Baines.
Augt. — 1819. Was baptized Mary Goddard, born July 29th, 1819,
daughter of Sarah Goddard and Edwd. Williams. Sponsors John Moland
and Margaret Cromwell,
                                        by me P. Baines.
Aug. 20, 1819. Was baptized Maria Ganby, Daughter of John and
Elizabeth Ganby, born Aug. 12, 1819. Spons. Mary Short,
                                        by me Thos. Brindle.
Aug. 23, 1819. Was baptized Sarah Keevil, daughter of Mary and Robt.
Keevil, born March 14, 1815, and on the same day Mary Ann Keevil,
daughter of the same Mary and Robt. Keevil born July — 1817,
                                        by me Thos. Brindle.
* [*see after entry for 22 Sept.*].

Aug. 26, 1819. Was baptized Honoria Helton, daughter of Mary and
Stephen Helton, born May 16, 1819,
                                        by me Thos. Brindle.
Aug. 29, 1819. Was baptized Bridget Howe, daughter of Dionisius and
Martha Howe, born 7 Feby. 1819. Spons. Mrs Hippisly,
                                        by me Thos. Brindle.
Septr. 13, 1819. Was baptized Richd. Shortill, Son of Richd. and Eliz.
Shortill, born Sept. 6, 1819. Spons. Maurus Quin and Mary Murray,
                                        by me Thos. Brindle.

Septr. 22, 1819. Was baptized Joseph Peter Langley, the Son of Benjamin[28] and Hannah Langley, born Septr. 20, 1819. Spons. Lewisa Dixon and John Cady [? Cody],

by me Thos. Brindle.

*Aug: 23, 1819. Was baptized Eleanora Exeter. Godmother Mrs Hippisly. Born 22 of Augt. 1819,

by me Thos. Brindle.

Septr. 26, 1819. Was baptized Jane Fautsch, Daughter of Michael and Eliz. Fautsch, born 24th of Septr. 1819. Spons. Mary Ann Ketchin and John Kentchin,

by me Thos. Brindle.

Septr. 27. Was baptized Louisa Brown, daughter of Thos. and Mary Brown, born Septr. 23, 1819. Spons. Ann Hippisly,

by me Thos. Brindle.

Octr. 15, 1819. Was baptized Charles O'Conor, Son of John and Ellen O'Conor, born Octr. 4, 1819. Spos. [sic.] Sophia Fettle and James Taff

by me Thos. Brindle.

Octr. 15, 1819. Was baptized (sub conditione) Letitia O'Conor, Sister to the above C. O'Conor,

by me Thos. Brindle.

Octr. 21, 1819. Was baptized John Ryan, Son of Michael and Mary Ryan, born Octr. 16, 1819. Spons. Stephen Quin and Jane Wall,

by me Thos. Brindle.

Novr. 7, 1819. Was baptized John Johnson, Son of John Johnson and Mary Moor, born July 8, 1819. Spons. Ann Sulivan and Danl. Hallacy,

by me Thos. Brindle.

Octr. 31, 1819. Was baptized (sub conditione) Clare, the Daughter of John and Eliz. Baily, born Augt. – 1819. Spons. Miss – and Mr Walter Irvine,

by me Thos. Brindle.

Novr. 14, 1819. Was baptized Andrew Magill, Son of William and Mary Jane Magill, born Octr. 26, 1819. Spons. Susana Duggan and Edmund Welsh,

by me Thos. Brindle.

Sarah Elizabeth Jordan – See Register at June 1820 [*Baines's hand*].

Decr. 5, 1819. Was baptized (sine ceremoniis) Mathew Crowley, Son of Math. and Eliz. Crowley, born Decr. 2, 1819. Spons. Ann and Thos. Welsh,

by me Thos. Brindle.

Edwd. Mitchell – See register at June 1820 [*Baines's hand*].

Decr. 12, 1819. Was baptized John Brogen, Son of John and Bridget Brogen, born Decr. 9, 1819. Spons. Mary Clark and John Boland,

by me Thos. Brindle.

[28] Catholic schoolmaster; see *C.R.S.*, 65, note 412 to Introduction.

Decr. 19, 1819. Was baptized Thos. Ryan, Son of John and Margaret Ryan, born Decr. 2, 1819. Spons. Ann Wailand, and Wm. Cullan,

by me Thos. Brindle.

Decr. 28, 1819. Was baptized John Doyle, Son of John and Mary Doyle, born Decr. 15, 1819. Spons. Ann Hippisly,

by me Thos. Brindle.

Decr. 31st. Maria Francoise Zitte — See register at June 1820 [*Baines's hand*].

Jany. 2, 1820. Was baptized Winifred Fenning, Son [*sic.*] of Loftus and Mary Fenning, born Decr. 6, 1819. Spons. John Morris,

by me Thos. Brindle.

Jany. 5th. See Register at June 1820, Elizabeth Freeman. [*Baines's hand*].

Jany. 9, 1820. Was baptized Eliz. O'Brian Dunscomb, Daughter of Mark and Eliz. Dunscomb, born Jany. 1, 1820. Spons. James Heagarty and Honora Heagarty,

by me Thos. Brindle.

Jany. 15, 1820. Was baptized Mary Ann O'Neil, daughter of Edward and Mary O'Neil, born Jany. 4, 1820. Spons. Mary Dobbs,

by me Thos. Brindle.

Jany. 16, 1820. Was baptized Eliz. Quin Ryan, daughter of Pat. and Joanna Ryan, born Jany. 13, 1820. Spons. Eliz. and Edwd. Quin.

by me Thos. Brindle.

Jany. 22, 1820. Baptized conditionally Denis Howe, Son of Denis and Martha Howe, born Jan. 1st, 1820.

by me Thos. Brindle.

Jany. 30, 1820. Were baptized William and John Macdonald, Sons of John and Eliz. Macdonald, born on the same day. Spons. Mary Magee and Eliz. Cornelius,

by me Thos. Brindle.

Jany. 28, 1820. Was baptized George Basil Eyston, son of Charles Eyston and Teresa Mary Eyston his wife, the same day he was born. Godfather Charles Butler Esqr., Godmother the Widow Lady Throcmorton, by proxy of Charles Eyston Esqr. and Mrs Metcalf.

by me P. Baines.

Feb. 6, 1820. Was baptized Mary Ward, daughter of James and Frances Ward, born Jany. 17, 1820. Spons. Robt. and Ann Prangley [?],

by me Thos. Brindle.

Feby. 6, 1820. Was baptized Ann Dobson, Daughter of Joseph and Eliz. Dobson, born Jany. 30, 1820. Spons. Teresa Heskins, prox. for Henry and Mary Dobson,

by me Thos. Brindle.

Feby. 20, 1820. Was baptized George Lambert, Son of John and Ann Lambert, born Feby. 18, 1820. Spons. Ann Hippisley,

by me Thos. Brindle.

Laura Shell — See Register at June 1820 [*Baines's hand*].

Feby. 25, 1820. Were performed the ceremonies of baptism by Mr P. Baines over Charles Peacock, Son of [*blank*] Peacock, who was baptized Feby. 16, 1820,
by me Thos. Brindle.

March 3, 1820. Was baptized Mary Ann Frances Cecilia La Bigne, Daughter of Aimable Prosper and Mary Ann La Bigne, born Feby. 27, 1820. Spons. [*blank*]
by me Thos. Brindle.

March 4, 1820. Was baptized Joseph Dunscomb, Son of Mark and Eliz. Dunscomb born Novr. 9 [? 3] 1817. Spons. Mrs Hippisley,
by me Thos. Brindle.

March 7, 1820. Was baptized Ann Collings, Daughter of Charles and Mary Collings, born Jany. 24, 1820. Spons. Mrs Lucy Willoughby,
by me Thos. Brindle.

Brindle's hand:
March 22, 1820. Was baptized Patrick Flannigan, Son of Francis and Mary Flannigan, born 16 of March 1820. Spons. Mrs. Hippisley,
by [*blank*] Postlewhite.[29]

Baines's hand:
March 28th. Charles Ed. Wilkes. See register at June 1820.

Next ten entries in Brindle's hand:
April 5, 1820. Were baptized Kezia Mary and Michael Magrah, Daughter and Son of Thos. and Kezia Magrah, the former born Feby — 1812 and the latter July — 1816. Spons. Han'h Currey,
by me Thos. Brindle.

April 7, 1820. Was baptized David Wall, Son of Mary and Edward Wall, born May 1, 1817. Spons. Joana Ryan,
by me Thos. Brindle.

April 16, 1820. Was baptized Mary Lane, Daughter of Thos. and Ellen Lane, born Aug. — 1819. Spons. Ann Foley and John Nunan,
by me Thos. Brindle.

May 7, 1820. Was baptized Ann Magary, Daughter of John and Mary Magary, born May 2, 1820. Spons. John Flanagan and Ann Whitiker,
by me Thos. Brindle

May 21, 1820. Was baptized Catharine Bailie, Daughter of Thos. and Mary Bailie, born April 21, 1820. Spons. Thos. and Catharine Walsh,
by me Thos. Brindle.

May —, 1820. Was baptized Ellen, daughter of Francis and Hanah Allworth, born April 13, 1820. Spons. Margaret and Daniel Casey,
by me Thos. Brindle.

June 4, 1820. Was baptized Charlotte, daughter of John and Eliz. Gilbert, born June 14, 1818. Spons. Thos. Sullivan and Elenor McCartney,
by me Thos. Brindle.

[29] Joseph Postlewhite S.J., chaplain at Wardour, Wilts.; cf. Foley, VII, p. 618; Oliver, p. 385.

June 4, 1820. Was baptized Jane, daughter of John and Eliz. Gilbert, born May 1, 1820. Spons. Thos. Sullivan and Elenor McCartney,
by me Thos. Brindle.

June 7, 1820. Was baptized Charles McCartney, Son of Daniel and Mary McCartney born June 1, 1820. Spons. Cornelius Obrian,
by me Thos. Brindle.

June 15, 1820. Was baptized Eliz. Riley, daughter of Cornelius and Sarah Riley, born May 14, 1820. Spons. John Morris and Eliz. Pallet,
by me Thos. Brindle.

Omitted in their proper places [*eight entries by Baines*].

June 1819. Baptized Mary Parfitt, born June 3d, daughter of Silas and Mary Parfitt. Godmother Catharine Neil,
by me Peter Baines.

— 1819. Baptized Joseph Orange, born July 30th, son of Joseph and Catharine Orange. Sponsors John Coleman and Ann Edmunds,
by me P. Baines.

Novr. 23d 1819. Was baptized Sarah Elizabeth Jordan, born Novr. 17th, daughter of Thos. and Sarah Jordan. Sponsors Wm. Hopkins and Mary Clements,
by me Peter Baines.

Decr. 8th 1819. Baptized Edwd. Mitchell, born Sepr. 8th, son of William and Catharine Mitchell. Sponsor David Ryan,
by me Peter Baines.

Decr. 31st 1819. Baptized Marie Francoise Zitte, daughter of Wm. Thos. and Marie Francoise Terese Thomas Zitte. Sponsor Elizabeth Ladell,
by me Peter Baines.

Jany. 5th 1819. Baptized Elizabeth Freeman, daughter of Isaac and Lucy Freeman. Godmother Elizabeth Osmund,
by me Peter Baines.

Feby — 1820. Baptized Laura Ann Shell, born Feby. 21st, daughter of Christopher and Laura Rosalie Cecilia Shell. Sponsors John Lawly and Mary Havez,
by me Peter Baines.

March 28th 1820. Was baptized, without the ceremonies, Charles Edwd. Wilks, son of James and Eliza Catharine Wilks. Godmother Sarah Dealy,
by me Peter Baines.

Henceforth in Baines's and Brindle's hands, as signed:

June 21st 1820. Was baptized George Cave, son of John and Ellen Cave. Godmother Elizabeth Cave,
by me Peter Baines.

July 16th 1820. Was baptized Ellen Jane Rend, daughter of William and Ann Rend. Sponsors Michael Sheen, by proxy of Wm. Rend, and Mary Louis,
by me Peter Baines.

July 20th 1820. Was baptized Mary Ann Earls, daughter of Thos. and Ann Earls. Sponsors Hugh Reynolds and Ann Gilhespie,
by me Peter Baines.

July 21st 1820. Was baptized Ann Barbara, daughter of John and Henrietta Palmer, born July 16th. Sponsors Mathew Campbell and Barbara Cooper, proxy Honor Hagerty,

by me Peter Baines.

July 21st 1820. Was baptized Joseph, son of James and Mary Porch,[30] born July 18th. Sponsor Bridget Harding,

by me Peter Baines.

July 30th 1820. Was baptized Joseph son of — and — Barker, born July July 21st. Sponsors Mary Healy and John Farrell,

by me Peter Baines.

Augt. 2d 1820. Was baptized Ellen, daughter of Thos. and Elizabeth Donahoe. Sponsors Daniel and Catharine Cummins,

by me Peter Baines.

Augt. 2d 1820. Was baptized Emilia, daughter of Michael Ryan and Catharine Ahern. Godfather Maurice Quin, Godmother Cath. Hall,

by me Peter Baines.

Augt. 6, 1820. Was baptized James, son of Thos. and Barbara Abberville. Sponsors Joseph Spencer and Eliza Dixon,

by me P. Baines.

Augt. 6th. Was baptized Margaret, daughter of James and Frances Flinn. Sponsors James Dowding and Mary Dowding,

by me P. Baines.

Augt. 15th. Was baptized John, son of Thos. and Barbara Abbeville. Sponsors Henry Cody and Mary Head,

by me P. Baines.

Augt. 15. Was baptized Ethelred Bridget, daughter of John English Esqr. and Mrs Frances English his wife. Sponsors [blank],

by me P. Baines.

Aug: 20, 1820. Was baptized Ann, Daughter of Mary and Patrick Ward, born Aug. 9, 1820. Sponsors Eliz. and Joseph Donnahough,

by me Thos. Brindle.

Sept. 6, 1820. Was baptized Henry, Son of Mary and John McClaskey, born June 13, 1820. Sponsor Mrs Short,

by me Thos. Brindle.

Septr. 9, 1820. Was baptized Emelia, Daughter of John and Elizabeth Newman, born Septr. 7, 1820. Sponsor Hannah Curry,

by me Thos. Brindle.

Septr. 10, 1820. Was baptized Joachim Joseph, Son of William and Teresa Heskin, born Aug. 20, 1820. Sponsors Joseph Dobson and Sarah Barns,

by me Thos. Brindle.

Septr. 10, 1820. Was baptized Bridget, Daughter of John and Ann Murphy, born Septr. 1, 1820. Sponsors James Dawson and Mary Murry,

by me Thos. Brindle.

Septr. 15, 1820. Was baptized Elizabeth Bush, Daughter of Joseph and Ann Bush, born Septr. 5, 1820. Sposor [sic.] Mrs Hippisly,

by me Thos. Brindle.

---

[30] A shoemaker named Porch occurs in the *1819 Directory*, p. 86.

Septr. 22, 1820. Was baptized Margaret, Daughter of Mary and John Swafield, born Septr. 3, 1820. Sponsor Elizabeth Donaough,

by me Thos. Brindle.

Septr. 27, 1820. Was baptized Julia, Daughter of William and Bridget Weston, born April 18, 1820. Sponsor Cath. Baily,

by me Thos. Brindle.

Octr. 1, 1820. Was baptized Fabian Michael, Son of William and Esther Allner, born Septr. 28, 1820. Sponsors Michael Shea and Martha Steene,

by me Thos. Brindle.

Octr. 8, 1820. Was baptized Mary Dawson, Daughter of James Dawson and Alice Moclar, born Octr. 5, 1820. Sponsors John Naani and Ann Foley,

by me Thos. Brindle.

*Octr. 16th 1820. Was baptized, without the ceremonies, William Barrett, son of Thos. and Ellen Barrett,

by me P. Baines.

*[see second Oct. 16th entry, following Nov. 12th.]

Octr. 29th 1820. Was baptized Mary Whillen, daughter of James and Christiana Whillen. Godmother Catharine Orange,

by me P. Baines.

Novr. 10th 1820. Was baptized George Hafford, son of George and Rose Hafford. Sponsor Mary Short,

by me P. Baines.

Novr. 12th 1820. Was baptized Henry Strata, son of Anthony and Elizabeth Strata. Sponsors Peter Michel and Barbara Tyler,

by me P. Baines.

*Octr. 16, 1820. Was baptized John Lawler, Son of John and Grace Lawler, born Octr. 8, 1820. Spons. Maurus Quin and Bridget Henkins,

by me Thos. Brindle.

Decr. 2d 1820. Was baptized Elizabeth Ensay, daughter of William and Elizabeth Ensay. Godmother Elizabeth Quin,

by me P. Baines.

Decr. 8, 1820. Was baptized William Barrett, Son of Thomas and Ellen Barrett, born Octr. 15, 1820. Spons. Ann Fare and Wm. Edwards,

by me Thos. Brindle.

Decr. 24th 1820. Was baptized Patrick Peter McNolty, son of John and Sarah McNolty. Sponsors Peter Smith and Harriet Smith,

by me P. Baines

Decr. 26th 1820. Was baptized Teresa Louisa Fresoldi, daughter of Joseph and Martha Fresoldi. Sponsor Anthony Fresoldi,

by me P. Baines.

1821

Jany. 18th 1821. Was baptized Elizabeth Shires, daughter of John and Sarah Shires. Sponsors Michael Ryan and Jane Wall,

by me P. Baines.

Jany. 18th 1821. Was baptized Thomas Magraw, son of Thomas and C. Magraw. Sponsor Mary Coleman,
                                                    by me P. Baines.
Jany. 19th 1821. Was baptized* Denis McCarthy, son of Patrick and Ellen McCarthy. Sponsors John Donavan and Jane Fenning,
                                                    by me P. Baines.
* sine ceremoniis

Jany. 28. Supplied the ceremonies to the above. P.B.

Feby. 6th 1821. Was baptized Isabella Jane Eyston, daughter of Charles and Teresa Eyston. Sponsors Charles Courtney Esq. and Jane Eyston,
                                                    by me P. Baines.
Feby. 13th 1821. Was baptized William Casey, son of Daniel and Margaret Casey. Sponsors Joseph Spencer and Louisa Dixon,
                                                    by me P. Baines.
Feby. 16th 1821. Was baptized Alexander Coleman, son of John and Mary Coleman, Godmother Susan Byrne,
                                                    by me P. Baines.
Feby. 23d 1821. Was baptized Peter Welsh, son of Peter and Catharine Welsh. Godmother Lucy Freeman,
                                                    by me P. Baines.
Feby. 26th 1821. Was baptized Anthony Mylady, son of Mathew and Emely Mylady. Sponsors Anthony Mylady and Mary Martin,
                                                    by me P. Baines.
March 4th 1821. Was baptized Marianne Thomas, daughter of William and Frances Thomas. Godmother Lucy Freeman,
                                                    by me P. Baines.
March 11th 1821. Was baptized (sub conditione) Ann Slack
                                                    by me P. Baines.
March 22, 1821. Was baptized Henry, Son of Henry and Joanna Thompson, born 19 of Feby. 1821. Spons. Sarah Maria Nokes and Maurice Quin,
                                                    by me Thos. Brindle.
March 25, 1821. Was baptized, William West born Feby. 24, 1821. Son of Jacob and Eliza West. Spos. Eliz. Edwards and James Barrett,
                                                    by me Thos. Brindle.
March 25, 1821. Was baptized William, Son of John and Cath. Hancock, born Feby. 24, 1821. Spons. Bernard Fenning and Eliz. Obrian,
                                                    by me Thos. Brindle.
May 20, 1821. Was baptized James Fanning, son of Bernard and Jane Fanning, born April 28, 1821. Spons. Lydia May and Loftus Fanning,
                                                    by me Thos. Brindle.
May 25, 1821. Was baptized Cornelius Smith, Son of William and Elizabeth Smith, born May 21, 1821. Spons. Lucy Freeman,
                                                    by me Thos. Brindle.
May 25 [? 26] 1821. Was baptized Eliza Smith, Daughter of William and Eliza Smith, born July 12, 1818,
                                                    by me Thos. Brindle.

May 27, 1821. Was baptized Mary Calverwell, Daughter of Thos. and Mary Calverwell, born April 28, 1821. Spons. Hannah Curry,
by me Thos. Brindle.
June 6, 1821. Was baptized John, the Son of John and Elizabeth Piggot, born June 4, 1821. Spons. Mary Thomas,
by me Thos. Brindle.
June 23, 1821. Was baptized James Grace, Son of James and Eliz. Grace, born June 21, 1821. Spons. Lucy Freeman,
by me Thos. Brindle.
June 24th 1821. Was baptized Eliza Carrol, born May 31 last, daughter of John and Margaret Carrol,
by me P. Baines.
July 1st 1821. Was baptized John McKinney, son of William and Anna McKinney, born June 15th last. Godmother Mary Short,
by me P. Baines.
July 11, 1821. Was baptized Eliza, Daughter of Eliza Linton, born June 7, 1821. Spons. Sarah Barns,
by me Thos. Brindle.
July 8th 1821. Was baptized Charles James Wilkes, son of James and Elizabeth Catharine Wilkes, born July 5th. Sponsors Joseph Spencer and Sarah Dealy,
by me P. Baines.
July 10th 1821. Was baptized John Osmunde, son of – and Mary Osmunde. Godmother Elizabeth Osmunde,
by me P. Baines.
July 15th 1821. Was baptized Ann Quin, daughter of Maurice and Elizabeth Quin, born the 12th inst. Sponsors John Ingram and Anna Langley,
by me P. Baines.
July 19th 1821. Was baptized George Brown, son of George and Ann Brown, born May 18th last. Sponsors Maurice Quin and Sarah Clark,
by me P. Baines,
July 21st 1821. Was baptized Mary Flanaghan, born Oct. 12th last, daughter of John and Elizabeth Flanaghan. Godmother Mary Haily,
by me P. Baines.
July 22, 1821. Was baptized John Labarte, son of John and Maria Labarte. Sponsors John Labarte and Jane Ryol,
by me P. Baines.
July 22d 1821. Was baptized Cecilia Elenora Ann Kelly, daughter of William and Maria Kelly. Sponsors Alexander Rorley [?] and Ann Green,
by me P. Baines.
July 27th 1821. Was baptized* Elvira Springford, daughter of Henry and Sarah Springford. Sponsor Mary Parfitt,
by me P. Baines.
* without the ceremonies

Augt. 12th 1821. Was baptized Marianne Peacock, daughter of John

and Margaret Peacock. Godmother Alice Rutherford,
by me P. Baines.

Augt. 13, 1821. Was baptized Wm., Son of John and Ann Kentgen. Spons. Louisa Dixon and Joseph Spencer, born Aug. 3, 1821,
by me Thos. Brindle.

Augt. 19th 1821. Was baptized John Gain, son of William and Sarah Gain,
by me P. Baines.

Augt. 20th 1821. Was baptized William Collins, son of James and Mary Collins (without ceremonies),
by me P. Baines.

Septr. 2, for the above Child the ceremonies were performed. Spons. Charles Coakley and Lucy Ann Cody. Child born Augt. 2d, 1821,
by me Thos. Brindle,

Septr. 2, 1821. Was baptized Ellenor Mine, Daughter of Jeremiah and Ellenor Mine, born Augt. 28, 1821,
by me Thos. Brindle.

Septr. 21, 1821. Was baptized Arthur Farrell, Son of Peter and Eliz. Farrell, born 18 of Septr. 1821. Ann McGinnis and Arthur McGinnis Spons.,
by me Thos. Brindle.

Septr. 23, 1821. Was baptized Eliz. Foutchs — Daughter of Eliz. and Michael Foutchs, born Septr. 21, 1821. Spos. John and Maria Kentgen,
by me Thos. Brindle,

Septr. 30, 1821. Was baptized Joannah Cowley, Daughter of John and Ellen Cowley born Septr. 16, 1821. Spos. Ann Joyce and John Dullivan,
by me Thos. Brindle.

Octr. 25, 1821. Was baptized Ellen, Daughter of John and Ellen Connor, born Oct. 4, 1821. Spons. Jane Wall and Alexander Raw,
by me Thos. Brindle.

Octr. 19th 1821. Was baptized Michl. Henley, Son of William and Harriet Henley. Godmother Martha — (without ceremonies),
by me P. Baines.

Octr. 20th 1821. Was baptized Mary Ann Ward, daughter of James and Catharine Ward. Sponsors John Donevan and Elizabeth Mellard,
by me P. Baines.

Octr. 27th. Was baptized Charles Horgnils, son of — and L. Horgnils (his mother). Sponsors Joseph Spencer and Euphrosine Avril,
by me P. Baines.

Novr. 2d, 1821. Was baptized Francis, son of John and Maria Prirring [or Piran, *added in pencil by Brindle*] born Octr. 27th (without ceremonies),
by me P. Baines.

Novr. 4th 1821. Was baptized John,* the son of Patric and Sarah Mahune. Godmother Mary Pitte,
(* born Octr. 18th of this year) by me P. Baines.

Novr. 11, 1821. Was baptized Sarah Riley, Daughter of John and [Ellen

Riley *crossed out in pencil and* Ann Taylor *written above it*] born Novr,
4, 1821. Spons. Anna Riley and Bridgit Henkins,
                                                              by me T. Brindle.
* see 15th on next page [*next entry but one; note in Baines's hand*].

Novr. 17, 1821. Was baptized Thomas, Son of Thomas and Mary
Blakeley, born Novr. 2, 1821. Spons. Ann Hippisly,
                                                              by me Thos. Brindle.
* Novr. 15th. Was baptized Alfred Felix English, son of John English
Esqr. and Mrs Frances English his wife, born the same day. Sponsors
Denys Scully Esqr. and Miss Elizth. Dalton, by proxy of Thos. Eyre
Esqr. and Miss Georgiana Cary,
                                                              by me P. Baines.
Novr. 24, 1821. Was baptized William, Son of Jane and James
Mulsmack, born Octr. 3, 1821. Sps. Jery. McCarthey,
                                                              by me T. Brindle.
Novr. 29, 1821. Was baptized Michael, Son of Patrick and Dora Shea,
born Novr. 5, 1821. Spons. Maria Lalor,
                                                              by me Thos. Brindle.
Decr. 3, 1821. Was baptized Matilda Galloway, Daughter of Thos. and
Ann Galloway, born Novr. 16, 1821. Spons. Hannah Galloway,
                                                              by me T. Brindle.
Decr. 4, 1821. Was baptized Eleanor Cartlen, Daughter of Patrick and
Sarah Cartlen, born Novr. 24, 1821. Spos. Sarah Brooks,
                                                              by me T. Brindle.
Decr. 6, 1821. Was baptized Christopher Julian, Son of Christopher and
Laura Shell, born Novr. 27, 1821. Spons. Julian and Mary Havez,
                                                              by me Thos. Brindle.
Decr. 9th 1821. Was baptized John, son of Thos. and Ann Brown.
Sponsors Hugh Johnson and Lucy Freeman,
                                                              by me P. Baines.
Decr. 13th 1821. Was baptized Anne Josephine Creagh, daughter of
James Creagh Esqr. and Mary Anne his wife. Sponsors James Nagle
Esqr. (by proxy of James Creagh Esqr.) and Mrs Susannah Nagle,
                                                              by me P. Baines.
Decr. 13, 1821. Was baptized George Taylor Dobson, Son of George
and Lucy Dobson, born Novr. 8, 1821. Spons. Louisa Dixon and
and Joseph Spencer,
                                                              by me Thos. Brindle.
Decr. 17th 1821. Was baptized Edward, son of Charles and Mary
Coakley. Sponsors, Maurice Quin and Ellen Crowley,
                                                              by me P. Baines.
Decr. 23d 1821. Was baptized Frances Ellen, daughter of John and
Henrietta Palmer, born the 17th day of Decr. this year. Sponsors Mr
Francis Gainsford[31] and Miss Ellen Fryer,
                                                              by me P. Baines.

[31]   See Baines's journal, 7 & 9 July 1818 (*C.R.S.*, 65, p. 236); also *C.R.S.*, 65,
p. 88 & note 454.

Here follows a blank page

1822

Jany. 6th 1822. Was baptized Thomas, son of John and Bridget Grogan. Sponsors Alexander Rorty and Catharine Beechwood,

by me P. Baines.

Jany. 25, 1822. Was baptized John, the Son of Ed. and Mary O'Neill, born Jany. 22, 1822. Spons. Ann Hippisley,

by me T. Brindle.

In Baines's hand, apart from signature:
Jany. – 1822. Was baptized Elizabeth Williams, daughter of William and Ann Williams. Godmother Mary Swins,

by me John Morris.[32]

Ceremonies supplied Jan. 27th.

Henceforth in Baines's and Brindle's hands, as signed:
Jany. 27th 1822. Was baptized Louisa Fasana, daughter of Dominic and Sarah Fasana. Sponsors Joseph and Martha Fasana,

by me P. Baines.

Jany. 27th 1822. Was baptized Henry, Son of Cath. and Thos. Bennet,

by me P. Baines.

Jany. 27th 1822. Was baptized Marianne, Daughter of Mark and Elizabeth Dunscombe. Sponsors Hugh Johnson and Lydia May,

by me P. Baines.

Feby. 10th. Was baptized Mary Gahagan, daughter of – and – Gahagan. Sponsors Sarah Gahan and William Gahan,

by me P. Baines.

Feby. 12, 1822. Was baptized John, Son of Thos. and Ann Earls, born Decr. 6, 1821. Spons. Patrick Earls and Sarah Shire,

by me T. Brindle.

Jany. 19. Was baptized (sine ceremoniis) Arthur, Son of Thomas and Mary Adams, born Feby. 23, 1821.

by me Thos. Brindle.

Feby. 17th. Ceremonies supplied by me P. Baines.

Feby. 17th 1822. Was baptized (sub conditione) Edwin, son of Thos. and Mary Adams. Sponsor Margt. Brodrick,

by me P. Baines.

Feby. 17th 1822. Was baptized Catharine, daughter of John and Bridget Provis. Sponsors John Palmer and Elizabeth Quin,

by me P. Baines.

Feby. 24th 1822. Was baptized Thomas, son of James and Charlotte Murphy. Sponsors Joseph Spencer and Louisa Dixon,

by me P. Baines.

March 13, 1822. Was baptized Ann White, Daughter of John and Elizabeth White, born March 8, 1822. Spons. Maria Norris,

by me Thos. Brindle.

---

[32] Perhaps the secular priest, then at Worcester, mentioned in Foley, VII, p. 526, or the Rev. John George Morris (*ibid.*).

March 17, 1822. Was baptized Joseph, Son of William and Ann Fincher, born Novr. 10, 1821. Spons. — (Sine ceremoniis),

by me Thos. Brindle.

March 17, 1822. Was baptized Caroline, daughter of John and Mariana Moach. Sponsors Charles Giralli and Sophia Giralli,

by me P. Baines.

March 17th 1822. Was baptized Ellen Mary, Daughter of Edmund Harvey and Mary Harvey. Sponsors Maurice Quin and Anna Langley,

by me P. Baines.

March 19, 1822. Was baptized Henry, Son of Thomas and Mary Bailie, born 16th March 1822. Spons. Patrick Walsh and Mary Ann Beaumont,

by me Thos. Brindle.

March 19, 1822. Was baptized Charles, Son of John and Sarah Shire, born Feby. 24, 1822. Spons. Thos. Earls and Mary Davies,

by me Thos. Brindle.

March 20, 1822. Was baptized Joseph Shortall, Son of Richd. and Elizabeth Shortal, born March 18th, 1822. Ceremonies supplied March 24th. Sponsors Maurice Quin, Frances Kearns,

by me Thos. Brindle.

March 22d 1822. Was baptized Mary Frances Christina Langton, daughter of Michael Theobald Langton Esqr. and Mary his wife, being born the same day. Sponsors Jeremiah Ryan Esqr. and Mrs Frances Galet,

by me P. Baines.

March 24th 1822. Was baptized Rosina, daughter of Charles and Sophia Geraldi. Sponsors John and Marianne Moach,

by me P. Baines.

March 24th 1822. Was baptized Teresa Marianne Alner, daughter of William and Esther Alner. Sponsors Wilm. Rose and Ursula Laws,

by me P. Baines.

March 24th 1822. Was baptized Thomas, son of Michael and Margaret Ryan. Sponsors Edwd. Keough and Ann Earles,

by me P. Baines.

April 19th. Was baptized Mary, daughter of James and Ellen Murray. Sponsor Mary Grogan,

by me P. Baines.

April 21st. Was baptized (conditionally) William Taylor, a boy of 4 years old, son of Wilm. and Ann Talyor [sic]. Sponsors Hugh Johnson and Ann Curry,

by me P. Baines.

* See next page [note in Baines's hand re 4 entries, dated 3rd to 19th May, inserted between those for 30 July and 18 August].

Barber's hand (2 entries):
1822, May 18th. Was baptized Robert Carpenter, a boy of 2 years old, son of George and Louisa Carpenter. Sponsors Cornelius Landers, Elenor Hazard,

by me L. Barber.

Same day. Was baptized Mary, daughter of John and Margaret Frazer.

Born 13th of May. Sponsor Margaret Brazell,

by me L. Barber.

Henceforth in Baines's and Brindle's hands, as signed:

May 27th 1822. Was baptized Elizabeth, Daughter of Thos. and Bridget Bird, born May 9, 1822. Spons. Sarah Hooper,

by me Thos. Brindle.

June 20, 1822. Was baptized Andrew McCue, Son of Andrew and Mary Tryat [?] McCue, born June 4, 1822. Spons. James Hagarty and Elizabeth Helena Sheen [? Shears],

by me Thos. Brindle.

July 13, 1822. Was baptized William Cary, Son of William and Mary Cary, born June 22d 1822. Spons. Ann Hippisly,

by me Thos. Brindle.

July 30, 1822. Was baptized James Quin, Son of Stephen and Hannah Quin, born July 25, 1822. Spons. Honora Cann [?] and Michael Hart,

by me Thos. Brindle.

* May 3d 1822. Was baptized Martha Lucas, daughter of Charles and Martha Lucas. Sponsors Stephen Quin and Marianne Moratti,

by me P. Baines.

May 5th 1822. Was baptized Harriet, daughter of John and Hester Crowley. Sponsors John Burn and Anna Allworth,

by me P. Baines.

May 5th 1822. Was baptized Elizabeth, daughter of John and Sarah Hale. Sponsors Edwd. Trowbridge and Mary Higstone,

by me P. Baines.

May 19th 1822. Was baptized Ann, daughter of Thos. and Teresa Askins. Sponsors Thomas and Mary Osmond,

by me P. Baines.

Augt. 18th 1822. Was baptized Elizabeth daughter of William and Martha Murray,

by me P. Baines.

Augt. 21, 1822. Was baptized Mary Ann Riordan, Daughter of Sarah and Timothy Riordan, born June 12, 1822. Spons. Eliz. Baily and Thos. O'Niel,

by me Thos. Brindle.

Augt. 25th 1822. Was baptized Edwd., son of John and Mary Macgarrey. Sponsor Edwd. Harris,

by me P. Baines.

Sepr. 1st 1822. Was baptized Sarah, daughter of Wilm. and Elenor Thorpe. Sponsors Thos. and Frances Dilworth,

by me P. Baines.

Septr. 4, 1822. Was baptized Henry, Son of Joseph and Jane Lee. Born Augt. 29, 1822. Spons. Mary Dowding and Thos. Cavenah,

by me Thos. Brindle.

Septr. 4, 1822. Was baptized Catharine, Daughter of Joseph and Jane Lee. Born Augt. 29, 1822. Spons. Jane Wall and Ed. Keough,

by me Thos. Brindle.

Sepr. 18th 1822. Was baptized John, son of Thos. and Mary Calverwell. Sponsor Ann Curry,

by me P. Baines.

Septr. 24, 1822. Was baptized Joseph Moger, Son of William and Mary Moger, born Aug. 20, 1822. Spons. James Moger and Mary Quin,
                                                      by me Thos. Brindle.
Octr. 11, 1822. Was baptized Har't Henly, daughter of Har't and William Henly, born 30 of Sept. 1822. Spons. Fraces [*sic*] Flinn and John Barrett,
                                                      by me Thos. Brindle.
Octr. 13, 1822. Was baptized Robt. Fare, Son of John and Mary Ann Fare, born Septr. 19, 1822. Spons. John and Cath. Martyn,
                                                      by me Thos. Brindle.
Octr. 17, 1822. Was baptized (sine ceremoniis) Frances Reed, Daughter of [*remainder of entry blank*],
                                                      by me Thos. Brindle.
Novr. 8, 1822. Was baptized (sine ceremoniis) James Keough, Son of Thos. and Mary Keough, born Octr. 10, 1822,
                                                      by me Thos. Brindle.
Novr. 13, 1822. Was baptized John Kenworth, Son of Alban and Catharine Kenworth, born [*blank*] 1821. Spons. Eliz. Clarke,
                                                      by me Thos. Brindle.
Novr. 14, 1822. Was baptized Thos. Dexeter, Son of Ed. and Ann Dexeter, born 12 of Octr. 1822. Spons. Mary Short,
                                                      by me Thos. Brindle.
Novr. 23, 1822. Was baptized Eliz. Flinn, Daughter of James and Mary Flinn, born Novr. 18, 1822. Spons. Eliz. Price and James Hagarty,
                                                      by me Thos. Brindle.
Novr. 23, 1822. Was baptized Ann Caroline Barrett, Daughter of John and Ellen Barrett, born Feby. 14, 1822. Spons. Valentine Back,
                                                      by me Thos. Brindle.
Novr. 24th 1822. Was baptized Sophia, daughter of John and Mary Shea. Sponsor Maria Howell,
                                                      by me P. Baines.
Novr. 26th 1822. Was baptized Frances Teresa, daughter of Charles Eyston Esqr. and of Maria Teresa his wife. Sponsors Thos. Moore Esqr. and Mary Courtney,
                                                      by me P. Baines.
Decr. 15, 1822. Was baptized (sine ceremoniis) John Eusebius Rand, Son of Wm. and Ann Rand, born Decr. 14, 1822. Spons. Maria Connor and Richd. Roche,
                                                      by me Thos. Brindle.
Decr. 19, 1822. Was baptized Bridget Taylor, Daughter of James and Mary Taylor, born 5 Decr. 1822. Spons. Ann Hippisly,
                                                      by me Thos. Brindle.
Decr. 22d 1822. Was baptized Thos., Son of Peter and Margaret Brazell. Sponsors Edward Keough and Maria Sivino,
                                                      by me P. Baines.
                              1823
Jany. 12, 1823. Was baptized (sine ceremoniis) William Moran, Son of Jane and Wm. Moran, born Decr. 13, 1823 [*sic*],
                                                      by me Thos. Brindle.

Feby. 2d 1823. Was baptized Agnes Mary, Daughter of Maurice and Elizabeth Quin. Sponsors John Palmer and Jane Curtis,
by me P. Baines.

Feby. 23d 1823. Was baptized* James, son of William and Margaret Gamble (born the 10th. inst.). Sponsors John Crowley and Fanny Ward,
by me P. Baines.

(*without ceremonies)

Feby. 26, 1823. Was baptized Mary Teresa Cowell, Daughter of James Gifford Cowell and his Wife Mary Letitia Frances Cowell, born Jany 20, 1823. Spons. Mary Bushell and Birmingham Nugent,
by me Thos. Brindle.

March 8th 1823. Was baptized Emilia Caroline, daughter of Mary Dodson and Henry Abram, born March 19, 1822. Spons. Mary Short and John McNolty,
by me Thos. Brindle.

March 9th 1823. Was baptized John, son of John and Margaret Peacock. Sponsors John Peacock and Eliza Paillet,
by me P. Baines.

March 9th 1823. Was baptized Abigail, daughter of John and Ann Byrne. Sponsor Charles Coakley,
by me P. Baines.

March 16th 1823. Was baptized James, son of Jacob and Elizabeth Eustace. Sponsors George Home [? Horne] and Elizabeth Barry,
by me P. Baines.

March 16th 1823. Was baptized Catharine, daughter of James and Mary Moren. Sponsor Mary Short,
by me P. Baines.

March 16th 1823. Was baptized (conditionally) James, Son of James and Mary Moren. Sponsor Stephen Quin,
by me P. Baines.

March 16th 1823. Was baptized Thos., son of John and Maria Labarte. Sponsors David and Mary Crowley,
by me P. Baines.

March 21, 1823. Was baptized William Thomas, Son of William and Mary Thomas, born March 13, 1823. Spons. Martha Moon,
by me Thos. Brindle.

March 23, 1823. Was baptized Ellen McCabe, Daughter of John and Mary Ann McCabe, born March 4th, 1823. Spons. Mary Short and James Haggerty,
by me Thos. Brindle.

March 30th 1823. Was baptized Emanuel James, son of Joseph and Mary Meade. Sponsors Henry Cody and Louisa Bailey,
by me P. Baines.

April 7, 1823. Was baptized Eliz. Vaughn, Daughter of David and Margt. Vaughn, born April 6, 1823. Spons. Margt. Brazel and Peter Brazel,
by me Thos. Brindle.

April 12, 1823. Was baptized James Long, son of Eliz. and John Long, born March 7, 1823 (sine ceremoniis),

by me Thos. Brindle.

Barber's hand:
May 17th 1823. Was baptized Mary Elizabeth Spencer, daughter of Joseph and Elizabeth Spencer, born May 16th 1823. Sponsors Martin Biddlecomb and Jane Sturdy,

by me L. Barber.

Brindle's hand:
May 17, 1823. Was baptized Ann Elizabeth Dudden, daughter of Wm. and Ann Dudden, born May 12, 1823. Spons. Wm. Kelly and Eliz. Caroline Green,

by Robt. Pope.[33]

Henceforth in Brindle's and Cooper's hands, as signed:
May 18, 1823. Was baptized Georgina Verstein, Daughter of George and Mary Verstein, born 23d of April 1823. Spons. Wm. Manners,

by me Thos. Brindle.

May 31, 1823. Was baptized Cornelius, Son of Thos. and Frances Dilworth, born May 14, 1823. Spons. Mary Whittaker and Philp Sullivan,

by me Thos. Brindle.

June 25, 1823. Was bapitzed (sine ceremoniis) Susana Portill, Daughter of James and Hannah Portill, born Septr. 5, 1820,

by me Thos. Brindle.

June 25, 1823. Was baptized (sine ceremoniis) Robt. Portill, Son of James and Hannah Portill, born March 5, 1823,

by me Thos. Brindle.

June 27. Was baptized (sine ceremoniis) Ann Palmer, Daughter of Wm. and An Palmer, born June 25, 1823,

by me Thos. Brindle.

Ceremonies of the Above supplied by Mr Ralph Cooper [*Cooper's hand*].

June 28, 1823. Was baptized Honora Acock, Daughter of Richd. and Elizabeth Acock, born 26 of June 1823. Spos. Ann Hippisly,

by me Thos. Brindle.

June 30th 1823. Was baptized Bartholomew Augustin Brown, son of Bartholomew Augustin and Mary Brown, born June 20th 1823. Sponsors Peter Mosse and Anne Hippisly,

by me Ralph Cooper.

June 30, 1823. Was baptized Mary Eliza Laughnan, Daughter of Connel Andrew and Isabella Mary Ann Laughnan, born June 13, 1823. Spons. Mary Byrne and Wm. Shearman,

by me Thos. Brindle.

July 18th. Mary, Daughter of Edward and Jamaima Shehan, was born Feb. 16th 1817 and baptized by me July 18th 1823,

Ralph Cooper.

---

[33] Dom Robert Alexius Pope (*vere* Hoole) O.S.B.; cf. Birt, p. 142.

Jan. 20th 1819. Was born Naomy, daughter of Edward and Jamaima Shehan, and baptized July 18th 1823.

by me Ralph Cooper.

October 17th 1820. Was born John, Son of Edward and Jamaima Shehan, and baptized by me Ralph Cooper, July 18th 1823.

October 16th, 1822. Was born Ann, daughter of Edward and Jamaima Shehan, and baptized July 18th 1823,

by me Ralph Cooper.

July 15th 1823. Was born Sebastian Swithune Allnar, Son of William and Esther Allnar. Sponsors Rich. Grey and Sarah Harman and baptized by me Ralph Cooper, July 20th 1823.

July 21, 1823. Was baptized Harriett Jenner Eccles, Daughter of John Henry and Harriett Eccles (olim Harriett Jenner), born June 19, 1823. Spons. Henry and Mary Brettorgh,

by me Thos. Brindle.

July 22d 1823. Was baptized (sine ceremoniis) Ed. Hill, Son of John and Mary Hill, born Septr. 29, 1820,

by me Thos. Brindle.

July 22, 1823. Was baptized (sine ceremoniis) John Hill, Son of John and Mary Hill, born Novr. 30, 1822,

by me Thos. Brindle.

Aug. 4, 1823. Was baptized Mary Hill, daughter of John and Mary Hill, born May 25, 1814,

by me Thos. Brindle.

Augt. 5, 1823. Was baptized William, Son of Solomon and Maria Duffitt, born Aug. 2, 1823. Spos. Martha Moon and Jos. Spencer,

by me Thos. Brindle.

Augt. 14, 1823. Was baptized Edmnd. Henry Denny, Son of Danl. and Maria Denny, born July 25, 1823. Spons. Mary Frances Havez and John Chaulonneau,

by me Thos. Brindle.

Aug. 10th 1823. Was baptized Leonora Elizabeth Kelly, daughter of William and Anna Maria Kelly, born Aug. 3d 1823. Sponsors Patrick Madding and Elizabeth Green,

by me Ralph Cooper.

Aug. 25th 1823. Was baptized Elena Lawley, daughter of Joseph and Charlotte Lawley, born July 29th 1823. Spons. Fidele Lawley and Laura Shell,

by me Ralph Cooper.

1823, Aug. 26th. Was baptized John Shay, Son of Patrick and Dorothy Shay, born on the 2d of August 1823 and Sponsors being Michael Lalor and Mary Short,

by me Ralph Cooper,

Aug. 31, 1823. Was baptized James Tognoni, Son of John and Hannah Tognoni, born May 9th 1823, Josue Moretti and Mary Anne Moretti being Spons.,

by me Ralph Cooper.

Septr. 2, 1823. Was baptized Mary Teresa Clifford, Daughter of the Honble. Charles Thomas Clifford and his wife Teresa Clifford (olim Maxwell), born Septr. 1st 1823. Spons. Charles, Lord Clifford (Proxy M. Langton Esqr.) and Teresa Appolonia Constable Maxwell (proxy Mrs Langton),

by me Thos. Brindle.
Sep. 14th 1823. Was baptized Anne Fautsch, Daughter of Michael and Elizabeth Fautsch, born Sep. 10th 1823. Spons. John Kentgens and Mary Anne Kentgens,

by me R. Cooper.
Septr. 20, 1823. Was baptized Wm. Gane, Son of Wm. and Sarah Gane, born Octr. 31, 1823. Spons. Peter Brazell and Sarah Magrath,

by me Thos. Brindle.
Septr. 27, 1823. Was baptized Elizabeth, Daughter of Edward and Mary O'Neill, born Septr. 23, 1823. Spons. Rogr. Hagan,

by me Thos. Brindle.
Septr. 27, 1823. Was baptized Hugh McClockey, Son of Henry and Ann McClocky, born Septr. 15, 1823. Spons. Rogr. Hagan,

by me Thos. Brindle.
Oct. 10th 1823. Was Baptized Thos. William Stephens, Son of Thos. and Mary Stephens, born June 24th 1817. Spons. Patrick Welsh and Catharine Welsh,

by me Ralph Cooper.
Octr. 24, 1823. Was baptized John Coney, Son of John and Mary Coney, born Octr. 2d 1823. Spons. Ann Connor and Cornel Landers,

by me Thos. Brindle.
Oct. 30th 1823. Was baptized James Collins, Son of James and Mary Collins. Spons. James Harrington and Elis. Fautch. (Born Oct. 26th 1823.)

by me Ralph Cooper.
Nov. 2st [sic] 1823. Was baptized John Crowley, born on 16th of October and supplied with the ceremonies on the following Morning. Parents John and Helen Crowley. Spons. Thos. Choice and Marg. Baily.

by me Ralph Cooper.
Novr. 9, 1823. Was baptized Mary Barbara Cousins, Daughter of Henry and Elizabeth Cousins born Octr. 30, 1823. Spons. Barbara Cooper and John Palmer,

by me Thos. Brindle.
Cooper's hand:
Catharine Wray was baptized Oct. 30th (Sine Ceremoniis) – (died soon after).

Henceforth in Brindle's and Cooper's hands, as signed:
November 16th 1823. James Long was supplied with Baptismal Ceremonies, Son of John and Eliz. Long. Spons. Patrick Johnson and Helen Ohier,

by me Ralph Cooper.
November 19th 1823. Was baptized (Sine Cerem.) Elizabeth Bailie,

by me R. Cooper.

1823, October 31st. Was baptized James Manning. And supplied with Ceremonies Novber 23d. Born 18th of October 1823. Parents John and Mary Manning. Spos. Joseph Varga and Sarah Magrah,

by me Ralph Cooper.

Decr. 3, 1823. Were baptized John and Patrick Field, sons of John and Ann Field, born Novr. 30, 1823. Spons. Mrs. Hippisly,

by me Thos. Brindle.

Decr. 7, 1823. Ceremonies supplied to Eliz. Bailie, Daughter of Thos. and Mary Bailie. Spons. Robt. Walsh and Mary Ann Beaumant (Child born Novr. 5th 1823.),

by me Thos. Brindle.

Decr. 14, 1823. Was baptized James FitzPatrick, Son of Philip and Mary FitzPatrick, born Novr. 23, 1823. Spons Jos. and Eliz. Spencer,

by me Thos Brindle.

Decr. 16, 1823. Was baptized Robt. Henry Brown, Son of George and Hannah Brown, born Novr. 26, 1823. Spons. Ed. O'Neil and Joan Henwright,

by me Thos. Brindle.

Decr. 18, 1823. Was baptized Alfred Basil, Son of John and Frances English his Wife, born Decr. 18, 1823. Spons. George Eyston Esqr. (Proxy Jo. Eyston Esqr.) and Miss Eliz. Dalton (proxy Miss Mary Jane Eyston),

by me Thos. Brindle.

Decr. 19, 1823. Was baptized Mary Lions, daughter of Joseph and Margt. Lions, born Octr. 11, 1823. Spons. Joseph Williams and Sarah Magrath,

by me Thos. Brindle.

Dec. 26th 1823. Was baptized Maria Louisa Threshod [*sic*], Daughter of Joseph and Maria Threshold, born July 21st 1823. Sponz. Angelo Threshold and Maria Anne Moretti,

by me R. Cooper.

Decr. 27, 1823. Was baptized Hellen Tallis, Daughter of George and Ann Tallis, born Octr. 24, 1823. Spons. Teresa Tucker and Ed. Keough,

by me Thos. Brindle.

Decr. 28, 1823. Was baptized Mary Ann Burchell, Daughter of George and Sarah Burchell, born Feby. 1823. Spons. Charles Porch and Mary Rickets,

by me Thos. Brindle.

Decr. 28, 1823. Was baptized Maria Doyle, Daughter of Patrick Doyle and Maria Lelor, born Decr. 7, 1823. Spons. Pat. Shea,

by me Thos. Brindle.

Jany. 6th 1824. Helena Rolfe was supplied the Ceremonies. Daughter of Abel and Anne Rolfe. Having been baptized at Horton by Mr Birdsall [*in Cooper's hand*] .

Jany. 12th 1824. Was baptized Helen Read (Sine Cer.).

Jan 16th. The Above Child was Supplied the Cerem., Mary Short and

John Short being Sponz. The Father Francis and Mother Helen Read,
by me Ralph Cooper.
Jany. 15, 1824. Was baptized Edward Gadis, Son of Robert and Julia
Gadis, born December 15th 1823. Sponz. Joseph Spencer and Hanah
Dixon,
by me R. Cooper.
Jany. 25, 1824. Was baptized Charles, Son of Charles and Mary Coakley,
born Jany. 15, 1824. Spons. Margt. Baily and David Crowley,
by me Thos. Brindle.
Jany. 25, 1824. Was baptized Elizabeth, Daughter of John and Sarah
Hales, born Jany. 15, 1824. Spons. Mary Kingston and Joseph Abbot,
by me Thos. Brindle.
Jany. 27, 1824. Was baptized Bridget, Daughter of Dennis and Elizabeth
Lannaghan, born Jany. 21, 1824. Spons. Patrick Dealey,
by me Thos. Brindle.
Feby, 1, 1824. Was baptized Augustine, Son of James and Eliza Wilks,
born Jany. 31, 1824. Spons. Louisa Dixon and Ed. Keough,
by me Thos. Brindle.
Feby. 1, 1824. Was baptized Agnes, Daughter of James and Eliza Wilks,
born Jany. 1, [sic, see previous entry] 1824. Spons. Hannah Dixon and
Joseph Spencer,
by me Thos. Brindle.
Feby. 8, 1824. Was baptized Thos. Shortall, Son of Richd. and Eliz.
Shortall, and born Feby. 1, 1824. Spons. M. Quin and Frances Quin,
by me Thos. Brindle.
Feby. 15th 1824. Was baptized Michael Byrne, Son of John and Anne
Byrne, born 13th of Jany. 1824. Spons. Daniel Tagny and Mary Hinkins,
by me R. Cooper.
Feb. 17th 1824. Was baptized (sine Cer.) Joseph Skannal* and on the
above day also, James Joyce (Sine Cer.),
*[See 7 March]   by me R. Cooper.
Feb. 24th 1824. Was baptized Elizabeth Byrne (Sine Cerem.)
by me R. Cooper.
Feb. 27th 1824. Helen Smith, daughter of Wm. and Helen Smith, was
supplied the ceremonies. Mary Short God Mother. Also was baptized
conditionally
by me R. Cooper.
Feb. 29th 1824. Was baptized Margaret Ward, born Feb. 10th 1824.
Son of James and Frances Ward. Sponz. Wm. Gambell and Susanna
Smith,
by me R. Cooper.
Feb. 29th 1824. Mary Ryan, born Feb. 8th, was baptized. Daughter of
Michael and Margaret Ryan. Sponz. Henry Cody and Eliza Barry,
by me R. Cooper.
March 7th 1824 was baptized Anne MacKarti, daughter of Charles and
Caroline MacKarti, born Feb. 18th. Sponz. Dennis [illegible — ?
Dusckin] and Frances Wall,
by me R. Cooper.

March 7th 1824. Was Supplied with Ceremonies Joseph Skannal*. Sponz. Lydia – and Hugh Johnson,
*[see 17 February] by me R. Cooper.
March 15th 1824. Was baptized Esther Obrien, Daughter of Peter and Mary Obrien, born Feby. 19th 1824. Sponz. Richard Shortill and Arabella Kelly,

by me R. Cooper.
March 28th 1824. Was baptized William Edwards, Son of Wm. and Sarah Edwards, born March 24th 1824. Wm. Rose and Elizabeth Abbot Spons.,

by me R. Cooper.
April 5, 1824. Was baptized Charles Murray, Son of John and Mary Murray, born March 19, 1824. Spos. Stephen Quin and Ellen Crowley,
by me Thos. Brindle.
April 20, 1824. Was baptized Dorothea Mary Louisa La Bigne, Daughter of Aimable Prosper and Mary Ann La Bigne, born April 1, 1824. Spons. Monsieur Louis Jacques La Bigne and Miss Dorothea Bellingham. (Proxies John Palmer and Ann Hippisley),

by me Thos. Brindle.
April 18th 1824. Was supplied with ceremonies Catharine Macknolti, born 31st of March 1824 and baptized April 13th. (Sine Cer.). Daughter of John and Sarah Macknolti. Spons. James Macknolti and Catharine – (proxies John and Letitia Macknolti),

by me R. Cooper.
April 20th 1824. Was baptized (Sine Cer.) (at Horton near Sodbury) James Gregory Thompson, born 12th of March 1824. Son of James and Anne Thompson. Spons. Elizabeth Rodway,

by me R. Cooper.
April 23, 1824. Was baptized John, Son of John and Rose Bennon, born March 27, 1824. Spons. Martha Steen and Jos. Moratti,

by me Thos. Brindle.
April 25th 1824. Was supplied with ceremonies Sarah Reed, Daughter of Richard and Margaret Reed, born on the 18th Feb. and baptized (Sine Cer.) April 13th 1824, Sponsor being Margaret Reynolds,

by me R.M. Cooper,
April 25th 1824. Was baptized Sarah Smith, born April 3d 1824 daughter of Hugh and Sarah Smith, Spons. being James Calahan and Deborah Calahan,

by me R.M. Cooper.
April 27th 1824. Henriette Gosselin la Mère, le Père Louis Adamo, l'Enfant Louis Henry Gosselin. This child was baptized on the above day, Godmother being Anne Hipisley (the Child was born [blank] 1824),

by me R. Cooper.
April 27th 1824. Was baptized Michael Melone, born 24th April 1824. Cornelius and Anna Melone Parents. Sponss. James Brown and Honoria Cronine,

by me R. Cooper.

30th of April 1824. Was baptized (Sine Cer.) Mary Enright,
> by me R.M. Cooper.

May 9th 1824. Was baptized Sophia Elizabeth Murphy, daughter of James and Charlotte Murphy, born April 10th 1824. Sponss. Salvadore Michione and Anna Maria Benfield,
> by me R.M. Cooper.

May 18, 1824. Was baptized Osmund William, Son of Christopher and Laura Shell, born May 10, 1824. Spons. Sarah Magrath,
> by me Thos. Brindle.

May 22d 1824. Was baptized Margaret Caroline Felicia Langton, Daughter of Michael Theobald Langton Esqr. and of his Wife Mary Langton, born May 21, 1824. Spons. Lieut. Colonel Charles Stonor[34] (Proxy Jer'ah Rayn Esqr.) and Mrs Ryan, the Child's Maternal Grand-Mother,
> by me Thos. Brindle.

May 24, 1824. Was baptized Hugh Crawford, Son of David and Margt. Crawford, born May 8, 1824. Spons. Eliz. Ordley,
> by me Thos. Brindle.

May 24, 1824. Was baptized Emma Brown, Daughter of Thos. and Ann Brown, born May 3, 1824. Spons. Richd. Shortall and Eliz. Batten,
> by me Thos. Brindle.

May 25, 1824. Was baptized (sine Ceremoniis) Mary Symes, Daughter of Charles and Emma Symes, born May 23d 1824,
> by me Thos. Brindle.

June 7, 1824. Was baptized John, Son of Jeremiah and Joana Dealy, born May 6, 1824. Spons. John Harding and Mary Meland,
> by me Thos. Brindle.

June 14th 1824. Was supplied with ceremonies Mary Henright, daughter of Jeremiah and Esther Henright. Spons. Josua Moretti and Mary Anne Moretti,
> by me R. Cooper.

July 1st 1824. Was baptized Anne Teresa Mitchell, born 9th of Jan. 1824, daughter of William and Caroline Mitchell. Spons. Helena Young,
> by me R. Cooper.

July 7th 1824. Was baptized Elleanora Luisa, daughter of Joseph and Eliza Spencer, born July 6, 1824. Sponsors John Doughty and Luisa Doughty,
> by me Thos. Brindle.

July 10, 1824. Was baptized Catharine, daughter of Peter and Mary Cunningham, born July 8, 1824. Spons. Mrs Ann Hippisly,
> by me Thos. Brindle.

July 11, 1824. Was baptized Martin, Son of John and Bridget Grogan, born June 8, 1824. Sponsors Martin Egan and Honoria Egan,
> by me Thos. Brindle.

July 12, 1824. Was baptized Teresa daughter of Charles and Martha

---

[34] Of the Spanish army; son of Henry Stonor of San Lucar (J. Stonor, *Stonor*, genealogical table facing p. 320).

Lucas, born June 28, 1824. Sponsors Mary Ann Marath and Joseph
Virga [?],

by me Thos. Brindle.

July 11th 1824. Were baptized twin Sisters (Sine Cer.) Joanna Fair and
Mary Anne Fair,* being born the same day,
*[see also 8 August]   by me R.M. Cooper.

July 15th 1824. Was baptized Thos. Randle, Son of Thos. and Rosa
Randle, born June 22d 1824. Sponzor Peter Cunningham,

by me R. Cooper.

July 18th 1824. Was baptized Caroline Kinching, born 8th of July
1824, daughter of John and Anne Kinching. Sponzors Wm. Kelly and
Hannah Dixon,

by me R. Cooper.

On the above day was baptized Elizabeth Keoughbourke, Daughter of
Thos. and Mary Keoughbourke, born 5th of July. Spons. Michael
Kearney and Anne Hippisley,

by me R. Cooper.

On the same day was also baptized Margaret Creon, daughter of George
and Margaret Creon, born on the 27th of June. Spons. Arabella Kelly,

by me R. Cooper.

25th of July 1824. Was baptized Edward Kentgens, Son of John Jones
and Mary Anne Kentgens, born 11th of July 1824. John Kentgens and
Anne Kentgens, Sponsors,

by me R. Cooper.

On the above day was baptized David Crowley, born 22d of July 1824.
Son of John and Esther Crowley. Spons. David Crowley and Hannah
Longley,

by me R. Cooper.

On the above day was baptized Helen Quin, born 22d of July 1824,
daughter of Stephen and Ann Quin. Spons. Alexander Rorty and
Elizabeth Abbot,

by me R. Cooper.

On the above day was baptized Elizabeth Anne Ohens, daughter of
William and Anne Ohens. Born 1st of June 1824. Spons. Anne Hipisley,

by me R. Cooper.

On the above day was also baptized Philip Riley, Son of Bernard and
Mary Riley, born 17th of July. Spons. Sarah and Michael Magrath,

by me R. Cooper.

July 31, 1824. Was baptized Elizabeth, daughter of Michael and Lea
Gorman, born July 2, 1824 (sine ceremoniis),   by me Thos. Brindle.

July 31, 1824. Was baptized Pauline Frances Chilton English, daughter
of Robt. English and his Wife [blank] English, born the same day.
Sponsors John English and Winifred English,   by me Thos. Brindle.

August 1st 1824. Was baptized Thomas Moger, born July 27th 1824,
son of Mary and Wm. Moger. Anne Moger and Martin Moger Spons.

by me R. Cooper.

Aug. 6th 1824. Was baptized Charles John Piren, Son of John and Mary Piren, born Aug. 5th 1824. Spons. Ann Galway and Cornelius Landers,
by me R. Cooper.
Aug. 8th 1824. Joanna Helena Fair and Mary Anne Fair, twin Sisters,* were supplied the Ceremonies. Spons. John Martin and Anne Sullivan to the first and Wm. Martin and Helen Barnet Spons. to the Second,
*[see also 11 July]
by me R. Cooper

Augt. 11th 1824. Was baptized Helena Cecilia, daughter of John and Henrietta Maria Palmer, born Aug. 7, 1824. Sponsors Cumberland William Manners[35] and Helena McCarthy,
by me Thos. Brindle.
Aug. 20th 1824 [altered from 1820]. Was baptized Patrick Doyle, Son of Patrick and Anne Doyle, born Aug. 18th 1824. Sposs. Patrick Grime and Mary Mackhugh,
by me R.M. Cooper.
Aug. 15th 1824. Was baptized John Cullins, born July 28th 1824, Son of John and Hannah Cullins. Sponss. Patrick Dauling and Frances Wall,
by me R. Cooper.
Aug. 24th 1824. Was baptized Edward Joseph Hebden, born Aug. 23d 1824, son of Edward and Anne Teresa Hebden. Spons. Lucy Willoughby and Wm. Berington,
by me R. Cooper.
Aug. 29th 1824. Was baptized Helen Keating, born Aug. 15th 1824, daughter of Thomas and Margaret Keating. Spons. James Terris and Catharine Terris,
by me R. Cooper.
Aug. 30th 1824. Was baptized Edward Davis, born August 8th 1824, son of Thomas and Catharine Davis. Spons. Anne Church and Richar [sic] Shortall,
by me R. Cooper.
September 5th 1824. Was baptized Ferdinand Baily, son of Alexandrina and David Baily, born August 4th 1824. Spons. Lucy Willoby,
by me R. Cooper.
September 5th 1824. Was baptized John Hening, born 31st of August 1824. Son of Timothy and Mary Hennings [sic]. Spons. Richard Shortill and Anne Hipisley,
by me R.M. Cooper.
September 6th 1824. Was baptized Thos. Green born Son of Thos. and Mary Green. Spons. Elizabeth Smith,
by me R.M. Cooper.
September 12th 1824. Was John Walshannuck baptized, born Sep. 6th 1824. Son of James and Jane Walshannuck. Spons. James Walshannuck and Martha Moon,
by me R.M. Cooper.
September 13th 1824. Was baptized John James Malligan, born December

---

[35]   See Baines's journal, note 75 (in C.R.S., 65, p. 213).

7th 1823. Son of James and Sarah Malligan. Sponsr. James Haggarthy and his wife Honoria Haggarthy,

by me R.M. Cooper.

In a different hand, presumably Platt's:
September 19, 1824. Was baptized Emma Mulligan, born 4th of June 1820. Daughter of James and Sarah Mulligan. Sponsr. Thos. O'Neill, Honoria Haggarty,

by me Robert Platt.[36]

Henceforth in Brindle's and Cooper's hands, as signed:
October 3d 1824. Was baptized Mary Anne Connor, daughter of John and Helen Connor, born September 22d 1824. Spons. John Toner and Mary Arundell,

by me R.M. Cooper.

Octr. 7, 1824. Was baptized James, son of Solomon and Maria Duffet, born Octr. 4, 1824. Spons. Joseph Spencer and Martha Moon,

by me Thos. Brindle.

Octr. 10, 1824. Was baptized Mary Callwell, daughter of Thos. and Mary Calwell [*sic*], born Septr. 6, 1824. Spons. Peter Brazil and Maria Cyvans,

by me Thos. Brindle.

Octr. 13, 1824. Was baptized Joseph, Son of Ed. and Ann Dexeter, born Septr. 11, 1824,

by me Thos. Brindle.

Octr. 17, 1824. Was baptized Michael, Son of Hugh and Ann Reiley, born Septr. 30, 1824. Spons. Eliza Lambert

by me Thos. Brindle.

November 1st 1824. Was baptized Eliza Howard, born Oct. 16th 1824. Daughter of John and Elizabeth Howard. Peter Braize and Sarah Gaine, Sponss.,

by me R.M. Cooper.

November 2d 1824. Was baptized Wm. Thorp, born October 23d 1824. Son of Wm. and Helen Thorp. Spons. Anne Connor and George Head,

by me R.M. Cooper.

November 8th 1824. Was baptized Charles Leigh, born Oct. 1824. Son of Joseph and Jane Leigh. Spons. Stephen Quin and Arabella Kelly,

by me R.M. Cooper.

Dec. 5th. Wm. Bird was baptized. Born Novr. 10th. Son of Thos. and Bridget. Spons. Alexander MacDonald and Catharine Hancock,

by me R.M. Cooper.

Jan. 1st 1825. George Blinkworth was baptized (sine cer.), born in November 1824,

by me R.M. Cooper.

1825 [*entry illegibly deleted, followed by baptism dated 9 June 1819, here printed on p. 159*].

---

[36] Recently ordained and newly arrived from Rome to take charge of the Axminster mission (Oliver, pp. 381-2).

Mortuary Register from December 3rd 1809 [*at opposite end of register, turned upside down, starting in Calderbank's hand.*]

Names	Age	Residence	Death		
Thos. Dutton	65	Twerton	Decr	13th	1809
Mrs Anne Welch	67	Aylsbury	Jany	15th	1810
Anne Geoghan		Bath	Jany	4th	1810
Miss Maria Constable	16	Burton³⁷	Feby.	24th	1810
Margt. McGill	84	Bath	March	7th	
Barbara Pierce	47	Bath	March 25.		
Mr V. Bauggini [?]	62	Bath	April	8th	
Master Fred Knapp		Bath	April	8th	
Mrs Mgt. Quinn	77	Weston	April 23.		
Michl. O'Brien	53	Bath	June	12th	
Jeremias Bergen		Bath	July	12th	
Dominic Antonio Quintas		Bath	July	13th	
[*blank*] Kelly		Bath	Aug.	23d	
Thos. Smith	infant	Bath	Septr. 10.		
Cath. Dto.	30	Bath	Septr. 11th		
Helen Barry	51	Bath	Septr. 16th		
Mr Ed. English	81	Bath	Octr.	1st	
Mr Jos.[? Jas.] Murphy	72	Bath	Novr.	5th	
Hannah Clapton	18	Bath	Decr.	1st	
Mr Jos. [? Jas.] Sanderson	39	Liverpool	Decr.	3rd	
John Dempsey	81	Bath	Decr.	19th	
Ainsworth's hand:					
Mary Gill	49	Bath	Feb.	1st	1811
Matthew Arundel	1½	Bath	Feb.	3d	1811
Henrietta Fryer	14	Bath	Feb.	5th	1811
Calderbank's hand:					
Mrs Mary Knapp	36	Bath	Feby.	17th	1811
Christina Loveless	1½[?]	Bath	Feby.	19,	1811
Mary Dealy		Bath	March 15,		1811
Mrs Chetwynde	75	Bath			
John Rozanna		Bath	May	4th	1811
Elizth. Best		Bath	May	12th	1811
Virginia Cayeau	7	Bath	May	30th	1811
Wm. Bonsford [? Bourford]	infant	Bath	June	24,	1811
Anne McDale	70	Bath	July	14th	1811
Mary Rose	65	Bath	Septr. 2nd		1811
Thos. McGuire	17	Bath	Septr. 13,		1811
John Wogan		Bath	Septr. 15,		1811
Bridget Guillan	50	Bath	Septr. 29,		1811
Rowley Ryan	37	Bath	Octr. 30th		1811
Wm. Kingman	72	Bath	Octr. 30th		1811
Jas. Groves	23	Bath	Novr. 27,		1811
Peter Higgins	40	Bath	Decr.	3d	1811
Dr John Toole	50	Dublin	Decr.	6th	1811

³⁷ Burton Constable, Yorks. (East Riding); see *C.R.S.*, 1, p. 216; *C.R.S.*, 12, p. 109 and for this family, H. Aveling, *Post-Reformation Catholicism in East Yorkshire* (E. Yorks. Local History Society, York, 1960); *C.R.S. Monograph 2.*

Names	Age	Residence	Death	
Mary Crowley	92	Bath	Decr. 11th	1811
Thos. Ketcherside	69	Bath	Decr. 25,	1811
Anthony Smith		Bath	Jany. 30,	1812
Ainsworth's hand:				
Anne Bradshaw	67	Bath	March 27th	1812
Calderbank's hand:				
Mrs C. O'Brien[38]		Bath	March 15,	1812
Richd. O'Connor		Bath	April 8,	1812
John Alpin		Bath	April 10,	1812
Jas. Lyons		Bath	April 21st	1812
Margt. Lowther	31	Bath	June 2nd	1812
Timothy O'Brien Esq.[39]	68	Bath	Augt. 13th	1812
Owen Mooney	68	Bath	Novr. 23,	1812
Jas. Bugley [?] Esqr.	71	Bath	Decr. 16th	1812
John Ferrers [?]	45	Bath	Decr. 29,	1812
Wm. Lawton	7	Bath	Jany. 9th	1813
Edwd. Wogan		Bath	Jany. 10th	1813
Michael Lawton	4	Bath	Decr. 26,	1812
Elijah Odber	42	Bath	Jany. 10,	1813
[*blank*] Nutall		Bath		
Mrs Margt Trapp[40]	74	Bath	Jany. 27,	1813
G. Butler Esqr.[41]		Bath	Jany. 30th	1813
Wm. Fisher	35	Bath	March 14,	1813
H. Clifford Esqr.	44	London	April 22,	1813
Helen Donahue	69	Bath	May 9th	1813
Philip Mulican [?]	36	Bath	May 14th	1813
Mary Short	4	Bath	May 23d,	1813
Edwd. Short	2	Bath	June 6,	1813
Dorothy Molland	67	Bath	June 13th	1813
George Taylor Esqr.[42]	44	Bath	July 5th	1813
Mrs Elizth. Bishop[43]	75	Bath	July 19th[?]	1813
Mr Garret Farrel	68	Bath	Nov. 23,	1813
Paul Barbe		Twerton	Jany. 3,	1814
Mrs I. Clarkson		Bath	Jany. 3,	1814
John Kelly	50 [?]	Bath	Jany. 12,	1814
Judith Wall		Bath	Feby. 3,	1814
Revd. R. Ainsworth[44]	50	Bath	Feby. 5th	1814

[38]   Christian name Catherine (*C.R.S.*, 12, p. 117).

[39]   In *C.R.S.*, 12, p. 118.

[40]   In *C.R.S.*, 12, p. 120, as "Trapps".

[41]   *ibid.*, as "late of Bath"; Christian name George.

[42]   *ibid.*, p. 121; also *C.R.S.*, 63, *passim* and J. Gillow, *The Haydock Papers* (1888) p. 132 where he is wrongly stated to have died "about Christmas, 1813".

[43]   *C.R.S.*, 12, p. 121, as "late of Bath". A Bath death not included in this mortuary list is that of the Rev. John Sanderson in October 1813 (*ibid.*, p. 122; Foley, VII, p. 684).

[44]   See *C.R.S.*, 65, pp. 72, 80-81. Buried in the vaults beneath the Old Orchard Street chapel (now a masonic hall).

Names	Age	Residence	Death		
J.[?] Stonor[?] Esq.	43	Bath	Feby.	11,	1814
Mary Coffee	52	Bath	March	16,	1814
Michael Carr	76	Bath	March	16,	1814
Mrs Margt. Plunkett	90	Bath	April	8th	1814
Marquis de Sommery[45]	43	Bath	April	13,	1814
Mr Alexander Henry John					
Vincent de Cayeau	25	Bath	April	28,	1814
Mr Piere Francois Benoit	25	London,	May	11th	1814
Berthe		formerly			
		of Calais			

Rishton's hand;

Walter Lacon Esq.[46]	75	Bath	May	25th	1814
Mary Burke	25	Bath	July	16th	1814
Jeremiah Donaghue	30	Bath	Septr.	11th	1814
Philip Nunan Esqr.	62	Kerry	Septr.	23rd	1814
Ellenor Lawton	34	Bath	Octr.	23rd	1814
Richd. Batterby	7	Bath	Novr.	13th	1814
Chas. Metralcourt	75	Bath	Novr.	12th	1814
James Collingridge	75	Wootton[47]	Novr.	24th	1814
Thos. Maran	38	Ireland	Jany.	4th	1815[48]
Anne Quin	42	Ireland	Apl.	29th	1815
Anne Church	73	Bath	May	14th	1815
Wm. Brady	48	Bath	May	20th	1815
Cath. Henriet Cole	35	Bath	May	31st	1815
Simon Ryan	60	Bath	June	3rd	1815
Bernard Dowlan	76	Bath	June	22nd	1815
Thos. O'Brian	17	Bath	July	1st	1815
Nicholas Dowling	88	Bath	July	5th	1815
John Brady	43	Bath	May	10th	1815
John Sullivan		Bath	July	15th	1815
John Short	75	Englishbatch	July	10th	1815

Calderbank's hand:

Susan Holland	33	Bath	Augst.	2,	1815
Margt. Slade	62	Bath	Augst.	9,	1815
Henry Cooper	Infant	Bath	Aug.	10,	1815
Mary Const. Dalton	70	Bath	Aug.	12,	1815
Miss Cathne. Fleming	68	Bath	Sept.	15,	1815
Saml. Odber	70	Bath	Octr.	11,	1815
Charles Callahan	63	Bath	Nov.	11th	1815

[45]   Buried in vaults (memorial tablet).

[46]   Buried in vaults (memorial to Armand Dumesniel, Marquis de Sommery and his wife, Adelaide).

[47]   Wootton Bassett, Wilts.

[48]   An 1815 death not in this mortuary list is that of Mary Chichester who died in Queen Square, Bath, and to whom there is a monument in the Catholic chapel at Marton, Yorks. (E. Riding); see Sir N. Pevsner, *Yorkshire: York and the East Riding* (1972) p. 312. The lower part of the monument records that her daughter Mary MacDonnell, Lady Constable, died in Bath ten years later and was buried in the vaults beneath the Old Orchard St. chapel (where there is also a memorial to her).

Names	Age	Residence	Death		
Mary Manning	32	Stranger	Novr.	12,	1815
Elizth. Hutchinson	73	Bath	Novr.	18th	1815
Win'd Feltham		Bath	Decr.		1815
Mary Rowe	4	Bath	Jany.	11,	1816
Martha Townsend	69	Bath	Jany.	1,	1816
Wm. Blakeley	15	Bath	Jany.	22,	1816
Mrs Frances Crouch[49]		Bath	Feby.	5,	1816
Edwd. Murphy	58	Bath	March 23,		
Mr John Webb	55	Weston [?]	April	7th	

Here follow, crossed-out, the Callahan [spelt Callan], Feltham [Felton] and Townsend entries, already entered above. These, and the next two, are in Rolling's hand:

Names	Age	Residence	Death		
Mary Wall	35	Bath	April	27-16 [i.e. 1816]	
Mr B. Brickman	71	Bath	May	3-16	
Calderbank's hand:					
Cathne. McGuir	19	Bath	July	6th	1816
Elizth. Dutton		Twerton	July		1816
Mary Green		Farmborough	July		1816
Henry Beaumont		Bath	Nov.		1816
Thos. Slade	55	Bath	Novr.		1816
John Bidcon [?]	63	Bath	Nov.		1816
Rishton's hand:					
Jas. Maguire		Bath	Nov.		1816
Calderbank's hand:					
Daniel Kirwen	55	Bath	Decr.	4th	1816
[blank] Brown		Bath			1816
Richd. Abbott	55	Bath	Decr.	24,	1816
Martha Silvey	42	Bath	Decr.	29,	1816
Honob. Agnes FitzWilliams[50]		Bath	Jany.	15,	1817
Edwd. Gillhespy	39	Bath	Jany.	15,	1817
Mary Bence	77	Bath	Jany.	20,	1817
Elizth. McCatey	57	Bath	Feby.	18,	1817
Margt. Palmer	43	Bath	Feby.	19,	1817
Timothy Lynch	63	Bath	Feby.	23d	1817
Mathew Molloy	43	Bath	April	4th	1817
John Mansfield Esqr.	64	Ireland	April	15,	1817
Mary Hughes	72	Bath	April	30th	1817
Mary Feasanna	37	Bath	July	3d	1817
Baines's hand:					
An Irishman	about 33	Northampton St., Bath	Aug. or beging. of Sep.		1817

[49] In *C.R.S.*, 12, p. 133.

[50] *ibid.*, p. 137.

Names	Age	Residence	Death
An infant of Mrs Strutter[51]		North Parade B.	abt. the 10th of Sepr. 1817
Mrs Butler		Walcot St. Bath	Octr. 1817
Mr Phelan[52]		South P. Bath	Octr. 28th 1817
Mr Ryan[53]		James St. Bath	Novr. 1st 1817
Mrs Hacket[54]		Margaret's P. Bath	Dec. 11th 1817
Augustine Melin[55]		Beaufort Sqr. Bath	Decr. 19th 1817
A Black Man[56]	young	Avon St.	
A man drowned in the river[57]	young		
Mrs Esther Hippisly		Bath St.	Novr. 1818
Mr Vigano	about 30	Abbey Church Yd.	Decr. 4th. 1818
James Pope		Walcot poor house	Decr. 5th 1818
Thos. Burns.		Avon St.	Decr. 4th 1818
Ann Hyde	80	Bath, Johnson St.	Jany. 12, 1819
Mrs Scott[58]	60	Bath, Queen St.	Feby. 26, 1819

Here follow 8 blank pages; death-entries continue in the next Register (unprinted). See also C.R.S., 12, p. 147 et seq.

Marriages
Heading and first entry in Ainsworth's hand.
1810, March 4th. Were married, according to the rites of the Church, John Swarbrick and Helen Rose; present as witnesses Revd. Wm. Coombes, Mr Williams and Mrs Catharine Brown,

by me Ralph Ainsworth.
Next eighteen entries in Calderbank's hand:
1810, June 18th. Were married, according to the rites of the Catholic Church, Mr Walter Gldhill [*sic* ? Gledhill] and Miss Elizabeth Knight, in the presence of Mr, Mrs Bezely [?] etc.

Jas. Calderbank.
1810, Aug. 26th. Were married, according to the rites of the Catholic Church Jno. Thompson and Ann Winbow, both of the parish of Horton, in the County of Glocester, by me

Jas. Calderbank.

[51]   See Baines's journal, 14 Sept. 1817 (in *C.R.S.*, 65). The vague dating of Baines's first two mortuary entries suggests that they were written-up some time later. A Bath death not recorded in this list was that of James Everard, 9th Lord Arundell of Wardour, on 14 July 1817 (*C.R.S.*, 12, p. 138).

[52]   Baines's journal, 28 Oct. 1817 (in *C.R.S.*, 65).

[53]   *ibid.*, 31 Oct. 1817.

[54]   *ibid.*, 11 Dec. 1817.

[55]   *ibid.*, 13-20 Dec. 1817. For a burial on 30 Dec. 1817 (not in this mortuary list) see journal under that date.

[56]   *ibid,,* 13 June 1818.

[57]   *ibid.*, 16 June.

[58]   For this and the preceding entry, see *C.R.S.*, 12, p. 143.

1810, Aug. 29th. Were married, according to the rites of the Catholic Church, Mr John English and Miss Frances Huddleston, in the presence of the Lady's two Sisters and many others, by me
Jas. Calderbank.

1811, June 22nd. Were married, according to the rites of the Catholic Church, Bartholemew Vaughan and Catharine Mary Norris, in the presence of Miss C. Murphy and Mr Ryan, by me
Jas. Calderbank.

1811, Septr. 1st. Were married, according to the rites of the Catholic Church, John Brenan and Anna Maria Hayter, in the presence of Mrs Phelan, by me
Jas. Calderbank.

1811, October 30th. Were married, according to the rites of the Catholic Church, John Tully and Catharine Murphy, in the presence of Mr N. Dowling and Mrs Dowling, by me
Jas. Calderbank.

1812, June 8th. Were married Joseph Ward and Frances Stytche, according to the rites of the Catholic Church, in the presence of Mrs. Clifford and all the family, by me
Jas. Calderbank.

1812, July 11th. Were married, according to the rites of the Catholic Church, John Rideout and Rosanna Purnell, in the presence of Julien Havez and Mary, by
R. Ainsworth.

1812, Septr. 9th. Were married, according to the rites of the Catholic Church, Mr Ferdinand Birkin [?] and Miss Mary Anne Deverel, in the presence of her Sister and Misses [?] Wats, by me
J. Calderbank.

1813, Jany. 20th. Were married, according to the rites of the Catholic Church, Henry Clifford Esqr. and Miss Anne Ferrers, in the presence of the respective families, by me
Jas. Calderbank.

1813, Octr. 29. Were married, according to the rites of the Catholic Church, Edwd. Gelepsie and Ann Thawman [?], in the presence of Miss F. Taylor, Henry Williams and his Daughter Mary, by me
J. Calderbank.

1813, Decr. 26. Were married, according to the rites of the Catholic Church, Mathieu Paul Louis Anne Prygny de Gueriaux, Capte. de Vaissiau dans la Marine Imperial, Chevalier de la Legion d'honneur, and Miss Sarah Marshall, in the presence of Le Contre Amiral Durand de Linois, Comte de L'Empire, Commandant de la Legion D'honneur, and Frances Sacherey de Beaurepaire, by
R. Ainsworth.

The above entry also occurs in the First Register, supra., p. 71.

1814, Feby. 22. Were married Henry Barnwall Esq. and Miss Jane Nugent, in the presence of the Lady's Brother and Aunt, by me
J. Calderbank.

*The next two entries (baptisms) also occur supra., p. 142, though with
some difference in the dating of the second entry.*

1814, March 9th. Was baptised Wm., Son of George and Sarah Stacey,
born Feby. 28. Sponsors Cornelius Dowding and Henrietta Loveless,
by me

J. Calderbank.

1814, March 23rd. Was baptised Denis Harry, Son of Edwd. and
Elizabeth Murphy, born Decr. 16, 1813. Sponsors Patrick Hoy and
Henrietta Loveless, by me

J. Calderbank.

1814, April 18. Were married, according to the rites of the Catholic
Church, Wm. Heskins and Theresa Osmund, in the presence of Mary
Edwin, John Smith etc., by me

J. Calderbank.

1814, May 28. Were married, according to the rites of the Catholic
Church, Thos. Osmund and Mary Edwin, in the presence of Noah
Osmund and his Sister Theresa, by me

J. Calderbank.

1814, June 26th. Were married, according to the rites of the Catholic
Church, John Talbot Esqr. and Miss Maria Talbot, in the presence of the
Lady's family and Miss Frances Talbot, by me

J. Calderbank.

The next seven entries in Rishton's hand:
1814, Octr. 12th. Were married Charles Eyston Esq. and Miss Teresa
Metcalf,[59] according to the Rites of the Catholic Church, in the presence
of their respective families, by

James Calderbank.

1814, Octr. 25th. Were married, according to the Rites of the Catholic
Church, Matthew Campbell and Mary Williams, in the presence of her
Father and her Sisters and others, by

James Calderbank.

1814, Novr. 25th. Were married, according to the Rites of the Catholick
Church, John Palmer and Henrietta Church, in the presence of her
Grandmother, Aunt and others, by

James Calderbank.

1815, Jany. 11th. Were married, according to the Rites of the Catholic
Church, Mr Michael Fautsch to Miss Elizabeth Caswell, in the presence
of Richard Phelan and his Son, by

James Calderbank.

1815, Feby. 2nd. Were married, according to the Rites of the Catholic
Church, William Allner to Esther Green, in the Presence of James Green
and Mary Anne Green, by me

Thos. Rishton.

1815, March 6th. Were married, according to the Rites of the Catholic
Church, George Thomas Maddox Esqr. and Miss Anna Teresa Maria

[59] See notes 90 & 95 to first register.

Cockayne, in the presence of her Mother and several Friends, by
James Calderbank.
1815, March 13th. Were married, according to the Rites of the Catholic
Church, John Peacock and Margaret Collins, in the Presence of Richd.
Clarke and Margaret Edwards, by
James Calderbank.
Next nine entries in Calderbank's hand:
1815, April 4th. Were married Joseph Park and Mary Thompson, in the
presence of Mr and Mrs Phelan, by me
Jas. Calderbank.
1815, April 5th. Were married John Wright Esqr. and Miss Mary
Catharine Cholmeley, in the presence of Mrs Charton and other friends,
by me
Jas. Calderbank.
1815, Octr. 1st. Were married, according to the rites of the Catholic
Church, Thomas Collins and Mary Browne, in the presence of her
Brother and Sister and others, by me
Jas. Calderbank.
1815, Octr. 23rd. Were married, according to the rites of the Catholic
Church, Edwd. Hebdin Esqr. and Mrs Henry Clifford, in the presence of
the Lady's family and Sir Richd. Bedingfield Bart., by me
Jas. Calderbank.
1816, Jany. 11. Were married, according to the rites of the C. church,
Wm. Charles Jerningham Esqr. and Miss Anne Moore, in the presence
of their respective families, by me
J. Calderbank.
1816, Feby. 24. Were married, according to the rites of the Catholic
church, Richd., Lord Viscount MountEarl,[60] and Mrs Mary Blennerhasset, in the presence of the Servants, by me
Jas. Calderbank.
1817, Jany. 26th. Were married John Phillips and Elenor Priestman,
according to the rites of the Catholic church, in the presence of Elizth.
Ward, by me
Jas. Calderbank.
1817, Feby. 16. Were married, according to the rites of the Catholic
church, Wm. Isaacs and Jane Moger, in the presence of two Witnesses,
by me
Jas. Calderbank.
1817, April 13th. Were married, according to the rites of the Catholic
church, Jas. Wilkes and Eliza. Melor, in the presence of her Mother and
several others, by me
Jas. Calderbank.

[60] Richard Quin, Baron Adare, Viscount Mount-Earl (5 Feb. 1816) and Earl of
Dunraven (1822). See "G.E.C", *Complete Peerage*, IV, pp. 547-8, according to
which this marriage took place on *26* Feb. 1816. If the Catholic ceremony did
precede the Anglican this was in contravention of Hardwicke's Act. See also note
119 to first register.

Henceforth in Baines's and Brindle's hands as signed:[61]
1817 [*blank*]. Were married, according to the rites of the Catholic Church, John Walsh and Catharine Finity, in the presence of Catharine Walsh and Mrs Corbin, by me

Thos. Brindle.

1818, Novr. 29. Were married by dispensation (being Advent Sunday) John FitzPatrick and Mary Mahony, according to the rites of the Catholic Church, in the presence of two witnesses, Joseph Fitzgerald and Eliza Moor,

by me Thos. Brindle

April 15th 1819. Were married, according to the rites of the Catholic Church, Walter Jones and Mary Madeleine Philippine Buron, in the presence of Mrs Willoughby and Miss F. Ferrers,

by me P. Baines.

May 15th 1819. Were married, according to the Rites of the Catholic Church, Aimable Prosper La Bigne and Mary Ann Shaw, in the presence of Guiseppi Huelli and Maria Shaw,

by me Thos. Brindle.

Septr. 3, 1819. Were married, according to the Rites of the Catholic Church, Oliver Grace Esqr. and Frances Mary Nagle, in the presence of Mr and Mrs Jo. English, Miss Huddleston and others,

by me Thos. Brindle.

Octr. 11, 1819. Were married, according to the Rites of the Catholic Church, Bernard Fanning and Jane Currin, in the presence of Mary and John Short,

by me Thos. Brindle.

Octr. 31, 1819. Were married, according to the Rites of the Catholic Church, James Holland and Ellen Kelly, in the presence of Bernard Fanning and Ellen Barker,

by me Thos. Brindle.

Jany. 31, 1820. Were married, according to the Rites of the Catholic Church, John Boland, and Mary Clark in the presence of John and Bridget Gragan,

by me Thos. Brindle.

Feby. 7, 1820. Were married according to the Rites of the Cath. Church, John Hussey Esqr. and Miss Christina Arundell,[62] in the presence of Miss Lacon, Mr, Mrs and Miss B. Arundell etc.,

by me Thos. Brindle.

May —, 1820. Were married, according to the rites of the Catholic Church, Patrick Shea and Dora Leler, in the presence of Michael and Ann Leler,

by me Thos. Brindle.

---

[61] Apparently incomplete – only two entries between April 1817 and April 1819.

[62] Daughter of Thomas Raymund Arundell and Mary Ann Elizabeth (*née* Smythe; see *supra*, p. 83). Miss B. Arundell may be the bride's sister, Mary Blanche Appolonia Arundell; cf. genealogy in E. Doran Webb (ed.) *Notes by the 12th Lord Arundell of Wardour on the Family History* (1916).

Novr. 21st 1820. Were married, according to the rites of the Catholic Church, Michael Theobald Langton Esq. and Miss Mary Ryan, in the presence of their respective families and of Col. Stonor[63] and — Murphy Esq.,
by me Peter Baines.

July 30th 1821. Were married, according to the rites of the Catholic Church, Mathew Malone and Mary Hulbert, in the presence of John Shire and Charlotte Pierce,
by me P. Baines.

Septr. 18, 1821. Were married, according to the rites of the Catholic Church, Chas. Dormer and Eliza Charlotte de Coettogon, in the presence of John Palmer and Mary Redwood,
by me Thos. Brindle.

Feby. 18, 1822. Were married, according to the rites of the Catholic Church, Henry Cozons and Eliz. Kent, in the presence of Barbara Cooper and James Haggarty,
by me Thos. Brindle.

Augt. 28, 1822. Were married, according to the rites of the Catholic Church, William Edwards and Sarah Abbot, in the presence of William Rose and Elizabeth Abbot,
by me Thos. Brindle.

Octr. 26, 1822. Were married, according to the Rites of the Cath. Church, Solomon Duffitt and Eliz. Maria Moon, in the presence of Jo. Palmer and Mary Short,
by me Thos. Brindle.

Jany. 16th 1823. Were married, according to the rites of the Catholic Church, Giovanni Thewenetti and Emely Appleford, in the presence of Richd. Appleford, Charlotte Appleford and Eliza Hay,
by me P. Baines.

Feby. 1st 1823. Were married, according to the Rites of the Catholic Church, Joseph Lawley and Charlotte Perry, in the presence of Miss Bond and John Palmer,
by me Thos. Brindle.

Feby. 10, 1823. Were married, according to the Rites of the Catholic Church, Michael Hart and Susana Hill, in the presence of Benjn. Evans and Mary Wickley,
by me Thos. Brindle.

April 23, 1823. Were married, according to the rites of the Cath. Church, John Cody and Mary Ann Head, in the presence of Joseph Dowding and Charlotte Head,
by me Thos. Brindle.

Octr. 6, 1823. Were married, according to the rites of the Cath. Church, John Foyle and Cath. Bayston, in the presence of Michl. Moore and Eliz. Connor,
by me Thos. Brindle.

[63] See note 34.

Octr. 14, 1823. Were married, according to the rites of the Cath. Church,
Ed. Newport and Eliz. Shirley, in the presence of [*blank*],
by me Thos. Brindle.
Novr. 8, 1824. Were married, according to the rites of the Catholic
Church, John Day Esqr. and Miss Emely Hartsinck, in the presence of
Thos. Day Esqr., Saml. Day Esqr. and Stephanie de Sommery and
Mary Frances Brun, by me
Thos. Brindle.

Here follow ten blank pages.

In Calderbank's hand (for a convert not listed below, see foot of p. 137):
Rec'd into the Catholic Church

1811, April	20th	Rob't Smith	age 29
Augst.	10,	Maria Moon [? Moore]	14
		Anne Braddon	15
Octr.	2nd	Elizth. Hyde	28
	30,	Wm. Kingman	72
Novr.	3d	Elizth. Green	29
About the same time Mrs Herin			28

by me J. Calderbank.
1812, Septr. 24th. Miss Caroline and her Sister, Miss Susan Scott, the
the former aged 23, the latter 18,
by J. Calderbank.

October 20th		Margaret Slade	59	
		Henrietta Deverall	18	
		Louisa Deverell	16	
		Sarah Hutchings	16	
		Wm. Edwards	14	
		Jas. Nagle	14	
1813, Feby.	6,	Martha Sinnett	28	
	13th	Wm. Woods	18	
	26th	Mary Anne Heffernan	22	
March	13,	Wm. Fisher	35	
April	9th	John Timberley	18	
	19th	Pricilla Marsh	15	
	20th	John Ridout	56	
		Sarah Vancombe	40	
May	29th	Lucretia Atto [?]	19	Black
June	3rd	Elizth. Mockman	28	
1814, March	31,	Mary Anne Vaisey	26	
1814, April	9,	Mary Ane [sic] Green	14	
		Sister to Do.	13	
1814, May	18,	Mary Woods	29	
1814, June	9th	Miss Anne Darbyshire	22	

In Rishton's hand;
1814, Octr.   1st.   Anne Baker

1814,Octr.	23rd	Mary Palmer	68
1814,Octr.	31st	Mary Parfit	33
1815,Feby.	3rd	John Parfit	35
1815,Feby.	4th	Esther Green	26
1815,Feby.	9,	Sarah Hutchings	20
–		Elizabeth Fautsch	29
1815,March	8th	Thos. Jenkins	80
1815,March	17,	Jemima Albion	22
		George Head	36
		Benjamin Langley[64]	27
		William Harling	17
		Martha Townsend	67
		Master Nelly	16
Apl.	22nd	Jane Noble	36
May	12th	Anne Davies	45
		Margaret Ford	24
		Mary Connor	47
		Mary Terry	64
May	22nd	Miss Maria Jane Johnson	33
June	3rd	Martha Dutton	35
		Mrs Elizabeth Davis	73
		Thos. Edwards	46
		John Baily	35
July	8th	Isite O'Brian	26
	17,	Elizabeth Edwards	45

In Calderbank's hand:

Augst	22,	Esther Hypsley	
Octr.	31,	John Webb	57
1816		Louisa Guista	
		Mrs Bailey	
		Mrs Arundell	
		Henry Beaumont	
Decr.	24,	Miss Elizabeth Johnson	16
1817,Jany.	18,	Grace Lalor	28
May	13,	Miss Mary Anne Lyescobe	22

In Calderbank's hand:
In capella catholica Bathoniae, die 25, mensis Octobris 1812, ab Illustrissimo et Reverendissimo D.D. Petro Bernadino Collingridge, Episcopo Thespiensi, confirmati fuerunt:-

Matilda Hatch	Maria Joseph
Elisabetha Gerish	
Sarah Abbott	Elenora Agnes
John Palmer	Jacob
Catharina McGuire	Elisabetha

[64] See note 28.

Henrietta Smith   Theresa
Gulielmus Coady   Petrus
Theresa Osmund   Elisabetha
Anna Maria Rozanna
Maria Sullivan
Elisabetha Wheelan   Maria Magdalena
Ellena Martin   Anna Maria Magdalena
Henrieta Barry   Maria Magdalena
Martha Moon
Robertus Moon
Richardus Clarke
Thomas Bridge   Josephus
Maria Molyneux   Anna
Maria Havez   Elisabetha
Gulielmus Martin   Josephus
Anna Bradden   Maria
Anna Moger   Maria
Maria Moon   Elisabetha
Elisabetha Quinn   Maria
Anna Leonard   Maria
Dorothea Lalor   Margaretta
Maria Dowding   Elisabetha
Frances Flinn   Elisabetha
Maria Lovett   Theresa Josephus
Joanna Pike   Maria Josephus
Gulielmus Ludwick   Thomas
Margaretta Slade   Theresa
Gulielmus Edwards   Thomas
Sarah Hutchings   Maria
Susanna Scott
Carolina Scott
Henrietta Deverell   Anna
Louisa Deverell   Maria
Joannes Sullivan   Michael
Emilia Dimony   Maria
Jacobus Nagle
Catharina Brown   Theresa
Thomas Barry
Eliza Barry   Maria Anna Theresa
Robertus Moon
Maria [?] Louis   Anna
Maria Lalor   Elisabetha
Ludovicus Carré
Margaretta Carter   Maria
Elisabetha Lalor   Maria
Elisabetha Hyde   Anna
Maria Cotell
Thomas Coldfield

Georgina Richmond	Maria Clementina
Catharina Browne	Maria
Maria Carey	Maria
Joannes English	Petrus
Pulcheria Somerini	Maria Carolletta Agnes
Joanna Bolts	Maria
Eliza Fryer	Maria
Helena Moylan	Maria
Anna Kentgens	Maria
Helena Denie	Maria
Sarah Dungay	Anna
Sarah Carr	Agnes
Helen Fryer	Maria

In Baines's hand;
In capella Catholica Bathoniae, die 21, mensis Junii 1818, ab illustrissimo et reverendissimo Dno. Petro Collingridge Episcopo Thespiensi, in districtu occidentali vicario apostolico, confirmati fuerunt:-[65]

Joseph Mary Hoskins
George John Croft
Harriet Henely
Mary Burns
Mary O'Connor
John Whickham
Mary Isat O'Brien
Mary Cath: Taylor
Elizabeth Gill
Eliz. Mary Edwards
Mary Fletcher
Michael Henry Cooper
Catharine Brown
Mary Terry
Robt. Kirksby
Isaac Thatcher
Mary Thatcher
Ann Baker
Elizabeth Mary Redwood
John McGeary
Esther Mary Alner
Mary Teresa Hall
Mary Abbot
Elizabeth Paillet
Jane Hall
Pat. John Kearns

[65] See Baines's journal, same date (*C.R.S.*, 65, p. 235). Neither this nor the two following lists give any clear indication of confirmation-names but in some cases reference, *via* the index, to baptismal entries reveals additions to original Christian names, e.g. Eliz. added (in margin) to Mary Edwards.

Thomas Culverwall
Mary Joseph William Thomas[66]
Sarah Teresa Leonard
Ann Kiplar
Catharine Agnes Carr
Mary Ann Eliz. Wood
Mary Taylor
Jane Langhern
Mary Parfitt
Ann Davies
Teresa Sarah Maria Nokes
Benjamin Langley
Ellen Byrne
Mary Mack
Ann Mary Magdalen Martin
Mary Ann Green
James Harris
Ann Mary Short
Margaret Winifred English
Elenor Crawley
Frances Hormsby
John McNolty
Catharine Paillet
Joseph Cody
Mary Ann Bodman
George Joseph Smyth
Joseph Fasana
John Anthony Cody
John O'Connor
John Flanaghan
Elizabeth Ann Derbyshire
Joseph Agnes Cecilia Sommery[66]
Mary Leonard
Cath. Teresa Stanbridge
Victor William Bailey
Mary Ann Lewis
Martha Steene
Margaret St John
Isaac James Nokes
Patk. Ryan
Victoire Elizabeth Bailey
John Laurence Short
Monica Madelina Willoughby
Bridget Moonan
John Moon
Michael Hart

[66] Confirmation-name apparently preceding Christian names.

William Joseph Rose
George Wilson
Mary Ann Hunt
Robt. John Meloy
James Haggerty
Catharine Madden
Teresa Ann Still
Maria Louisa Quick
Mary Teresa Head
Susannah Teresa Westall
Ellen Gill
Elizabeth Caroline Gill
Cecilia Laura Havez
Sarah Harman
Mary Teresa Gill
Ann Harris
Mary Ann Kentgens
Catharine Neil
Ursula Roderigus
Elizabeth Harris
Elizabeth Welby
Ann Caroline Welby
Elizabeth Barrett
Anna Maria Cath. Green
Magdalene Mary Ann Heffernan
Elizabeth Foutsche
William Brown
Mary Verstein
Catharine Mary Martin

In Brindle's hand;
In Capella Catholica Bathoniae, die 30, mensis Decembris 1821, ab
illustrissimo et Reverendissimo Dno. Petro Collingridge, Episcopo
Thespiensi, V.A. etc., confirmati fuerunt:-
Maria Howell
Sarah Mary Hollis
Hannah Mary Maudy
Marth [*sic*] Mary Baltch
Monica Mary Errington
James Augustin Croft
Esther Henrietta Dealy
Anastasia Cady
Jane Wherret
Louis Theophilus Aubery
Mary Anne La Bigne
Christina Irvine
Mary Ann Louisa Baily

Alice Gough
Mary Eliz. Alley
Henry Benedict Cady
Monica Theresa Bellingham
Joseph Knapp
Mary Ashmore
Frederic Errington
Alexander Peter Christie
Fanny Dillan
James Bernard Short
Sarah Ann Morse
Bridget Agnes Barry
Marie Marguerite Monpiez
Robert Vincent English
Mary Ann Agnes Wood
Joseph James Abbot
Mary Ann Beaumont
Mary Ann Eliz. Brabyn
James Joseph Head
Sarah Ann Page
Eliz. Mary Cary
Mary Elizabeth Quin
John Andrew Edwards
Charles Peter Fryer
Ed. William Fryer
Dorothea Scholastica Bellingham
James John Sheil
Hannah Mary Teresa Button
Sarah Ann Burgess
Ann Canfield [? Caufield]
Jane Catharine Riel
Mary George
Ed. Joseph Ryan
Lucy Mary Frances Smythe
Mary Ann Moretti
James Joseph Dowding
Catharine Sophia Rousell
Mary Ann Teresa Head
Thomas Sweeney
Nicholas Cornelius Paillet
James John Bailey
Mary Ann Margaret Horler
Jane Mary Hickson
Mary Agnes Kentgens
William Kelly
Mary Murphy
Elizabeth Cecilia Gill
Marth Mary Griffiths

In Brindle's hand:
In Capella Catholica Bathoniae, die 6, mensis Junii 1824 (Dominica
Pentecostes) ab illustrissimo et Reverendissimo Dno. Petrus Baines,
Episcopo Sigeense, V.A. Coadjut., confirmati fuerunt;-
Mary Ann Hodges
Antonia Pierina Clementina Solliers
Teresa Margt. Morse
Ann Mary Moyer [? Moger]
Margt. Mary Cavenagh
Sarah Mary Freeman
Bridgt. Mary Witts
Maria Agnes Connery
Sarah Mary Bourne
Ann Teresa Weetnam
Mary Ann Lucy Hayter
Mary Teresa Thornhill
Ann Teresa Thornhill
Elizabeth Agnes Thornhill
Elizabeth Agnes Lacy
Elizabeth Cecilia Green
Margt. Mary Brezel
Ann Ann Burn
Mary Mary Figgins
Emma Mary Phipps
Ann Agnes Batterburry
Honira Mary Carr
Sophia Mary Magdeline FitzPatrick
Rebecca Mary Shippings
Sarah Elizabeth Magrath
Elizabeth Restieaux
Harriet Mary O'Flaherty
Margt. Agnes Fryer
Elizabeth Cecilia Martin
Sarah Mary Hoskins
Frances Mary Kaines
Mary Flinn
Elizabeth Mary Frances Thompson
Elizabeth Agnes Woolcote
Mary Rial
Mary Teresa Euriel
Mary Caisy
Mary Ann Teresa Dobson
Mary Aloysia Arthur
Helen — Baily
Henrietta Catharine Dobson
Mary Lynche
Ann Mary Lapedge
Mary Martha Dexeter

Sarah Mary Carter
Ann Mary Clarke
Mary Shortall
Elizabeth Agnes Hornsby
Elizabeth Agnes Conlon
Christina Mary Swift
Jane Elizabeth Swift
Hannah Mary Dixon
Jean Baptiste Joseph Raimond
Louis Joseph de Gollerile
Jeremiah John Morrison
Thomas Joseph Phelan
Michael Joseph Magrath
Michael Laurence Magrath
John Burn
James Matthias Moger
John Quin
Joseph John Quin
Michael George Cady [? Cody]
James John Flinn
William Joseph Henty
Francis James Edwards
John Baptist Coakley
Owen William Real
Henry James Edwards
Patterick Hannington
William Dominick Powell
Henry Paul Fryer
Jeremiah Matthew Morrison

END OF SECOND REGISTER

INDEX

Entries may occur more than once to a page of text; footnote-references are abbreviated as *n*. Catholic priests have the prefix "Rev". (or "Abbé") or appropriate suffixes: O.S.B., O.F.M., S.J. (or ex-S.J., the Society of Jesus having been suppressed from 1773 to 1814). A particular name does not necessarily denote only one person, nor do separate entries (Mr, Mrs, Miss in some; Christian names in others; or the same woman's married and maiden surname) necessarily represent different persons. "Mrs", at this period a courtesy-title for middle-aged spinsters, need not always signify a married woman (see *C.R.S.*, 65, p. 240, and *supra*, p. 18, note 34) and "Mr" (or a Christian name or initial with no prefix) may occasionally conceal an unidentified priest. Latinised Christian names are italicised and, where Christian and confirmation-names are not readily distinguishable both (or all) are indexed, marked with an asterisk. Some English Christian names have been abbreviated or systematised, so obviating the indexing of irrelevant variants; thus Eliz represents Eliza, Elisabeth and Elizabeth, Elen replaces Elenor (variously spelt) and Ellen, while Ann, Helen, Sara, Susan and Teresa also cover Anna and Anne, Helena, Sarah, Susanna(h), Teresia and Theresa. Names apparently different may appertain to the same individual, but where their initial letters differ, they are here distinguished, e.g. Esther, Hester (and also Helen, Ellen, Helena, Eleanor). Of the names already abbreviated in the MSS., a few are ambiguous, e.g. "Ed." (Edmund, Edwin, or Edward) and such have not been altered. Occasionally surnames are preceded by single letters (sometimes "N", possibly because the Christian name was unknown) but unless the latter is discoverable (see p. 15, note 20) "N" is treated as an initial. Where only a first name, or nickname, is given (e.g. Mary N.; Hopperkin) it is indexed under its initial letter, as are unnamed entries (Groom, Stranger, German Clock-Man), save that persons described as maids (or maidservants) and manservants are placed with "Servants". Surnames beginning M', Mc and Mic are gathered under Mac. The few children born out of wedlock are cross-indexed under both parents' surnames and cross-references are also provided to phonetic alternatives (Burn, Byrne; Reilly, Ryley, etc.) and to other variants of surnames (many of which are standardised) and place-names; nevertheless idiosyncratic spelling and execrable handwriting may still render odd entries misleading. As every page relates to Bath, the index concerns itself only with specifically-mentioned places, streets, buildings, etc. within the city; these appear alphabetically under "Bath". Other places in England are indexed both individually and under their counties, with the historic (pre-1974) county-names. French and Irish persons and places are both alphabetised and grouped under "France" and "Ireland" respectively. French surnames with the prefixes *de* and *d'* are indexed under the main name but *de la* and *du* occur under those words.

160, 171; Martin, 160; Mary, 142, 151; Thos, 134, 142, 151, 157, 160; Wm, 46

Brogen, Bridget, 161; John, 161

Brooke, Jane, 105

Brook(e)s, Charlotte, 117; Charlotte Mary,* 68; Mary Ann, 84; Nancy, 84; Sara, 170

Brookshire, Geo, 4, 11. See also Brockshaw.

Broudrick, see Broderick.

Brown(e), —, 92, 189; Ann, 153, 168, 170, 182; Bartholomew Augustin, 176; *Catharina Maria Cecilia,* * 68; Cath, 51, 56, 61, 75, 83, 89, 126, 153, 190, 198, 199; Eliz, 69, 85, 89, 96, 116, 132; Eliz Ann,* 67; Elen, 110; Emma, 182; Hannah, 179; Henry, 179; Geo, 168, 179; Jas, 85, 123, 181; John, 9, 170; Louisa, 161; *Louisa Maria Magdalena,* * 68, Lucy, 97; Maria Helen (or Elen), 75, 122; Martha, 69; Mary, 62, 69, 78, 107, 111, 118, 132, 138, 142, 161, 176, 193 (& brother & sister); Mary Ann, 143; Mrs, 5; Nicholas, 110; Thos, 13, 15, 16, 19, 21, 24, 29, 51, 56, 57 (& wife), 64, 75, 82, 83, 89, 116, 124, 153, 161, 170, 182; Wm, 51, 56, 120, 132, 201

Broxbourne, Herts., 1n

Brufy, Eliz, 52

Brun, Mary Frances, 196

Bruno, Marie Jeanne, 62, 75

Bryan, Bryen, Brian, Brien, —, 115; Alice, 50; Danl, 82; Dominick, 87; Jas, 52, 87, 120; John, 50, 64; John Wm, 50; Mary, 82, 87; Mich, 6, 9, 24, 29, 35, 50, 57, 81; Mr, 36; Mrs, 32; Rebecca, 52.

Buck, Frances, 73; Stephen, 73; Thos, 73

Buckinghamshire, 186

Buckley, Danl, 110, 136; Jane, 74, 125; Mr (butler), 2

Buet, Ann, 18, (cook-maid), 23, 29

Bugden, Wm, 93, 113

Bugley(?), Jas, 187

Bulbeck, Martha, 6, 7, 13, 23, 29

Bull, Ann, 139

Bullen, Vincent, 15

Bun, Bernard, 84; Jane 84; Richd,. 84

Burchell, Geo, 179; Mary Ann, 179; Sara, 179

Burgen, Bergen, Burgin, Helen, 89; Jas, 89; Jeremiah, 84, 88, 186; John, 89

Burgess, Sara Ann,* 202

Burk(e), Alice, 76; Brigit, 74; Caroline,

158; Cath, 66, 91; Edwd, 102 119, Edmund, 107; J., 150; Jas, 128, 133, 134; Jane J., 124; Jemima, 102, 107, 119, 128; John, 55, 76, 107; John Russell, 150; Lucia, 102; Mary, 71, 126, 149, 150, 158, 188; Mich, 149; Miles, 149, 158; Mr, 66; Mrs, 57, 71; Theobald, 18; Sir Thos, 110

Burn, Burne, Byrne, —, 51, 72 (deleted); Abigail, 175; Ann, 175, 180, 203; Bernard, 125; Cath, 3, 8, 48, 70, 128; El, 200; Eliz, 180; Jane, 118, 127; John, 173, 175, 180, 204; Martha, 3, 10, 11, 13n, 47-8; *Maria Magd,* 66; Mary, 142, 176; Mich, 93, 180; Mrs, 13, 24, 28, 36, 57, 109; Susan, 167. See also Smith Burn.

Burns, Jas, 153; John, 153; Mary, 153, 199; Thos, 190

Buron, Mary Madeleine Philippine, 194

Burrell, Mary, 4

Burrough, Ann, 82; Isabella Mary, 72; Jos, 72, 82; Mary, 72; Mary Ann, 77; Wm, 82

Burt, see Birt.

Burton Constable, E. Yorks., 186 & n

Bush, Ann, 165; Eliz, 165; Jos, 165

Bushell, Mary, 175

Butler (unnamed; Mr Dicconson's), 23

Butler, Ann, 158; Cath, 6, 7; Chas, 162; Elen Mary Ann,* 68; Eliz, 73; Geo, 52 (& wife), 56, 187 & n; Mary, 123 & n; Mich, 27, 35, 55; Miss, 34, 56; Mr, 3, 8, 13, 23, 40, 56; Mrs, 2 (& maid), 3, 8, 13, 23, 34, 56, 190

Butt(s), Cath, 41; Mr, 3, 8, 13; Mrs, 3, 8, 13, 23, 28, 36, 58; Thos, 18

Button, Hannah Mary Teresa,* 202

Byrne, see Burn.

Cacy, see Casey.

Cady, Anastasia, 201; Henry Benedict,* 202; John(?), 161; Mich John(?), 204*. See also Cody.

Caezby(?), Sara, 142

Caffeari(?), Hector St Cyr, 148; Mary, 148; Nicholas Philippe Constant, 148

Caghlan, Richd, 54

Cahagan, Cahegan, Laurence, 21, 33; Mrs, 115

Cahall, Patk, 65; Ruthe, 65

Cahegan, see Cahagan.

Cairns, Jeremiah, 144

Caisy, see Casey.

Calaghan, Calahan, see Callaghan, Collighan.

Calais, 108
Calderbank, Jas, O.S.B., 66, 69, 70, 89-102, 114-5, 117-20, 124-7, 129, 131-52, 186-93, 196-9
Callaghan, Callahan, Calaghan, etc., Amelia, 88; Chas, 180; Deborah, 181; Jas. 181. See also Collighan.
Callan, Callen, Mrs, 97, 119; Sara. 69
Callers, John, 127; Mgt, 69
Calley, Edwd, 70
Calne, Wilts., 141
Calonne, Chas Alexander, Count de, 61
Cal(l)well, Mary, 185; Thos, 185
Calverwell, John, 173; Mary, 168, 173; Thos, 155, 168, 173
Cambel(l), see Campbell.
Cambruzzo, Mary, 152; (or Rebottaro), Jos, 152
Camel, see Cammel, Campbell
Cameron, Eliz, 41; John, 41
Camerton, Som., 38
Cammel, Math, 107, 108, 114. See also Campbell.
Campbell, Cambel, Cambell, ——, 153, Ann, 109; Bridget, 97; Cath, 32; Eliz, 78, 125, 159; Henry, 146; Hugh, 97; Jas, 97; John, 124; Mary, 146, 153, 159, 192; Math, 104, 146, 150, 153, 159, 165, 192; (or Balsh), Frederic, 109
Camplin, Cath, 8, 9, 13, 24, 29, 33; Eliz, 13, 24; Mary, 8, 29
Cane, Bridget, 131, 132, 136; Wm, 107
Canfield(?), Ann, 202
Cann(?), Honora, 173
Can(n)ing, family, 6n; Edw, 3, 16, 22, 23, 29; Francis, 151; Jane, 151; Mary, 56; Mrs, 35, 36, 56; Thos, 1nn, 56, 75, 89
Canor, Chas, 155; Elen, 155; John, 155
Canvan, John, 135; Mary, 135; Wm, 135
Capel, Edw, 150; Mary, 149, 150; Wm, 150
Cappelle, Marie, 63
Carbonnier, Marguerite, 63
Car(e)y, Edw, 143; Eliz Mary,* 202; Georgiana, 153, 170; Jas, 9; Maria, 199; Mary, 143, 173; Peter, 9; Thos, 143; Walter, 46; Wm, 173
Carlas, Carlis, Betsy, 5; Frances, 64; Mary, 14; Richd, 18. See also Corlas.
Carpenter, Geo, 172; Jane, 108, 119, 128; Louisa, 172; Mgt, 22; Mrs, 25; Robt, 172
Carr, ——, 54, 99; Ann, 54; Cath Agnes,* 200; Harriette Cath; 98; Honira Mary,* 203; John, 41; Mary,

99; Mich, 41, 136(?), 137, 188; Sara, 41, 199
Carré, Ludovicus, 198
Carrell, Carrol(l), Ann, 42, 43, 55, 149; Ed, 128; Eliz, 168; Frances, 108; Henry Mich, 69, 108; Jas, 42, 107-8, 149; Jane, 55; John, 42, 55, 58, 69, 168; Judith, 107-8, Mgt, 168; Mary, 113, 119, 147, 149, 150, 151; Mich, 105, 108; Patric, 59; Richd, 107-8; Wm, 151
Carter, Mgt, 198; Mary, 84; Sara Mary,* 204
Cartlen, Elen, 170; Patk, 170; Sara, 170
Carty, Matty, 78; Tate, 78
Carver, Jas, 135
Cary, see Car(e)y.
Casaux, Caysau, Henriette de, 142; John Francis Dugout, Marquis de, 131; Leon Augustin de, 131; Paul George de, 131
Case(?), Mich, 136
Casey, Cacy, Caisy, Casy, Danl, 156, 158, 163, 167; Elen, 7; Eliz, 19, 156; Helen, 4, 64(?); Jas, 159; John, 14, 19, 32, 88; Mgt, 156, 158, 163, 167; Mary, 19, 87, 88, 203; Mich, 88; Mr, 6; Sally, 88; Sara, 159; Wm, 167
Casry(?), Jas, 123
Cassell, Ann, 118
Castellas, Abbé de, 63 & n
Castello, see Costello.
Castle, Castel, Amy, 4, 25, 64; Danl (& wife), 58
Castle Coombe, Wilts., 138
Caswell, Eliz, 192
Casy, see Casey.
Catharine ——, 35 ("Mr Crowtch's Maid"), 181
Caufield(?), Ann, 202
Cavanagh, see Kavannah.
Cavarly, see Caverley.
Cave, Eliz, 164; Elen, 164; Geo 164; John, 164
Cavena(g)h, see Kavannah.
Caverley, Eliz, 77; Mary, 82, 98
Cayeau, Alexander Henry John Vincent de, 188; Virginia, 186
Cellaro (? Cellars), Cath, 93
Chaddock, Jas, 74; Joanna, 74; Sara, 74
Challoner, Saml, 46
Champion, François, 63; Marie Jeanne, 63
Chapel, Mary, 90; Richd, 90; Wm, 90
Chapin, Mrs, 66
Chapman, Mr, 46n
Charker, Anastasia, 129

Crawford, Craufuird, David, 182;
Emilie, 66; Hugh, 182; Mgt, 182;
Walter Kennedy (Dr.), 66
Crawley, El., 200. See also Crowley.
Creagh, Craigh, Ann Josephine, 170;
Jas, 170; Mary Ann, 170; Mich,
148.
Creon, George, 183; Mgt, 183
Creven, David, 137; Mary, 137
Croft, Geo John,* 199; Jas Augustin,*
201
Crofton, Henry, 95; John, 95; Mary,
95
Cromwell, Mgt, 160
Cronin, Cronine, Croning, Honoria,
181; Mary, 111; Robt, 111; Wm,
111
Crook, Hannah, 160
Crosby, Ann, 135; John, 135; John
Edwd, 135
Crouch, Croutch, see Crowch.
Crow, Wm, 158
Crowch, Crouch, Croutch, etc.,
Frances, 25, 189; Mr, 35 (maid of),
36, 57; Mrs, 36, 57; Richd, 25, 127,
128
Crowl(e)y, David, 175, 180, 183; Eliz,
161; Elen, 148, 170, 181; Esther,
152, 173, 183; Harriet, 173; Helen,
178; Joanna, 50; John, 173, 175,
178, 183; John Cornelius, 152;
Mary, 149, 175, 187; Math, 161;
Patk, 152; Timothy, 53, 60. See
also Crawley.
Cruse, Chas, 21; Joanna, 21; Maria, 21;
Wm, 21
Culbert, Deborah, 130; Elen, 48; John,
48; Julia, 48; Wm, 130
Cullan, Cullen, Patk, 159; Wm, 162
Cullins, Hannah, 184; John, 184. See
also Collins.
Culverwell, Thos, 200
Cumberland, 121n
Cummings, Cummins, Andrew, 100;
Cath, 165; Danl, 165
Cunningham Jas Francis,* 67; Mary,
182; Peter, 182, 183
Cuppa, Miss, 5
Curly, Kerly, Kirly, etc., —, 92;
Francis, 24, 29, 52, 53, 73, 87, 124;
Mgt, 98; Mich, 96; Mr, 57; N., 52;
Sara, 66, 96, 98
Curren, Currin, Honora, 84; Jane, 194
Curr(e)y, Ann, 172, 173; Hannah, 163,
165, 168
Curtin, Jas, 104, 128
Curtis, Cortis, Jane, 175; Maria Anna,
67; Mary, 149; Robt, 149; Sealy,
149
Curwen, Curwin, see Kirwan.

Cyvans, Maria, 185

d'Acary, see Acary.
Daigan, Mary, 93; John, 93. See also
Degan.
Dale, Eliz, 67; Mary Ann, 61, 100;
Miss, 3, 24, 47, 57, 64
Daley, see Daly, Deal(e)y.
Dalton, Bridget, 122 & n; Constantia,
22, 28, 34 & n; Eliz, 170, 179;
Jo., 133; Julia, 88; Lucy, 88, 133;
Mary Const., 188; Miss, 7, 22, 28;
Mr, 56; Mrs, 7, 22, 28, 40, 48, 50,
53; Peter (Count), 85; Richd Chas,
85; Robt, 7, 22, 28; Rosalia, 85,
88; Wm, 29, 88
Daly, Daley, Dayly, Ann Mary,*, 67;
Cornelius, 77; Denis, 26; John, 98;
Mary, 26; Stephen Jeremiah, 26.
See also Dealy.
Daman, John (Jean), 15, 47
Dane, Jas, 121
Daniel(s), Jas, 148; John, 37, 148;
Mary, 37, 39; Winifred, 148. See
also Macpherson, Mary.
Darbyshire, Ann, 196; Eliz Ann,* 200
Darcy, Mrs, 5
Darell, Barb, 29; Cath, 86; Elen, 86;
Miss, 29; Mrs, 29; Philip, 86. See
also Dorel.
Darling, Godwin, 24, 32; Mary, 24, 33,
47, 58, 122; Wm, 24, 32, 33, 121
Darnley, Jas, 129
Darrell, see Darell.
Dauling, Patk, 184; See also Darling,
Dowling.
Dauober(?), see Dawber.
Davey, Wm, 21. See also Deavy.
Davis, Davies, Ann, 13, 20, 25, 28, 197,
200; Cath, 184; Edwd, 184; Eliz, 5
& n, 23, 28 (Mrs Chetwynd's ser-
vant), 89, 197; Eliz Lucy,* 68; Jas,
117 (servant), 154(?); Jas Jos,*
68; Janet(?), 154; Mary, 1, 172;
Stephen, 119; Thos, 184; (or
Dimpsey), Mary, 89. See also
Deaves.
Dawber, Thos, 23, 28 (Dicconsons'
servant)
Dawson, Jas, 166; (or Moclar), Mary,
166
Day, Chas, viiin, 68; Emely, 196;
Frances, 16; John, 70, 196; Maria,
67; Mary, 16 (alias Fleming), 19,
20; Miss, 3, 13 (& senr.), 23, 35,
64, 68; Mr, 3 (senr. & junr.) 13, 23,
36 (senr.), 47 (do.), 58 (&
daughter), 64 (& senr. & junr.), 68;
N. (Mr), 3; Saml, 196; Saml Bede,
O.S.B., 49n; "Surgeon", see Wm;

Quigley, Quigly, Cath, 17, 136; Jas (& wife), 4; Jane, 136, 147, 148; John, 8, 24; Mr, 24; Mrs, 8; Thos, 136, 147

Quin(n), Agnes Mary, 175; Ann, 168, 183, 188; Edwd, 15, 19, 64, 162; Eliz, 98, 102, 107, 113, 136, 137, 139, 143, 144, 152, 157, 162, 166, 168, 171, 175, 198; Elen, 128; Esther, 149; Frances, 180; Francis, 149; Geo, 98, 102, 136, 143; Hannah, 173; Helen, 75, 183; Jas, 69, 75, 104, 107, 110, 113, 173; Joanna, 102; John, 136, 204; Jos John,* 204; M., 180; Mgt, 186; Mary, 107, 148, 154, 174; Mary Ann, 75; Mary Eliz,* 202; Maurice (& Maurus), 107, 113, 139, 144, 148, 152, 153, 154, 157, 160, 166, 167, 168, 170, 172, 175; Nath, 23; Peter, 149; Simon, 98, 121, 139; Stephen, 161, 173, 175, 181, 183, 185; Thos, 141; Thos Linus, 157; Wm, 144, 155. See also Mount-Earl.

Quince, Jas, 121
Quinlan(d), Michael, 55, 73, 96
Quinn, see Quin.
Quintas, Quintus, Augustine John, 17; Dominic, 27, 40; Dominic Ant, 10, 17, 186; Mary, 10, 17
Quirk, Joanna, 110

Raarden, see Riordan.
Rabbitt, Honor, 88
Racket, Mary, 135
Radclyffe, Hon. Jas Clement, 40
Radener, Radenue, Cath, 62, 78
Radigan, Jane, 7. See also Redican.
Rafferton, Eliz, 26
Railly, see Reilly.
Raimond, Jean Baptiste Jos,* 204
Rand, Ann, 174; John Eusebius, 174; Wm, 174
Randal, Randell, Randle, etc., Ann, 97, 150; Cath, 11, 19, 21, 70, 82, 84, 88; John, 97, 150; Jos, 97; Mrs, 5, 14, 23, 28, 36, 47, 57, 64; Rosa, 183; Sara, 41, 70; Thos, 183
Ranedin, John, 55
Rassenno, see Rosanno.
Ratclyffe, see Radclyffe.
Rate, Ann, 153
Raw(e), Alexander, 169; Frances, 25; Richd, 142
Read, Reed, Frances, 174; Francis, 180; Helen, 179, 180; Jane, 71, 118; *Joanna Maria,* 68; Mgt, 181; Mary, 105; Richd, 181; Sara, 181; Stephen, 60

Ready, Mary, 19, 20; Mrs, 5, 64
Real, Owen Wm,* 204. See also Rial.
Realy, Mrs (deleted), 13. See also Reilly.
Rearden, see Riordan.
Rebottaro, Paschal, 152; (or Cambruzzo) Jos, 152
Redican(?), Eleanor, 77. See also Radigan.
Redman, Redmond, Ann, 136, 142; Jas, 136, 142; Jane, 142. See also Ridmond.
Redwood, Eliz Mary,* 199; Mary, 195
Reed, see Read.
Reef, Mary, 157
Reilly, Railly, Reyley, Riley, Ryley, etc., Ann, 83, 97, 170, 185; *Anna,* 89; Bernard, 159, 183; Bridget, 142; Cath, 42, 87, 104; Cornelius, 146, 147, 164; Elen, 169-70 (deleted); Eliz, 74, 83, 164; Helen, 74; Hugh, 185; Jas, 27, 97; Jane, 27, 141; John, 83, 89, 97, 169-70; Mgt, 15, 47; Mary, 83, 142, 183; Matthias, 128; Mich, 17 & n, 74, 185; Mr, 104; Reilly, Mrs, 13, 15, 104; Owen, 141; Patk, 141; Philip, 142, 183; Richd, 136, Sara, 164; Stephen, 26, 27; Wm, 89; (or Taylor), Sara, 169-70
Rend, Ann, 164; Elen Jane, 164; Wm, 164
Rendell, Ann, 158; Robt, 158; Wm, 158
Rennes, Fr., 79
Reorden, see Riordan.
Resana, see Rosanno.
Restieaux, Eliz, 203
Reyley, Reyly, see Reilly.
Reynolds, Hugh, 136, 164; Jas, 53; John (& wife), 58; Mgt, 35, 181; Martha, 39; Richd, 137, 144; Teresa, 53; Thos, 53; Wm, 58
Rezano, see Rosanno.
Rial, Riel, Ryol, Edwin, 152; Jane, 152, 168; Jane Cath,* 202; Mary, 203; Patk, 152. See also Real.
Rian, see Ryan.
Rice, Almande Mary, 85; Eliz, 85; Jas (& wife), 138; John Ant, 85; Thos, 43
Richards, Elen, 104; Jas, 104; Joanna, 104
Richardson, Ann, 32; Elen, 110; Jas, 110; John, 110
Richmont, Georgina de, 131, 199
Richy, Mary, 93; (or Gribbon), Mary, 93
Rickets, Riquetts, ——, 121; Mary, 179
Ride, Justine, 62, 75
Rideout, Ridout, John, 191, 196; Rosanna, 191

C.R.S., 65: *Corrigenda* (page-nos. italicised)

34, line 15: cavalier misspelt; *40*, line 7: owing; *46*, note 217: for "00" read 100; *56*, line 6: cross-reference to pp. 113-72; *65*: first word Other; *78*, line 16: declining; line 23: to; n. 393: for "00" read 74; *79*, nn. 400, 402: cross-refs. to pp. 91-7, 101-5; *80*, line 8: ones; *89*, 4 lines from end: benefit; *114* (C.13): before weeks', insert for 7; *116*, last line: lodging; *132* (8 Oct.): after for, insert staying; *148* (49th week): for "£1. s. 0d.," read £1. 1s. 0d.; *157* (27th wk.) & *161* (52nd wk.): insert *sic* before totals; *169* (last 10 entries): no date, 13 March, n.d., 16, 24, 25, n.d., 27, 29, n.d.; *174*, n. 80: for "the Account Book," read accounts; *207*, n. 41: for "00", read 82; *212*, n. 69: misprints; *224* (12 March) & *235* (24 June): for "To", read T.; *233* (12 June): ignorant; (13 June): promised.